WHO'S AFRAID OF POLITICAL EDUCATION?

The Challenge to Teach Civic Competence and Democratic Participation

Edited by
Henry Tam

First published in Great Britain in 2025 by

Policy Press, an imprint of
Bristol University Press
University of Bristol
1–9 Old Park Hill
Bristol
BS2 8BB
UK
t: +44 (0)117 374 6645
e: bup-info@bristol.ac.uk

Details of international sales and distribution partners are available at
policy.bristoluniversitypress.co.uk

© Bristol University Press 2025

British Library Cataloguing in Publication Data
A catalogue record for this book is available from the British Library

ISBN 978-1-4473-6695-9 hardcover
ISBN 978-1-4473-6696-6 paperback
ISBN 978-1-4473-6697-3 ePub
ISBN 978-1-4473-6699-7 ePdf

The right of Henry Tam to be identified as editor of this work has been asserted by him in accordance with the Copyright, Designs and Patents Act 1988.

All rights reserved: no part of this publication may be reproduced, stored in a retrieval system, or transmitted in any form or by any means, electronic, mechanical, photocopying, recording, or otherwise without the prior permission of Bristol University Press.

Every reasonable effort has been made to obtain permission to reproduce copyrighted material. If, however, anyone knows of an oversight, please contact the publisher.

The statements and opinions contained within this publication are solely those of the editor and contributors and not of the University of Bristol or Bristol University Press. The University of Bristol and Bristol University Press disclaim responsibility for any injury to persons or property resulting from any material published in this publication.

Bristol University Press and Policy Press work to counter discrimination on
grounds of gender, race, disability, age and sexuality.

Cover design: Nicky Borowiec
Front cover image: Adobe Stock/rob z

Contents

Notes on contributors		v
Preface		vii

Introduction
1	Citizens, we have a problem *Henry Tam*	1

PART I Why changes are needed
2	Political education in an unequal society *Diane Reay*	17
3	Classroom conflict, 'divisive concepts' and educating for democracy *Barrett Smith and Sarah M. Stitzlein*	35
4	The contested scope of academic freedom *Dina Kiwan*	50
5	Rethinking citizenship education for political literacy *Tony Breslin*	64

PART II What could be done differently
6	Populism, classrooms and shared authority *Kathleen M. Sellers and Kathleen Knight Abowitz*	81
7	Different approaches to teaching civic and national identity *Edda Sant*	96
8	Active learning of marginalised young people *Kalbir Shukra*	112
9	Universities' role in teaching practical politics *Titus Alexander*	127

PART III How to make a lasting impact
10	The evidence on educational methods for political engagement *David Kerr and Bryony Hoskins*	147
11	Citizenship education: building for the future *Lee Jerome and Liz Moorse*	163
12	Reversing democratic decline through political education *Murray Print*	180
13	Towards civic learning for all *Kei Kawashima-Ginsberg*	195

Conclusion
14   Lessons for democratic health   212
      Henry Tam

Index   226

Notes on contributors

Titus Alexander is a Fellow of the Bernard Crick Centre for Understanding Politics, Sheffield University; and the convenor of Democracy Matters.

Tony Breslin is a National Leader of Governance, Department for Education (England); he is the author of *Lessons From Lockdown* and *Bubble Schools and the Long Road From Lockdown*; and was formerly Chief Executive at the Citizenship Foundation, and Chair of the Association for the Teaching of the Social Sciences.

Bryony Hoskins is Professor of Comparative Social Science, Department of Sociology, University of Roehampton, London.

Lee Jerome is Associate Professor of Education, Middlesex University; the editor of the journal, *Education for Citizenship and Social Justice*; and the author of *Children's Rights Education in Diverse Classrooms* (with Hugh Starkey) and *The Rise of Character Education in Britain* (with Ben Kisby).

Kei Kawashima-Ginsberg is the Newhouse Director, CIRCLE (Center for Information and Research on Civic Learning and Engagement), Jonathan M. Tisch College of Civic Life, Tufts University.

David Kerr is the Head of Initial Teacher Training, University of Reading; he was formerly Research Director of the Citizenship Education Longitudinal Study.

Dina Kiwan is Professor in Comparative Education, and Head of Department of Education and Social Justice, University of Birmingham.

Kathleen Knight Abowitz is Professor, Department of Educational Leadership, Miami University of Ohio.

Liz Moorse is Chief Executive, Association for Citizenship Teaching (ACT), a charity that supports high-quality citizenship education in schools; she previously worked at the government body responsible for the curriculum as the national lead for citizenship: she has written widely on citizenship in the curriculum and represents the UK at the Council of Europe Education Policy Network for Democratic Citizenship.

Murray Print is Professor and Chair of Education, School of Education and Social Work, University of Sydney; he was the former Lead Writer and Team Leader, Australian Curriculum: Civics and Citizenship.

Diane Reay is Emeritus Professor of Education, University of Cambridge.

Edda Sant is Reader in Education Studies, Manchester Metropolitan University.

Kathleen M. Sellers is a Doctoral Candidate, Miami University of Ohio; McPherson Fellow, University of Wisconsin-Madison and University of Illinois, Chicago, Center for Ethics and Education.

Kalbir Shukra is Senior Lecturer and Head of Community Studies at Goldsmiths, University of London.

Barrett Smith is a teacher in Cincinnati Public Schools; Graduate Student, Education Studies, University of Cincinnati.

Sarah M. Stitzlein is Professor of Education and Affiliate Professor of Philosophy, University of Cincinnati.

Henry Tam is Director of Question the Powerful; he was formerly Director of the Forum for Youth Participation and Democracy, Education Faculty, University of Cambridge; and he is the author of *Time to Save Democracy* and *The Evolution of Communitarian Ideas*.

Preface

Who's Afraid of Political Education? is the fourth book in a series I have done with Bristol University Press/Policy Press on the theme of rebuilding democracy. With their support, we have been able to set out why and what kind of reform is needed (*Time to Save Democracy*), explain how state–citizen cooperation can be strengthened in practice (*Whose Government Is It?*), and share key lessons on inclusive approaches to secure community-based improvement (*Tomorrow's Communities*). In this next work, our attention turns to how people can learn to engage effectively as democratic citizens.

It is generally accepted that we should raise people's understanding to help them guard against, for example, being misled as to what would aid or impair their health, or persuaded to part with their money on dubious grounds. Yet when people cannot tell a sound claim about a political matter from a specious one, we are often told to accept that nothing could be done – because politics is contested and hence cannot be taught without bias. But medical and financial issues are contested too, and that has not excluded them from being addressed in education.

Some in politics, like quacks and scammers, have tried to pretend that 'impartiality' means there should be no differentiation between the veracity of rival claims, and whatever assertion they make must be given the same respect as any statement backed by actual evidence and expert judgement. In reality, it is vital to be able to judge the validity of what is said about government and public policy. Our wellbeing depends on it. And there is a wealth of knowledge we can draw on to show how citizens can learn, with true impartiality, to become more astute in assessing public claims and choosing options for influencing political outcomes.

In putting together *Who's Afraid of Political Education?*, I am indebted not only to the contributors to this book – who share with us their impressive expertise in this field – but also the many other researchers, educators and policy practitioners I have learnt so much from over the years. Their respective efforts in advancing civic competence are inspirational. And their collective wisdom on how education can strengthen democracy is indispensable.

Henry Tam
2023

1

Introduction

Citizens, we have a problem

Henry Tam

Political ignorance and democratic atrophy

Democracy is meant to protect us from arbitrary rule. It ought to give everyone a chance to ensure decisions that are binding on all of us reflect our shared concerns, and are not made to suit just a powerful few. However, democracy cannot function if people are unaware of how it is supposed to work or what they could do to make a difference. Looking at developments in the UK and the US, countries that have historically led the way in democratising their system of governance, the signs are not encouraging.

A considerable number of citizens do not even register to vote – 17 per cent in Britain, 24 per cent in the US. Of those who have registered, many do not turn out to vote; around a third or more are no-shows in UK general elections, and about 40 per cent do not vote in US presidential elections. While there are rightly mass protests against climate change, racism and economic hardships, there is little concerted efforts in resisting the erosion of democracy – even though an effective democratic system is what people need to effect the necessary reforms to deal with major societal problems.

Instead of moving us closer to the point where we have a genuinely equal say about who are to be our representatives or which major policy to adopt, democracy has increasingly been undermined by political manoeuvres designed to reinforce unfair power distribution. Gerrymandering in the US has meant that in many states the vote for a Democrat candidate counts less than that for a Republican candidate, as it would take many more votes for the Democrats to win seats, given the way electoral boundaries have been redrawn (Li et al, 2018). The imposition of photo ID requirements in elections in the US and the UK is highly likely to put more of the poorest, most marginalised citizens off from voting (O'Donoghue, 2016). The hasty introduction of a flawed voter registration system in the UK led to almost 2 million people dropping off the electoral register – mainly those who were among the most disempowered in society, such as students, the poor and minority ethnic groups in inner cities (Lowles, 2015). In 2022, the Conservative government in the UK moved to take away the independence of the Electoral Commission and give itself the power to determine what would or would not be acceptable in election campaigns (Palese, 2021).

Against this backdrop, we detect not a wakening to the need to reinvigorate democratic politics, but a widening acceptance of defective practices. For example, two things were notable in the 2011 referendum held in the UK for the proposed alternative voting system, which would have taken into account to a greater extent the preferences of voters:[1]

1. The main argument of those who wanted to preserve the existing system was not that it was more democratic, but simply that the new one would allegedly cost more money.
2. While 62.9 per cent of the votes cast went against introducing alternative voting, twice as many registered voters were not even concerned enough to vote either way (McGuinness and Hardacre, 2011).[2]

When the UK held another national referendum in 2016, this time on its membership of the European Union, voting had become even more disconnected from the core issues. In addition to the extensive false claims made about the advantages of leaving the EU, and the pervasive interference from Russia to promote Brexit to destabilise Europe, democracy was openly subverted by the advocates for Brexit, who assured voters that leaving the EU did not mean leaving the European single market, but once Brexit won the vote they declared it as a democratic mandate to leave the single market.[3] It became a mantra that to respect democracy, one should accept that the UK must leave the single market. That was akin to a political leader saying that a vote for him would be a vote to safeguard the Human Rights Act, and once elected, declaring that he now has a democratic mandate to abolish the Human Rights Act.

Meanwhile, blatant and regular lies have become routine political tactics with the likes of Trump (Cathey, 2021). From the day he entered the White House in 2017 to his attempt to overturn the legitimate election of Joe Biden as US president when his own term ended four years later, Trump was

---

[1] The proposed alternative vote system would determine which candidate wins based on who has the widest support when all preferences are taken into account, as opposed to the existing first-past-the-post system, which hands victory to the candidate who is the most favoured 'first choice', even if most people in that constituency do not want them to be their representative.

[2] 62.9 per cent of the 42 per cent of registered voters who voted cast their vote against the proposed system, that is, 26.4 per cent of registered voters voted against alternative voting, compared with 58 per cent of registered voters who did not vote at all.

[3] See, for example, 'UKIP and Brexit[ers] stating they will stay in single market': www.youtube.com/watch?v=A4y6BVPNe50

found to have made over thirty thousand false claims in his public statements (Kessler et al, 2021). Yet millions of Americans, instead of being alarmed by his continued incitement to reject their democratically elected government, have continued to express support for a political figure contemptuous of democratic integrity and who would use illegal means to dismiss countless authentic votes as 'fraudulent'.

At this point, despairing voices are raised about democracy itself because, in opening political decisions to the public, it allows people who are ignorant, misguided or deceived about complex issues to back options that are actually harmful to them and others in society.[4] For a long time, it was argued that this situation could not be rectified because it would not be possible to improve public understanding of the controversial matters that surround political problems. Allegedly, no one could have the authority and impartiality to explain to citizens what they should look for or guard against in considering political claims and proposals. But such a view is quite untenable when the coherence and validity of these claims are largely tied to assertions that are routinely subject to objective assessment. Political statements are made up of constituent components relating to legal judgements, scientific findings, technical projections, moral arguments and collected evidence, the reliability of which are scrutinised by a range of recognised experts and holders of designated public offices. Like all statements, some made by politicians may have to be treated as neither proven nor disproven for now, yet the majority would belong more closely to either the credible or the dubious end of the veracity spectrum.

Just because some politicians want to claim that homelessness is being reduced, measures such as vaccination against COVID-19 are unnecessary, or they have invested more in the education of pupils with additional needs, it does not mean that those claims cannot be found to be false. Similarly, some may use a political platform to deny that their campaign activities are funded by corrupt sources, they are fabricating stories about refugees to turn the public against them, or climate change poses a planet-wide threat – what they try to deny can nonetheless be established as true.

The extent to which democracy can help or hinder a society in governing itself in the interest of its members ultimately depends on how well citizens understand political claims, and what they know about using their civic

---

[4] From my own and others' experience in encouraging our fellow citizens to vote, I have encountered cases where people deciding to vote were not sure which party they should vote for because they had no idea who brought in the policies that affected them badly, and who had been opposing them. Some indicated they would vote for a candidate who seemed nice, oblivious of the fact that they supported policies that they deemed unacceptable.

influence on the basis of that understanding. One might assume that education must have a central role in meeting this need. Unfortunately, in practice, it is still widely presumed that politics is best left to adults to work out for themselves. Schools and colleges should, at most, pass on information about existing political institutions and electoral mechanisms, mention a selection of those universally acknowledged historical events (preferably without exploring too much the conflicting interpretations of their political significance), and teach a few generic skills in debating, reporting, or volunteering. Anything more would run the risk of being censured as 'biased' or 'indoctrination'.

In order to make the case for why and how political education[5] should be developed in support of democracy, we have brought together a team of leading experts to explain the challenges we face and what can be done to overcome them. We will focus primarily on the UK and the US, with examples drawn from other countries where these may illustrate particular problems and possible solutions.[6] Based on research findings, case studies and their own experience as educators, our contributors will set out, in Part I of this book, why a range of current assumptions and prevailing practices in education hinder democratic development and need to be changed; in Part II, what could be done differently with a number of specific practices[7] to enhance the understanding and skills needed for effective political engagement; and in Part III, how a lasting impact in improving citizens' learning for democratic participation can be achieved by adopting pedagogic approaches based on extensive research findings.[8]

---

[5] Education that enhances understanding of politics and the implications of being a member of a democratic society is referred to variously as 'political education', 'civic education', 'citizenship education', or 'education for democracy'.

[6] It is not our intention to offer advice to countries with their own distinct political backgrounds and educational systems, but given the influence of Anglo-American political culture around the world, people affected by the spread of neoliberal practices and 'culture war' politics will find many aspects of this book relevant to them as well.

[7] These include the development of shared authority with pupils, an open approach to teaching civic and national identity, active learning for marginalised youths, and universities' support for practical politics. They illustrate what can be achieved through the highlighted practices in areas often assumed to be inherently problematic. There are other areas relating to, for example, adult education, education about discrimination, international understanding, and so on that are not covered, primarily because of the overall length we need to keep to for the book.

[8] We draw from the ideas of a range of thinkers (such as Dewey, 1966; Freire, 1970; hooks, 1994; Crick and Lockyer, 2004), and take into account relevant findings (such as Arthur et al, 2008; Biesta, 2011; Hoskins and Janmaat, 2019; Peterson et al, 2020), in making our case for more effective political education.

Why changes are needed

In Part I of our book, we look at a number of key obstacles to political education. We begin with the neoliberal ethos of privileging private advancement over democratic cooperation, which has become a dominant force in Anglo-American politics for decades and is exemplified by the education system in England. In Chapter 2 'Political Education in an Unequal Society', Diane Reay explains why this exacerbates divisiveness and threatens the democratic cohesion of society. Schools in England are under pressure to focus overwhelmingly on individual competitiveness in examinations. Students are judged primarily on how much they are ahead of others in test and assessment results, while schools are ranked in league tables on the basis of the performance of their students. The democratic accountability of schools to local elected authorities is cut, while private and corporate interests are brought into the running of schools.

'Good citizenship' is reduced to the promotion of charitable giving and volunteering work, which tends to favour children from families with more disposable time and resources. Reay argues that we must develop a better alternative. This requires a systematic shift towards teamwork and critical thinking, so that students can learn to solve problems by asking pertinent questions and collaborating with others in finding the answers that best stand up to scrutiny. This, in turn, calls for structural changes to support the adoption of pedagogic approaches that value the cultivation of cooperative intelligence, as championed by thinkers such as Dewey (1966) and Freire (1970), and demonstrated by schools in countries like Finland and Estonia.

However, the task of strengthening education's role in the development of democratic citizens is increasingly hampered by moves to exclude 'contentious' issues in the classroom. In Chapter 3 'Classroom Conflict, "Divisive Concepts" and Educating for Democracy', Barrett Smith and Sarah Stitzlein look at the growing trends in the US where politicians are using the law to prevent the teaching of issues at odds with their ideological stance. By labelling as 'divisive' various ideas central to the critical discussions of topics such as race and sexuality, these politicians claim that for the sake of protecting students from conflicts and respecting the different viewpoints of parents, they would ensure the targeted ideas are kept out of school.

Smith and Stitzlein point out that the 'divisive concepts' under attack are actually central to civic deliberations, and to exclude them from classroom discussion undermines the development of a democratic culture. They explain that, instead of allowing partisan legislators to impose their preferences regarding what should or should not be taught, teachers should be given the support and protection to engage their students in considering issues, arguments and perspectives that need to be addressed in a civil and constructive manner. There is a real danger that teachers will otherwise retreat further and further from political education out of fear of prosecution, when they should be at the forefront of creating educational space for those with dissenting views to listen to each other and explore common ground. Democracy needs its members to learn about building strong relations that would enable them to engage with controversial matters and become, not more polarised, but more connected through shared understanding even when they disagree.

On the surface, the invocation of 'academic freedom' may appear to be an ally for political education. In reality, that notion has been used to disrupt educational institutions' efforts to foster democratic learning. Politicians in the UK and the US on their 'anti-woke' mission seek to protect certain views from criticisms and restrictions directed at them in educational institutions.[9] But the rationale they rely on is not the complete freedom of expression as they have no hesitation in demanding the banning of what *they* consider extremist or ideological views. For democracy to function, citizens need to understand how to differentiate between what should be freely expressed and what kind of communication would endanger others if not curtailed.

In Chapter 4 'The Contested Scope of Academic Freedom', Dina Kiwan examines the tension between the principle of academic freedom on the one hand, and diversity and inclusion on the other. Current debates have tended to focus on issues pertaining to free speech, rather than examining academic freedom in relation to the production of knowledge and the development of a democratic society. Kiwan reviews the issues highlighted through the sociopolitical context of universities and schools in the UK, critically analysing key governmental policy documents, and pointing to the need for a more thoughtful approach to deal with unfettered speech that can be utilised by those holding power in ways that harm traditionally marginalised communities.

Awareness of how power is distributed in society and exercised by those who have it is key to a well-functioning democracy. Although England's education system has become mired in market-centric individualism, which places personal success in money making far above that of aptitude in democratic cooperation, it is also where one of the most ambitious reform initiatives in support of the political education of citizens was launched. In Chapter 5 'Rethinking Citizenship Education for Political Literacy', Tony Breslin reminds us that the architect of that initiative, Bernard Crick, aimed at no less than a change in the political culture of the country so that people would think of themselves as active citizens, willing, able and equipped to have an influence in public life. Despite putting citizenship education on

---

[9] Such views have been ironically labelled by their defenders as 'politically incorrect', and the tendency to deny them a public platform is often referred to as the 'cancel culture'.

the map, Breslin draws attention to the factors that subsequently impeded Crick's project.

Demands for schools to play their part in promoting community cohesion and tackling extremism, along with a new concern with teaching 'British values', took the focus away from improving political literacy. Many teachers with qualifications in political studies and social sciences distanced themselves from citizenship as a subject. Others assumed that politics was too complex to be taught in schools. The lack of quality training and sustained support from government led to the marginalisation of citizenship learning. To recover Crick's goal, Breslin argues, the political dimension of democratic citizenship should be taught in a subject-specific *and* cross-curricular manner, with the skills for deliberation and cooperative engagement developed through practices that influence school policies and activities.

What could be done differently

We turn our attention in Part II to a number of areas where innovative practices could be adopted to achieve greater shared political understanding and participatory competence.[10] Complacency in the face of the widening gap between government and citizens is not sustainable. The rise of populism – on the Right and Left – signals that it will be increasingly difficult for political leaders to move their policy agenda forward without securing better engagement with the public. However, while demagogic populism may favour manipulative engagement to stir and steer people towards what authoritarian minded leaders want, democratic populism demands the informed participation of citizens in shaping public policies. To raise civic vigilance against the former and facilitate the development of the latter, citizens need to learn about how to acquire and exercise shared authority.

In Chapter 6 'Populism, Classrooms, and Shared Authority', Kathleen Sellers and Kathleen Knight Abowitz argue that prevailing modes of learning deny students-as-citizens the opportunity to ask and answer the essential civic question: 'What should we do?' They explore ways to overcome this problem through two theoretical perspectives. The first of these are Freirean critiques of banking education as well as his recommendations for problem-posing education. The second comes from the organisational power theories of Mary Parker Follett, a pioneer in theorising control in organisations as

---

[10] There are more innovative practices than we have space to cover. The ones selected for inclusion are particularly pertinent because they can readily make a positive difference to a number of prevalent problem areas such as alienation by remote authority, disputed sense of identity, marginalisation on the grounds of race, and lack of engagement know-how.

more humanely based in social processes rather than subordination. These are backed by practical examples of how educators can create innovative ways to share classroom authority in a variety of lessons.

Another challenge of political education is to ensure that people understand what it means to be members of their country in terms of their rights and responsibilities, and their shared identity as fellow citizens. This can raise problematic questions about how one thinks about one's country – its past actions, its current policies, its future plans, especially when these are considered in the context of what a democracy ought to do, rather than simply going along with what those with the loudest voice or greatest power may claim to be the 'national interest'.

In Chapter 7 'Different Approaches to Teaching Civic and National Identity', Edda Sant takes us through a number of approaches – with examples from diverse countries – that show what can help or hinder the development of political autonomy and pluralistic understanding needed for sharing the identity of being members of a democratic country. She explains why partisan approaches (both nationalistic and anti-nationalistic) cannot generate a common identity when people feel differently about who they are. Deliberative approaches tend to neglect real worldview clashes, and their reliance on rational analysis can marginalise people who are not used to formal reasoning practices. However, deliberations have a place when they supplement agonistic approaches that call for the pedagogies of articulation (talking through one's experiences), of differences (reflecting on the origins of assumptions), and of equivalences (getting together to share and express ideas in response to common concerns).

In addition to classroom lessons on how we think of ourselves as citizens, political education can be greatly advanced through active learning in the community. In Chapter 8 'Active Learning of Marginalised Young People', Kalbir Shukra explores how opportunities developed with local authorities, community groups and youth projects can facilitate young people, particularly those from minority ethnic groups, to raise their political consciousness, by engaging them in critical dialogue around the issues that affect their lives. Instructive examples include initiatives that enable young people to develop forms of representation, grow a sense of agency and make a difference. These cast light on how young people are effectively engaged and given a real voice in the context of their own lived experience and wider diasporic histories in challenging inequality.

Shukra points to three types of project that use interactive informal political education that give space to young citizens shaping agendas rather than seek to mould their thinking. The first involves self-organised political organisations that are community based and led by Black and minority ethnic adults. A second type is devised by mainstream, youth-oriented organisations to take account of Black and minority ethnic young people's concerns. The third type is led by local authorities and service providers when they want to empower young people to experience how they can shape plans and policies that affect them and their communities. A case study of a project of this type, the London Borough of Lewisham's Young Mayor Programme, shows how it helps public bodies and young people learn to acknowledge differences, respect dissent, and cooperate on finding solutions.

In Chapter 9 'Universities' Role in Teaching Practical Politics', Titus Alexander explains how the institutions for higher education can do substantially more than just provide degree courses in politics in order to help improve democratic engagement. Universities are well placed to support all their students (not just those studying politics formally) and members of partner communities in learning and applying practical political skills. Through symbolic acts and social practices on campus, there are opportunities to promote civil discussions about public issues and stimulate rethinking about prevailing assumptions. Staff can adopt pedagogical approaches to integrate critical reflection on societal matters in response to related topics being raised.

More widely, universities can offer more formal and informal programmes – as a few pioneers in the UK and the US have done – to give people a chance to learn about political processes and tactics, understand the power of different public offices, acquire the skills to exert their civic influence, and discover more about the threats and opportunities surrounding particular policy areas. Some universities have indeed set up issue-based centres and community partnerships to provide support in accessing and assessing research findings, assist with hosting community events, and facilitating policy development. Other examples include arrangements to promote collaboration across departments and with professional associations to improve the availability and utilisation of well-tested information in the evaluation of public claims and formulation of alternative proposals.

How to make a lasting impact

Having identified the key challenges to political education and drawn attention to a number of innovative practices that can help bring about improvements, we turn in Part III to consider the broader approaches that ought to be integrated into the education system to facilitate better democratic participation by citizens. In Chapter 10 'The Evidence on Educational Methods for Political Engagement', David Kerr and Bryony Hoskins examine research findings from Europe and America to see what learning methods tend to raise the level of engagement in political activities such as voting, protest and joining a political party. On their analysis, we need to apply both the principle of learning as acquisition – to transmit political knowledge from teachers to students as a first step in enabling young people to have a better understanding of politics – *and* the principle of learning as participation – to facilitate the co-creation of meaning that develops young people's competences that lead to future engagement.

They point out that to avoid some social groups of young people missing out, more should be done to ensure learning opportunities are fairly shared through methods that include:

- maintaining an open classroom climate where everyone can feel free to ask questions, express their own opinions, and perceive that their opinions are respected;
- overseeing inclusive activities such as class councils, school parliaments, and mock elections;
- contextualising debates in local politics and using interactive methodologies to enhance political knowledge, efficacy and participation.

In Chapter 11 'Citizenship Education: Building for the Future', Lee Jerome and Liz Moorse draw on their extensive review of citizenship education practices to identify what should be done to prepare young people more effectively to act as democratic citizens. They consider the impact of different school-based experiments and the feedback from experienced subject specialist teachers, and set out how good citizenship teachers need to address the emotional dimension, the role of knowledge and rational argument, and the case for citizenship to be enacted.

They put forward practical advice, illustrated by case studies, for how to secure long-term impact in five important areas:

1. Raising political literacy through better understanding of and working with public bodies and politicians.
2. Learning more about the spread of misinformation and conspiracy theories, improving media and digital literacy, and increasing awareness of how to check public claims and assess legitimacy of information sources.
3. Recognising problems of inequality and exploring how to pursue social justice.
4. Being alert to extremist rhetoric and propaganda, and working with others to tackle the spread of extremism.
5. Engaging with the threats posed by climate change, and collaborating with others to advance sustainability.

They also stress that alongside teaching the instrumental value of democracy as a means to secure better conditions, we should show how democracy is directly life-enhancing in terms of the openness, cooperation and solidarity it brings.

More recommendations are set out by Murray Print in Chapter 12, 'Reversing Democratic Decline through Political Education', which uses a model he devised that links political and civic learning to subsequent political and civic behaviours. He examines the evidence collected in Australia, the US and Europe, and explains why three factors need to be taken into account. The first of these concerns the development of a formal school curriculum by an expert, non-partisan group to structure learning about citizenship, democracy and participation. There is clear evidence that as students acquire more political knowledge, they develop more engaged political attitudes, and are more likely to participate actively in political activities from voting to running for office.

Second, attention should be given to the informal curriculum, which may consist of instrumental (student councils, student elections, assemblies, newspapers) and expressive (clubs, sports, bands and social activities) elements that can affect student political and civic learning. Research has found, for example, that the role of the student council was an important potential source of political education through practical participation, and the extent to which the school administration provided real opportunities for student governance was a key influence over students' involvement in political activities in school and beyond. Third, there is the role of situated learning, where support for open and respectful classroom discussion has been widely found to facilitate understanding of disputed public issues, appreciation of political conflict, and readiness to engage in politics on an informed basis.

We conclude our exploration of how to make a lasting impact in political education with Kei Kawashima-Ginsberg's 'Towards Civic Learning for All'. Drawing on her experience with initiatives in different states as well as the nationwide 'Roadmap to Educating for American Democracy', she points to an emerging consensus on what should be done to provide high-quality civic learning, which she defines as:

> one in which a young person, through a web of institutional and/or relational networks, is exposed to diverse and meaningful opportunities for democratic practice and form a strong working knowledge of the ways in which civic and political institutions function, and, therefore can leverage these systems for public good.

The way forward is encapsulated in five pathways:

1. Expand the meaning of 'civic learning', by using a classroom as a mini polity: educators are to help students build the necessary skills and commitment to share ownership of their learning space, so they can contribute to their collective thriving by learning to work together.

2. Civic education as connecting content, pedagogy and applied practice: students are to be given the chance to collaborate on identifying and solving problems in their school and community.
3. Thinking developmentally about civic readiness: educators are to leverage students' curiosity as an entryway into deep inquiry over time, so that students can revisit questions that are core to their civic knowledge and identity development.
4. Community schools and place-based collaborations: schools are to adopt a coalition-building and evidence-based approach to building consensus with community inputs to meet the needs of students and their families.
5. Educational policies and the role of parents and carers: schools are to inform and seek inputs from parents and carers about civics curriculum.

Democracy needs political education

Although there are many factors – from economic conditions and electoral mechanisms to media coverage and the positioning of political parties – that affect citizens' engagement with public affairs, one prerequisite for effective political participation has to be a reasonable comprehension of how issues ought to be assessed and what can be done to achieve an appropriate response. That is why education at all levels has a vital role to play in helping members of successive generations to learn to function as democratic citizens.

There are undoubtedly obstacles along the way. The prevalence of neoliberal culture has reduced learning – from schools to universities – to little more than an instrument for economic dealings. Education for civic competence has been marginalised, while funding for training and research in the teaching of democratic citizenship has shrunk. There is also a growing reluctance to discuss any topic that can draw accusations of bias, when 'bias' is often a term applied to what certain politicians object to when their stance or claims are questioned.[11]

But instead of backing away from raising political understanding – and allowing our collective governance to be further subverted to serve the interests of propagandists and demagogues, we must step up to defend objectivity in discourse, mutual respect in relationship building and cooperation in decision-making. There is no room for the politicisation of education when that involves teachers seeking primarily to promote or discredit certain politicians or parties through what they teach, or politicians

---

[11] When the pupils in one school in England planned to write to their MPs about their views of the prime minister (Boris Johnson) who was widely believed to have broken the law, which was subsequently confirmed by a police investigation, the Education Secretary criticised the exercise as inappropriate (Stone, 2022).

aiming to prevent facts and arguments being taught just because they inconveniently challenge their position. But such politicisation is not to be confused with political education that explains certain issues, such as the impact of climate change or the level of child poverty, with the support of robust evidence, even though they might be denied by certain politicians who prefer to dismiss concerns with such issues.

In the chapters that follow, we will learn about why certain changes need to be urgently made, how innovative practices can be adopted to bring about improvement, and what approaches can be built into the education system to secure lasting impact on political engagement. All educators and policy makers should reflect on the analyses and recommendations put forward, and take action accordingly.

References

Arthur, J., Davies, I. and Hahn, C. (eds) (2008) *Sage Handbook of Education for Citizenship and Democracy*, London: Sage Publications.

Biesta, G. (2011) *Learning Democracy in School and Society: Education, Lifelong Learning, and the Politics of Citizenship*, Rotterdam: Sense Publishers.

Cathey, L. (2021) 'Legacy of lies – how Trump weaponized mistruths during his presidency', ABC News, 20 January: https://abcnews.go.com/Politics/legacy-lies-trump-weaponized-mistruths-presidency/story?id=75335019

Crick, B. and Lockyer, A. (2004) *Education for Democratic Citizenship*, London: Routledge.

Dewey, J. (1966) *Democracy and Education*, New York: The Free Press.

Freire, P. (1970) *Pedagogy of the Oppressed*, London: Continuum.

hooks, b. (1994) *Teaching to Transgress: Education as the Practice of Freedom*, London: Routledge.

Hoskins, B. and Janmaat, J.G. (2019) *Education, Democracy and Inequality: Political Engagement and Citizenship Education in Europe*, London: Palgrave Macmillan.

Kessler, G., Rizzo, S. and Kelly, M. (2021) 'Trump's false or misleading claims total 30,573 over 4 years', *The Washington Post*, 24 January: www.washingtonpost.com/politics/2021/01/24/trumps-false-or-misleading-claims-total-30573-over-four-years/

Li, M., Rudensky, Y. and Royden, L. (2018) 'Extreme Gerrymandering and the 2018 Midterm', Brennan Center: www.brennancenter.org/our-work/research-reports/extreme-gerrymandering-2018-midterm

Lowles, N. (2015) 'The sham of voter registration in the UK', OpenDemocracy: www.opendemocracy.net/en/opendemocracyuk/sham-of-voter-registration-in-uk/

McGuinness, F. and Hardacre, J. (2011) 'Alternative Vote Referendum', House of Commons Library: https://commonslibrary.parliament.uk/research-briefings/rp11-44/

O'Donoghue, G. (2016) 'US Election 2016: Voter ID laws threaten lifelong voters', BBC: www.bbc.co.uk/news/election-us-2016-37569855

Palese, M. (2021) 'What is the Elections Bill? And why is it an issue?', The Constitution Society: https://consoc.org.uk/what-is-the-elections-bill-and-why-is-it-an-issue/

Peterson, A., Stahl, G. and Soong, H. (eds) (2020) *The Palgrave Handbook of Citizenship and Education*, London: Palgrave Macmillan.

Stone, J. (2022) 'Pupils shouldn't be criticising Boris Johnson in class, says education secretary', *The Independent*, 9 February: www.independent.co.uk/news/uk/politics/boris-johnson-nadhim-zahawi-b2011397.html

PART I

Why changes are needed

2

Political education in an unequal society

Diane Reay

Introduction

This chapter is about English education and its democratic deficit, although, when data specific to England is unavailable, the chapter draws on UK-level data. However, it is important to point out that England is increasingly an outlier relative to Scotland, Wales and Northern Ireland, with a more fragmented and privatised educational system that has left many teachers, pupils and parents feeling powerless in the face of rapid educational policy changes. As Tim Brighouse (2017), former London schools commissioner, asserted: 'England remains the poor relation of the four nations with its centralised system and weakened local government. If a sense of powerlessness is the enemy of democracy, England is more at risk than the other three countries.'

In England political education is something to be avoided. Throughout their schooling young people are rarely taught about politics. Instead, they are provided with a citizenship education where the focus is often on a depoliticised curriculum of personal 'responsibilisation' that concentrates on building character and social capital rather than political literacy and active citizenship (Kisby, 2017; Weinberg and Flinders, 2018). This creates what Conover and Searing (2000, p 108) call 'a privately orientated, passive understanding of citizenship'. The emphasis is placed on individual social and moral responsibility through volunteering and charitable giving rather than any active political engagement (Osler and Starkey, 2001; Power et al, 2021). One consequence is a lack of confidence in governments to address citizens' needs, and a belief that charities rather than the state are better at meeting people's needs. This could be viewed as a neoliberalising of citizenship education that encourages ad hoc individual action rather than collective political engagement. Involvement is primarily seen in terms of charitable giving and volunteering rather than actual political participation.

Recent research (DfE, 2022) found that even this anaemic form of citizenship education failed to reach a significant minority of English secondary school students; 24 per cent reported weekly lessons in citizenship education, while a further quarter had never received a lesson. The school workforce census of 2020 reported that only 16 per cent of the 2,876 schools surveyed had a trained citizenship education teacher (DfE, 2022). More concerning, Weinberg (2022) discovered that citizenship education, as it currently stands in English schools, accelerates class and race inequalities in young people's political participation. He concludes 'that all things considered, curricula lessons in politics and citizenship appear to inhibit the political ambition of ethnic minority and low SES [socioeconomic status] students' (Weinberg, 2022, p 205). One cause could be the growing emphasis on charity and volunteering, given that practices of charitable giving and volunteering are differentially enabled and facilitated by levels of resources. As such, they are easier to engage in if children and young people come from advantaged rather than disadvantaged backgrounds. A child receiving free school meals is more likely to view themselves as a recipient rather than a donor of charity. Furthermore, the growing proliferation of food banks in schools points to an institutionalisation of food insecurity within the education system and a normalisation of charity as a way of responding to such insecurity (Baker, forthcoming).

The focus on charity is one of a number of ways in which citizenship education deters young working-class people from political engagement. A major research study spanning six European countries (Hoskins and Janmaat, 2019) found that the English educational system was particularly ineffective in promoting political literacy and engagement among working-class students. They had less access than their middle-class peers to an open climate of classroom discussion and political activities in schools, forms of participation that Hoskins and Janmaat (2019, p 224) established were the most powerful modes of learning for political engagement. Even when working-class children were in the same year group as middle-class pupils, they still experienced less citizenship education. Furthermore, their class disadvantage was compounded if they attended predominantly working-class schools, or were placed in ability groups from an early age. As Hoskins and Janmaat (2019, p 231) concluded: 'the social sorting effects of such practices invariably result in working-class children being exposed to inferior learning opportunities in terms of fostering political engagement'.

The next section goes on to discuss the democratic deficit in wider society, but it could be argued that any democratic deficit in the wider political field is reflected in the state of citizenship education in English schools.

State of political play and the democratic deficit

The current historical period is marked by the aftermath of the 2008 Great Recession, continuing austerity and a context of rising inequalities.

At the same time, there is growing concern in the UK, and more widely, that there has been an erosion of the practices, values and commitments necessary to sustain a democratic society (Kahne et al, 2021). In the UK, state power strongly reflects elite interests, maintains class and racial inequalities, perpetuates dishonesty and greed, and has allowed disinformation and corruption (Lilleker, 2005; Gann, 2020). We have political representatives who are increasingly unrepresentative of the people they claim to speak for, with a representation gap that is particularly stark in the Conservative Party, where only 1 per cent of MPs come from working-class backgrounds (Quilter-Pinner et al, 2022). State power has always maintained class and racial inequality, but Brexit and the COVID-19 pandemic have revealed new, higher levels of corruption, cronyism and disinformation unparalleled in other developed northern states (Monbiot, 2021). As Monbiot (2021: 3) asserts, a once vaguely democratic nation is now sliding towards autocracy. The British public has become increasingly dissatisfied with both politics and their politicians over the past decade. But dissatisfaction has intensified since the election in 2019 of a populist and authoritarian Conservative government with little connection to traditional ideals of British democracy. In 2021, 80 per cent of UK citizens thought there was either 'a lot' or 'a fair amount' of corruption in British politics, with only 1 per cent thinking there was none (Richards, 2021). In terms of enabling a fairer, more socially just society, elite political will remains well behind public will on a number of key issues, including climate change, funding of private schooling, NHS funding and public sector pay (Toynbee, 2021). In short, our political elite are governing in their own narrow political self-interest, while a majority of the general public express a desire for an economically fairer society. It appears our political elites are even more in need of political education than the general public.

Yet, the democratic deficit apparent in the attitudes and actions of our governing elites is mirrored, to a lesser extent, among the general population. A need for informed political education is evident across all groups in English society. Research indicates that all sectors of society, including young people, have displayed increasing levels of intolerance towards 'the other' over the past four decades (Janmaat and Keating, 2019). The Introduction discussed the social class gap in relation to citizenship education, but across wider society there are glaring inequalities that further exacerbate the democratic deficit. In the 2017 election, social class differences in political engagement were stark. There was voter turnout of 35 per cent among young people who were either doing unskilled and semi-skilled work or were unemployed compared with a turnout of 65 per cent across the general population (Ipsos MORI, 2017). In particular, class and ethnic background plays an important role in the extent to which young people coming from different social groups have access to a political voice (Grasso and Giugni, 2021).

The state of English education

> Unlimited competition leads to a huge waste of labor, and to the crippling of the social consciousness of individuals. This crippling of individuals I consider the worst evil of capitalism. Our whole educational system suffers from this evil. An exaggerated competitive attitude is inculcated into the student, who is trained to worship acquisitive success as a preparation for his future career. (Einstein, 1949)

Studies of democratic deficit rarely focus on the role of educational institutions (Grasso et al, 2019), although see Allen (2017) and Mansell (2019) for exceptions. Yet, over the past 50 years, English education has become increasingly hollowed out by the prioritising of individualistic concerns over considerations of the common good. There has also been an intensification of the competition Einstein cautioned against over seventy years ago. Furthermore, public education has been virtually eliminated in England in the drive to introduce marketisation. In 2021, 91 per cent of secondary schools were academies, semi-privatised schools run by academy trusts, which are not-for-profit companies. Many draw on the rhetoric of emancipation and social mobility that characterises US charter schools catering for the poor (Stahl, 2019). However, in the US and the English education systems, meritocratic ideology entrenches and encodes social class distinctions through a multiplicity of rationing practices (Blood, 2022).

In pursuit of marketisation, academies, like American charter schools, have encouraged corporate and private interests to move into the educational system, enabling the control of wealthy private individuals over school policies. The underlying argument for markets in education has always been that competition drives improvement. As Kulz et al (2022: 12) argue: 'the academies programme is an instantiation of this position'. Such neoliberal education policy, with its prioritising of privatisation, competition and marketisation at the expense of providing a public education service, has resulted in the current 'misstructuring' of English education. The 21st century has ushered in an excess of school types, all with different funding regimes, modes of governance and varying levels of autonomy. We no longer have a democratically controlled state education system with a clear focus on shared social values. Instead, individualisation, competition, regulation and accountability are the hallmarks of English education, with negative consequences for civic engagement and democratic participation. English education has become increasingly fragmented and atomised, with a diminishing sense of collectivity and collaboration (Reay, 2017). This has had serious repercussions for both pupils' and teachers' sense of inclusion and democratic engagement. The OECD (2019) reported that in 78 per cent of education systems, students achieved more highly when they cooperated rather than competed with their peers. It also identified the UK as one of four countries, including the US and Brazil, where competition in schools was the most prevalent. Rather, the focus of learning has become one of fitting into 'the economic order of society' (Ideland et al, 2021), equipping students to compete against everyone else.

How this emphasis on individual excellence and hypercompetition is played out in English classrooms is evidenced in research carried out in 2019 (Reay, 2022). Forty five- and six-year-olds were interviewed about the learning incentive systems in their classrooms. While all children liked being designated a superstar, they also talked about being in the warning and caution zones as 'torture', 'shaming' and 'really upsetting'. As well as highlighting the pervasiveness of behaviour management across all stages of education, the research also revealed a harmful culture of self-centred excellence and ultra-competitiveness. Children talked about 'helping your friend being a form of cheating' and that they had to be 'the best of the best' in order to be seen as a really good learner. Over half the children said there could only be one or two superstars in a class, but that they felt a failure if they did not achieve superstar status. As Safstrom and Mansson (2021: 5) argue: 'focussing on the individual student's school performance devalues the public part of education such as fostering democracy and social change'. We have reached the deeply concerning position of achieving an educational system that prioritises discipline, control and individual excellence over creativity, critical thinking, collaboration and teamwork. However, Hoskins and Janmaat (2019) found in their survey of six European countries that it is working-class students in English schools who suffer the most from an excessive focus on discipline, as predominantly working-class schools prioritise highly managed disciplinary policies over the more liberal climate of open debate and discussion found in more advantaged schools. It is unsurprising then that in recent OECD international surveys (2019), England was bottom of the league table for skills that enhance democratic participation, namely critical thinking skills, creativity and deep learning. However, England was top of the league table for practices that impede democratic engagement, those of routine learning, repetition and drill (Knight, 2016). England's educational policy development has become a cautionary tale for other countries when it comes to how democratic citizenship can be nurtured or eroded.

As well as instantiating the privatisation of state schooling, academies are also part of a wider political 'turn to authoritarianism' (Kulz, 2017, p 2). In a further policy borrowing from the US, they often have the aggressive, zero-tolerance-style policies to be found in many US charter schools (Roberts, 2018). Such processes of authoritarianism are rooted in an intensification of monitoring and regulation, where behaviour, conduct and action are controlled through policies, practices and interventions designed to govern through conformity and the restriction of individual agency (Blood, 2022). As Raoul Martinez (2016) has argued:

> The combination of dress codes, rigid syllabi, set lessons, constant examination, hours of passive listening and an absence of internal democracy mean that schooldays are typically characterized by tight control. Study is geared to exams, which grants great power to those who set them and little autonomy to those who take them. Careful attention to a syllabus is rewarded over careful attention to one's curiosity. Regurgitation of facts is rewarded over originality, passionate engagement or independent thought. These arrangements prepare students for a society in which they have little say over the decisions that affect their lives. (Martinez, 2016, p 280)

Many English academies have an expanding control apparatus of behaviour hubs, isolation booths, and a range of behaviour and performance incentive schemes to manage poverty and deprivation rather than tackle it. Growing trends towards authoritarianism, hypercompetition and individualisation leave the English educational system in a poor position when it comes to closing the gap between the current democratic deficit and achieving a degree of healthy democratic engagement. In view of the divide we need to bridge, the next section discusses the feasibility of bridging the gap and then suggests possible ways forward.

Can we close the gap?

According to a House of Lords Select Committee on Citizenship and Civic Engagement (2018, para. 162): 'The Government has allowed citizenship education in England to degrade to a parlous state. The decline of the subject must be addressed in its totality as a matter of urgency.'

Before any educational system can act as a transformative force in relation to democratic ways of being, there must be a widespread understanding of the underlying structures that hold the status quo in place. A better comprehension of the factors that impede or facilitate active citizenship is vital. Changes at the level of curriculum and pedagogy are clearly necessary, in particular a shift in focus from individualised competition to collaboration and teamwork, alongside a move away from the excessive preoccupation with behaviour and discipline to an increasing emphasis on student participation through classroom debate and discussion. This must be accompanied by an emphasis on problem-solving and critical thinking skills in place of the current stress on repetition and drill. The current 'facts and phonics' approach to learning is failing all children (Wyse and Bradbury, 2022), but particularly those from working-class backgrounds.

The watered-down notion of citizenship that characterises much of citizenship education should be replaced by well-designed political education that emphasises and encourages active informed engagement in classrooms and beyond. However, such changes at the classroom level would need to be reinforced at the level of the education system and the wider economy. In order to have an educational system that facilitates rather than impedes democratic processes, changes must target all levels of the system. They would address macro concerns around structure, micro issues of teaching and learning in classrooms, as well as questions around the purpose of education, and the values that underpin it. The next section examines how the democratic potential of education can be enhanced through progressive pedagogic and curricular change before moving on to discuss the structural changes necessary.

Realising the potential of education through pedagogic and curricular change

Kahne et al (2021, p 2) make a strong case for the transformative potential of education, arguing that: 'Educational efforts have the potential to strengthen our weakened civic foundations by developing young people's understandings of and commitments to democratic norms and their abilities to practice them.' But there are worrying questions around whether our schools are able to act independently of partisan pressures in a period of the 21st century when it could be argued that one-sided political interests and ideologies have dictated educational policy and practice, including approaches to citizenship education (Morgan, 2017). There has been little political or professional response to our low international standing in relation to teaching critical thinking skills. A cross-national comparison of teachers' beliefs about the aims of civic education found that significantly fewer English teachers prioritised the promotion of critical and independent thinking (Reichert and Torney-Purta, 2019), compared to teachers in Nordic countries (64 per cent compared to 89 per cent in Denmark, 81 per cent in Finland and 84 per cent in Sweden). This is despite England faring far worse in terms of critical and individual thinking than the other three countries (OECD, 2019).

In *Pedagogy of the Oppressed* (1970), Paolo Freire wrote of education having one of two functions within society – as an instrument of conformity socialising younger generations into the logic of the existing system, in the present case, into compliance with neoliberal capitalism; or else, to operate as 'the practice of freedom', enabling children and young people to engage critically and reflexively with the society they are part of, and to learn how to participate in transforming it for the better. In contemporary England, education, with its emphasis on didactic rather than experiential ways of learning, approximates far more to 'the practice of compliance' than 'the practice of freedom' (Clarke et al, 2021).

bell hooks, the American feminist, has written about the idea of education as a collective practice of thinking together and making sense of the world. She asserts: 'To teach in a manner that respects and cares for the souls of our students is essential if we are to provide the necessary conditions where learning can most deeply and intimately begin' (hooks, 1994, p 13). Her educational model is based on intense personal relationships between students and teachers that aim to empower students to recognize their authority as legitimate knowers in the world. She claims that the most fertile ground for progressive social change is teaching critical skills to individuals rather than focusing on large-scale progressive social and political action. What is needed is an 'engaged pedagogy' that focuses on the self-actualisation, empowerment and wellbeing of students. For hooks, the most engaged and rewarding critical thinking is done with other people. It relies on collaborative efforts, like reasoning through problems in groups, to ensure that we are respectful and responsible to the interests and experiences of others as they relate to the issue at hand, and to ensure that as many potentially competing assumptions and perspectives can be raised to maintain the integrity of the critical thinking process (Sewell, 2013: 62). The practical wisdom (hooks, 2010) that grows out of critical thinking is both grounded in, and generates, empathy, care, compassion and understanding of both the self and others.

The need for structural change

Adopting socially just, inclusive pedagogies, such as those outlined by Freire and hooks, needs to be combined with educational reform to break down the hierarchical structures underpinning our educational system if democracy and democratic participation are to be enhanced. Currently, the class and racial inequalities sedimented into wider English society are reflected and reinforced in an educational system where reproductive rather than transformative practices work to suppress widespread civic engagement and validate and reward conformity and compliance with an inequitable status quo.

The English educational system has always been an elite hierarchical system. From its inception, English education has educated the different social classes for different social and economic purposes. Inequality is at the very core of our educational system, sedimented into its values and ethos. The private school system enables our political and economic elites to preserve their status and protect their privilege, creating citizens who see themselves as having more value and status than their state-educated counterparts (Beard, 2021). The latest research (Gamsu, 2021) shows that private schools have 3.7 times more income per student than the state sector. Private schools also remain as socially exclusive as they were 50 years ago, with just 1 per cent of their pupils on free bursaries (Verkaik, 2018). Their abolition would be one important step on the way to a more democratic, inclusive educational system.

But hierarchy and distinction making are increasingly hallmarks of our semi-privatised state system. Children and young people from different socioeconomic backgrounds are increasingly educated apart rather than together in schools that are predominantly middle or working class, or else in different ability sets within the same schools (Reay, 2017). As a consequence, our state educational system, no less than the private school system, is built on exclusion rather than inclusion – the educating of the different social classes in increasingly segregated spaces where ignorance, mistrust and stereotyping of 'the other' is a potent risk. Academies and free schools have exacerbated such processes of exclusion and segregation, and if we are to counter these, along with the development of hypercompetition, privatisation and harsh disciplinary cultures, one positive way forward would be to return academies to a form of local authority oversight that enables democratic pooling and a fair redistribution of resources. However, this should not be a return to a flawed past but a move forward that learns from the examples of educational systems that are successful in terms of educational attainment and achieving educational equality. The next section looks at two such examples.

Learning from others: international examples of good practice

Pasi Sahlberg (2021, p 233) argues that 'we should reconsider those education policies that advocate choice, competition and privatisation as the key drivers of sustained educational improvement. None of the best-performing education systems today rely primarily on them.' But he does not highlight the consequences of increased choice, competition and privatisation that lie in the growing polarisation within schooling, and the threat they pose for democracy.

Two of the best performing systems Sahlberg was referring to are in Finland[1] and Estonia (OECD, 2019). Both have prioritised collaboration,

---

[1] I suggest that there is a link between Finland's recent fall in the PISA rankings (Ahonen, 2021) and the introduction of a degree of deregulation into Finnish education. The drop has occurred during a period when Finland's regulations were relaxed to enable cities like Helsinki to pursue more free-market policies. These included introducing a degree of parental choice and enabling schools to select certain students on the basis of giftedness in areas such as music and languages (Dovemark et al, 2018).

excellent state provision and parity of schooling available over choice, competition and privatisation. They also combine high attainment with some of the most equitable outcomes of all the countries participating in PISA (Programme for International Student Assessment) (Tire, 2021; Ahonen, 2021). They both have a social class achievement gap that is a fraction of the one in England. Where our system valorises self-centred excellence, they prioritise the common good. In place of our incoherent, unfairly funded, fragmented system, they have comprehensive school systems that are well supported at national, regional and local levels. Both countries see the value of well-supported, highly trained and well-prepared teachers who merit considerable autonomy and respect. Their educational systems have a strong explicit focus on equality, and recognise the importance of providing adequate extra resources for both SEND (special educational needs and disabilities) and disadvantaged students. In response to the challenges of the 21st century, they have recently prioritised creativity and critical thinking in their curriculum offer. In the pressurised, inequitable, underfunded system we have in England, with the current preoccupation with performance, targets and accountability, there is little space for creativity, let alone critical thinking skills. Instead, we have growing mistrust and ignorance of those who are different from ourselves, as children continue to be educated in social class silos, and there is little attempt to ameliorate that mistrust and ignorance through either the provision of curriculum or pedagogic approaches.

Differences in policy and practice when it comes to citizenship education are also stark when we compare England with Finland. While curriculum reform in England has diminished formal programmes of study, the Finnish government has expanded how long citizenship education is taught as a separate compulsory subject across a child's education (Weinberg, 2019). Finland, along with Estonia, is one of only four countries in Europe that offers citizenship education as a compulsory separate subject throughout schooling, starting from primary level (Eurydice, 2017). In order to develop awareness of, and resilience to, fake news, it has extended the curriculum at both primary and secondary levels to include media literacy skills that combine fact checking with critical thinking skills (Quicke, 2020), an innovation that has kept the country at the top of international media literacy index for the past three years (Lessenski, 2021). Also, while England has moved towards more knowledge-based programmes of study, Finland has focused on providing more time and space for student participation. In 2017, England was one of only 9 out of the 42 education systems evaluated by Eurydice (2017, p 81) where the Department of Education issued no guidance on citizenship education to teachers. The expectation in Finland is that citizenship education should enable and enhance students' learning to become democratic individuals. In contrast, citizenship education in contemporary England has become less of a vehicle for political literacy and critical debate in schools, and more of a policy tool to address government concerns about national unity and developing 'character' and individual responsibility (Weinberg, 2019). As such, it approximates more to undemocratic than democratic education, imposition from above instead of engagement from below.

Education for democracy

As John Dewey warned over 80 years ago, we cannot assume that democracy is able to 'perpetuate itself automatically' (Dewey, 1939, p 225). He argued that it was imperative that individuals learnt to participate effectively and reflexively in civic and political institutions. In order for this to happen, Dewey asserted that schools must be able to cultivate democratic commitments and ways of being. In place of the contemporary focus on facts and phonics, we need to develop young people's problem-solving, critical thinking and teamwork skills. What we also learn from Dewey is that citizenship education, however good it is, is no solution to the ills of democratic governance on its own. Democratic inclusive curricula and pedagogies need to infuse all subject learning not just the citizenship education classroom (Claes and Hooghe, 2017). But beyond the curriculum, 'schools themselves should be democratically governed and allow pupils to play a role in this process so that they become socialized into the norms guiding democratic interaction and decision making' (Dewey, 1916).

For Dewey, democracy was first and foremost about working together cooperatively across differences:

> Democracy as a way of life is controlled by personal faith in personal day-by-day working together with others. Democracy is the belief that even when needs and ends or consequences are different for each individual, the habit of amicable cooperation—which may include, as in sport, rivalry and competition—is itself a priceless addition to life. (Dewey, 1939, p 228)

But for cooperative fellowship across social differences to happen in contemporary English society, there needs to be a reversion of the increasing social class segregation within the educational system and wider society, and a halt to the growing gap between rich and poor. In *Democracy and Education*, Dewey (1916) argued that the purpose of education should be oriented towards 'the common good'. He recognised that traditional forms of education would always fail to achieve this, with their primary goal of adjusting individuals 'to fit into the present social arrangements and conditions' (quoted in Carr and Hartnett, 1996, p 61). Social control rather than democracy was and still is the priority. In contrast, Dewey (1916, p 87) viewed democracy as providing 'a form of associated living, a conjoint, communicated experience'. Education thus provided a generative space in which students across differences of class background could, according to Dewey, 'learn to understand themselves as democratic individuals by becoming members of a democratic community in which the problems of communal life are resolved through collective deliberation and a shared concern for the common good' (Carr and Hartnett, 1996, p 63).

Conclusion

As Safstrom and Mansson (2021, p 8) point out: 'Market-driven schools tend to expel the "public" from public education and to exchange "public" with private interests and skills needed to be ahead of the other in competition.' But in 21st-century England, the need to reclaim the 'public' has never been greater. Post-Brexit and COVID-19, we have continuing austerity in England and abroad, a global refugee crisis, and a growing climate emergency that requires, above all, an educational system that fosters responsibility towards other people, regardless of their differences from ourselves. Moving towards a more caring, informed and tolerant citizenry necessitates putting the public and the political back into citizenship education. But, if we are to claim the common good, it also requires that democratic, inclusive and participatory ways of learning and interacting infuse all of the educational system at a time when the UK government is seeking to further inhibit democratic debate.

The latest DfE guidelines on tackling political and social issues in schools (Adams, 2022a) will stifle rather than encourage active political engagement, and discourage informed debate on issues, such as Black Lives Matter and the British Empire, that the Conservative government deem to be politically contentious. Even before the introduction of the new guidelines, a YouGov survey found that only 12 per cent of teachers surveyed felt empowered to teach so-called 'controversial' issues, such as colonialism, migration and identity (Adams, 2022b). As Mary Bousted, joint general secretary of the National Education Union, stated, the new guidance could 'induce such a level of uncertainty and caution in schools about "political issues" that they are even less likely to engage with them', leading to pupils being 'denied the opportunity to engage with the most challenging issues of our time' (quoted in Smith, 2022).

We need an ethos that is grounded in learning from all our 'others', not just the privileged few who think they know best. In fact, returning to a point made earlier in the chapter, our governing elite need political education as much if not more than the rest of the population. As Claes and Hooghe (2017) caution, excellent democratic education cannot compensate for the negative impact of political scandals and corruption. Even good citizenship education does not offer a solution to the wider structural problems embedded in the political system.

Excellent citizenship education would need to be allied with radical changes at the level of the education system. One progressive way forward would be to learn from what Danny Dorling (2016) called 'new Finnish cooperation rather than old English competition'. There are now almost a thousand cooperative schools in England, founded on values of self-help, democracy, collaboration, equality and solidarity. And while enacting such values is far more difficult than proclaiming a commitment to them (Sumroy, 2022), the principles underpinning the cooperative movement are more inclusive and democratic than the values of competition, self-interest, hierarchy and elitism that the current system is founded on.

More broadly, English society requires 'the levelling up' that is constantly promised but never delivered. England will not have a functioning democracy if vast swathes of the working classes are disaffected and disenfranchised, excluded politically and impoverished economically. As a lifelong political activist, campaigning for education equality and social justice for the working classes, both in education and wider society, I have seen the promise of a fairer society constantly disappear behind a receding horizon. But, despite a sense of acting to little avail, we need more not less grassroots activism and campaigning. It is clear we can neither rely on nor trust our political and economic elites when there is irrefutable evidence that they constantly act in their own narrow self-interest, both in education and beyond (Thomson, 2020).

Perhaps, with this three-pronged approach of excellent citizenship education, an educational system with cooperative values and practices, and vigorous efforts to build democracy up from the grassroots, it might just be possible to achieve a functioning democracy.

References

Adams, R. (2022a) 'Guidance on political impartiality in English classrooms "confusing" say teachers' unions', *The Guardian*, 17 February.

Adams, R. (2022b) 'Troy Deeney calls for more diversity in English schools' curriculum: footballer and father says children should be given a "balanced and inclusive understanding" of Britain', *The Guardian*, 23 February.

Ahonen, A. (2021) 'Finland: success through equity – the trajectories in PISA performance', in N. Crato (ed) *Improving a Country's Education: PISA 2018 Results in 10 Countries*, New York: Springer, pp 121–36.

Allen, A. (2017) 'The academy revolution is ousting governors', Democratic Audit, 26 January: www.democraticaudit.com/2017/01/26/the-academy-revolution-is-ousting-school-governors-we-need-to-hold-these-schools-accountable/

Baker, W. (forthcoming) 'Children's centres, families, and food insecurity in a time of crisis', *British Educational Research Journal*.

Beard, R. (2021) *Sad Little Men: Private Schools and the Ruin of England*, London: Harvill Secker.

Blood, K. (2022) 'The great education "permanent revolution"? Shape shifting academies and degrees of change (and "success")', in C. Kulz, K. Morrin and R. McGinty (eds) *Inside the English Education Lab: Critical Qualitative and Ethnographic Perspectives on the Academies Experiment*, Manchester: Manchester University Press, Ch 4.

Brighouse, T. (2017) 'How can we tackle hate crime with four school systems?', *The Guardian*, 27 February: www.theguardian.com/education/2017/feb/28/hate-crime-schoolbritish- values-tim-brighouse

Carr, W. and Hartnett, A. (1996) *Education and the Struggle for Democracy*, Buckingham: Open University Press.

Claes, E. and Hooghe, M. (2017) 'The effect of political science education on political trust and interest: results from a 5-year panel study', *Journal of Political Science Education*, 13(1): 33–45.

Clarke, M., Haines Lyon, C., Walker, E., Walz, L., Collet, J. and Pritchard, K. (2021) 'The banality of education policy: discipline as extensive evil in the neoliberal era', *Power and Education*, 13(3): 187–204.

Conover, P.J. and Searing, D.D. (2000) 'A political socialization perspective', in L. McDonnell, P.M. Timpane and R.W. Benjamin (eds) *Rediscovering the Democratic Purposes of Education*, Lawrence, KS: University Press of Kansas, pp 91–124.

Department for Education (DfE) (2022) Statistics on the Size and Characteristics of the Schools' Workforce in State-Funded Schools: www.gov.uk/government/collections/statistics-school-workforce

Dewey, J. (1916) *Democracy and Education: An Introduction to the Philosophy of Education*, New York: Macmillan.

Dewey, J. (1939) 'Creative democracy: the task before us', in J.A. Bodyston (ed) (1976) *John Dewey: The Later Works*, Carbondale, IL: Southern Illinois University Press, pp 224–30.

Dorling, D. (2016) 'England's schools make us the extremists of Europe', *The Guardian*, 23 February: https://www.theguardian.com/education/2016/feb/23/england-schools-extremists-europe-tests-excludes-elitism

Dovemark, M., Kosunen, S., Kauko, J., Magnúsdóttir, B., Hansen, P. and Rasmussen, P. (2018) 'Deregulation, privatisation and marketisation of Nordic comprehensive education: social changes reflected in schooling', *Education Inquiry*, 9(1): 122–41.

Einstein, A. (1949) Why socialism?, *Monthly Review*, 1(1): https://monthlyreview.org/2009/05/01/why-socialism/

Eurydice (2017) *Eurydice Brief: Citizenship Education in School in Europe*, Brussels: European Education and Culture Executive Agency (European Commission).

Freire, P. (1970) *Pedagogy of the Oppressed*, London: Continuum.

Gamsu, S. (2021) 'Why are some children worth more than others?: The private-state school funding gap in England', Common-Wealth: www.common-wealth.co.uk/reports/why-are-some-children-worth-more-than-others

Gann, N. (2020) 'Recapturing the castle: looking to the de-corporatisation of schools and a post-viral revival of educational values', FORUM, 62(2): 405–21.

Grasso, M. and Giugni, M. (2021) 'Youth doing politics in times of increasing inequalities', *Politics*, 42(1): 3–12.

Grasso, M., Farrall, S., Gray, E., Hay, C. and Jennings, W. (2019) 'Socialisation and generational political trajectories: an age, period and cohort analysis of political participation in Britain', *Journal of Elections, Public Opinion and Parties*, 29(2): 199–221.

hooks, b. (1994) *Teaching to Transgress: Education as the Practice of Freedom*, New York: Routledge.

hooks, b. (2010) *Teaching Critical Thinking: Practical Wisdom*, New York: Routledge.

Hoskins, B. and Janmaat, J. (2019) *Education, Democracy and Inequality: Political Engagement and Citizenship Education in Europe*, London: Palgrave Macmillan.

House of Lords (2018) *The Ties that Bind: Citizenship and Civic Engagement in the 21st Century*, HL 2017-2019 (118), London: UK Parliament.

Ideland, M., Jobér, A. and Axelsson, T. (2021) 'Problem solved! How edupreneurs enact a school crisis as business possibilities', *European Educational Research Journal*, 20(1): 83–101.

Ipsos MORI (2017) 'How the voters voted in 2017 election' Ipsos MORI: https://www.ipsos.com/sites/default/files/2017-06/how-britain-voted-in-the-2017-election_2.pdf

Janmaat, J. and Keating, A. (2019) 'Are today's youth more tolerant? Trends in tolerance among young people in Britain', *Ethnicities*, 19(1): 44–65.

Kahne, J., Rogers, J. and Kwako, A. (2021) 'Do politics in our democracy prevent schooling for our democracy? Civic education in highly partisan times', *Democracy and Education*, 29(2): 1–18.

Kisby, B. (2017) 'Politics is ethics done in public: exploring linkages and disjunctions between citizenship education and character education in England', *Journal of Social Science Education*, 16(3): 7–20.

Knight, J. (2016) 'England is bottom of the league when it comes to deep learning. And top for drill and practice. It's no coincidence', *Times Educational Supplement*.

Kulz, C. (2017) *Factories for Learning*, Manchester: Manchester University Press.

Kulz, C., Morrin, K. and McGinty, R. (eds) (2022) *Inside the English Education Lab: Critical Qualitative and Ethnographic Perspectives on the Academies Experiment*, Manchester: Manchester University Press.

Lessenski, M. (2021) *Media Literacy Index 2021: Double Trouble: Resilience to Fake News at Time of Covid-19 Infodemic*, Sofia: Open Society Policy Institute.

Lilleker, D. (2005) 'Political marketing: The cause of an emerging democratic deficit in Britain?', *Journal of Nonprofit & Public Sector Marketing*, 14(1/2): 5–26.

Mansell, W. (2019) 'Businessmen in near-complete control of schools educating more than 100,000 pupils, new analysis by Education Uncovered shows', Education Uncovered, 6 November: www.educationuncovered.co.uk/news/143236/businessmen-in-nearcomplete-control-of-schools-educating-more-than-100000-pupils-new-analysis-by-education-uncovered-shows.thtm

Martinez, R. (2016) *Creating Freedom: Power, Control and the Fight for our Freedom*, London: Canongate.

Monbiot, G. (2021) 'Dear Labour, fight for us now before the battle is lost', *The Guardian*, 8 December.

Morgan, N. (2017) *Taught, Not Caught: Educating for 21st Century Character*, London: John Catt Educational.

OECD (2019) *PISA 2018 Results (Volume III): What School Life Means for Students' Lives*, Geneva: OECD: www.oecd-ilibrary.org/education/pisa-2018-results-volume-iii_c414e291-en

Osler, A. and Starkey, H. (2001) 'Citizenship education and national identities in France and England: Inclusive or exclusive?', *Oxford Review of Education*, 27(2): 287–305.

Power, S., Frandji, D. and Vitale, P. (2021) 'The cultural making of the citizen: a comparative analysis of school students' civic and political participation in France and Wales', *Compare: A Journal of Comparative and International Education*, 51(8): 1226–40.

Quicke, A. (2020) 'Media literacy education in Finland', Nordic Policy Centre: www.nordicpolicycentre.org.au/media_literacy_education_in_finland

Quilter-Pinner, H., Patel, P., O'Grady, T. and Colligan, S. (2022) *Closing the Gap: Parliament, Representation and the Working Class*, London: IPPR.

Reay, D. (2017) *Miseducation: Inequality, Education and the Working Classes*, Bristol: Policy Press.

Reay, D. (2022) 'From worse to worse: Why is it so difficult to change English education for the better?', FORUM, 64(1): 9–18.

Reichert, F. and Torney-Purta, J. (2019) 'A cross-national comparison of teachers' beliefs about the aims of civic education in 12 countries: a person-centred analysis', *Teaching and Teacher Education*, 77: 112–25.

Richards, X. (2021) 'Just one in 100 Brits think UK politics has "no corruption", poll finds', *The National*, 11 November: www.thenational.scot/news/19711838.just-one-100-brits-think-uk-politics-no-corruption-poll-finds/

Roberts, J. (2018) 'No excuses for charter schools: how disproportionate discipline of students with disabilities violates federal law', *Oklahoma Law Review*, 70 (3): https://digitalcommons.law.ou.edu/olr/vol70/iss3/6

Safstrom, C. and Mansson, N. (2021) 'The marketization of education and the democratic deficit', *European Educational Research Journal*, 17(5): 621–30.

Sahlberg, P. (2021) *Finnish Lessons: What Can the World Learn from Educational Change in Finland?*, New York: Teachers College Press.

Sewell, J. (2013) 'bell hooks on critical thinking: the successes and limitations of practical wisdom', PhD thesis, Canada: University of Windsor.

Smith, E. (2022) 'DfE guidance on politically impartial teaching called "confusing" by teachers' unions', TheSchoolBus, 17 February: www.theschoolbus.net/news/featured-article/dfe-guidance-on-politically-impartial-teaching-called-confusing-by-teachers-unions/8939

Stahl, G. (2019) 'Critiquing the corporeal curriculum: body pedagogies in 'no excuses' charter schools', *Journal of Youth Studies*, 23(10): 1330–46.

Sumroy, A. (2022) '"We're not robots!": the interaction of cooperativism and neoliberalism for students at a co-op academy', *British Journal of Sociology of Education*, 43(2): 278–95.

Thomson, P. (2020) *School Scandals: Blowing the Whistle on the Corruption of our Educational System*, Bristol: Policy Press.

Tire, G. (2021) 'Estonia: a positive PISA experience', in N. Crato (ed) *Improving a Country's Education: PISA 2018 Results in 10 Countries*, New York: Springer, pp 101–20.

Toynbee, P. (2021) 'Fear for a party that sees Boris Johnson as too far to the left', *The Guardian*, 14 December.

Verkaik, R. (2018) *Posh Boys: How English Public Schools Ruin Britain*, London: Oneworld.

Weinberg, J. (2019) 'Who's listening to whom? The UK House of Lords and evidence-based policy-making on citizenship education', *Journal of Education Policy*, 36(4): 576–99.

Weinberg, J. (2022) 'Civic education as an antidote to inequalities in political participation? New evidence from English secondary education', *British Politics*, 17: 185–209.

Weinberg, J. and Flinders, M. (2018) 'Learning for democracy: the practice and politics of citizenship education in the United Kingdom', *British Educational Research Journal*, 44(4): 573–92.

Wyse, D. and Bradbury, A. (2022) 'Reading wars or reading reconciliation? A critical examination of robust research evidence, curriculum policy and teachers' practices for teaching phonics and reading', *Review of Education*, 10(1), e3314: https://doi.org/10.1002/rev3.3314

3

Classroom conflict, 'divisive concepts' and educating for democracy

Barrett Smith and Sarah M. Stitzlein

Increasingly, teachers in the US are afraid to take up contentious issues in their classrooms. These fears have been exacerbated by calls on the Right and the Left. On the Right, newly proposed and enacted laws seek to limit what and how some significant social, historical and political matters – described as 'divisive' in the legislation – are discussed in schools. A more generous reading of these policies suggests that they seek to stamp out discussions that might cause tension, disagreement, or discomfort in a spirit of seeking harmony and consensus. A more nefarious interpretation of these policies suggests that they are trying to restrict how concepts, such as race and equity, are taught in schools, prohibiting alternative, often more complex historical accounts that portray systemic injustice, or might raise feelings of shame. Because of their pressing and formal nature, we focus more on legislative action on the Right in this chapter. But some on the Left have made less formal suggestions that also chill classroom environments and limit the ability to teach citizenship well. These include calls for rather extreme forms of safety, where it is argued that students should be protected from topics that might upset them. It also includes silencing or 'cancelling' people who make some contentious claims, rather than working through the conflict they cause or talking about the substance of their claims.[1]

In either case, Right or Left, avoiding confrontations or silencing an array of views on controversial issues fails to prepare good citizens capable of navigating partisan divides. Political divisions have recently grown even more worrisome, as most Republicans and Democrats have admitted that members of the other party 'stirred feelings of anger and fear in them' (Pew Research Center, 2016). Rather than safe spaces free from political controversy or conciliatory spaces aimed at simply smoothing over divisions and the emotions they provoke, we need educative spaces where careful and

---

[1] Admittedly, though, some claims are not worthy of attention because they are untrue or seriously problematic in some other way.

constructive conflict takes place, modelling civility and good civic discourse for students (Stitzlein, 2021).

It is worth pausing to mention that these clashes and disputes about the practices and outcomes of schooling are not necessarily harmful. Taking time to collectively reconsider, deliberate and decide 'What should we do?' is a core element of democracy (Levine, 2016). Stakeholders' answers to this question will often be diverse and even conflicting. How we navigate these sorts of 'wicked' questions – where there are no clear or correct answers – should be a social, democratic process. It depends upon a relationality between citizens that communications scholars Keith and Danisch (2020, p 24) rightly proclaim as the 'heart of democratic culture'. This social fabric of relationality exists with inherent tensions, which moments of democratic decision-making often reveal and heighten. The key is to maintain that social fabric through the appropriate resolution of tensions. This skill requires practice, a commitment to civility, and an acknowledgment of shared fate, sacrifice and trust (Allen, 2004). The current climate of hyperpartisanship constrains and causes damage to our relational social fabric. Isolation into political echo chambers thins the threads and connections of our social fabric, jeopardising trust and a commitment to shared fate. Dissent and deliberation may be messy and imperfect, but that mess is not only a feature of democracy but also a strength that allows us to collaboratively create more robust and responsive solutions to the wicked questions we face.

This chapter will briefly review recent legislation that handcuffs teachers as they educate budding citizens. Such legislation is symptomatic of a larger political manoeuvre to control educational content, limit the influence of teachers, and reshape the knowledge and skills taught to developing citizens in schools. Recognising that political controversies are not best swept under the rug or silenced under the guise of political neutrality, this chapter offers an educative pathway forward, one intended to help us address partisan battles and foreground learning to be better citizens. It will illuminate some of the ways in which students can learn to use civility and dissent to navigate politically contentious topics, bridge hyperpartisanship, solve shared problems and revive democracy.

Divisive concepts, divisive legislation

Throughout 2021, state legislatures across the US worked to pass laws banning the teaching of certain concepts and histories in schools (Berkshire, 2021), despite 'firm opposition' from notable educational and historical organisations (American Historical Association, 2021). In the US, 'public' schools are funded by taxpayers, overseen by democratically elected boards, and open to all students. Proposed legislation targeted these schools, largely ignoring 'private' schools that are funded by tuition, overseen by organisations or religious groups, and selective in their admissions. Hence, our following discussion of 'schools' is focused mostly on public schools as targets of this legislation.

Many of the proposed laws were authored in response to the 1619 Project, a project sponsored by *The New York Times*, which recentres Black Americans in the historical narrative of the US, including highlighting their contributions and experiences related to the lingering consequences of slavery. In reaction, the legislation targeted certain ways of teaching about race, often misidentified as 'critical race theory' (CRT).[2] These laws labelled certain understandings of race and gender as well as racism and sexism as 'divisive concepts', which should be banned from public schools. For example, in some states 'divisive concepts' include 'white privilege' and 'systemic racism'. Rhode Island introduced a bill to mandate that 'any contract, grant or training program entered into by the state or any municipality include provisions prohibiting teaching divisive concepts and prohibit making any individual discomfort, guilty, anguish or any distress on account of their race or sex' (H 6070). Similarly, other states, like Iowa and Oklahoma, have prohibited teaching divisive concepts that cause students to 'feel discomfort, guilt, anguish, or any other form of psychological distress' about their own race/gender, or indoctrinating students (HF 802, Sec 2.1.a.8; SB 803, Sec.1.A.1.h). In proposed legislation in the state of Ohio, divisive concepts include teaching that the 'United States is fundamentally racist' or 'assigning fault, blame, or bias to a nationality, color, ethnicity, race, religion, or sex' (HB 327 Sec.3313.6027.A.1.b, A.3).

Some states developed pipelines for reporting and punishing teachers and/or schools who are perceived to be teaching divisive concepts (Marias, 2021; Greene, 2021a; NC Family Policy Council, 2021; Pulliam, 2021). And under the guise of increasing parental oversight of the curriculum, some states have proposed putting cameras in classrooms. This could enable outsiders to oversee when and how teachers invoke divisive concepts (Edelman, 2022). Citizens have even been encouraged to report violations of divisive concept laws by organisations that offer bounties for doing so. For example, Moms for Liberty in New Hampshire is offering $500 for the first person who 'successfully catches a public-school teacher breaking this law' (Greene, 2021b). Money, a common motivator in school districts, is wielded as a stick rather than a carrot, as some laws penalise districts with fines or loss of state funding for instances of teaching divisive concepts.

---

[2] Critical race theory generally posits that 'racism is ordinary, not aberrational' and emphasises racism as a systemic – rather than individual – historical and ongoing process within the US (Delgado and Stafancic, 2012).

Throughout 2021, heated demonstrations were stoked by faulty allegations that 'districts around the country have integrated CRT into school curricula' (Butcher and Gonzalez, 2020). While CRT is not widely taught at the primary or secondary level, some of its key ideas and vocabulary, such as equity, have increasingly made their way into classrooms and professional development seminars. The demonstrations, however, go too far in painting a false image of teachers as radical activists working to indoctrinate students into specific understandings of race and racism (Berkshire, 2021; Heim et al, 2021). Even if potential threats to teachers or schools do not materialize on a significant scale, there are wider detrimental effects. The larger narrative that the education system has been wholly infiltrated by a dangerous, anti-American ideology (Butcher and Gonzalez, 2020; Sullivan, 2021) erodes public trust in schools and teachers (Berkshire, 2021; Greene, 2021b). In short, this current movement may undermine and damage prospects for democratic education.

Divisive concept bills create a minefield for practising teachers. One particularly interesting example is Texas House Bill 3979,[3] 'Relating to the social studies curriculum in public schools'. This bill mandates that curricula 'develop each student's civic knowledge including an understanding of ... the history of white supremacy, including but not limited to the institution of slavery, the eugenics movement, and the Ku Klux Klan, and the ways in which it is morally wrong' (28.002.h-2.7). However, a teacher 'may not require or make part of a course the concept that: one race or sex is inherently superior to another race or sex ... slavery and racism are anything other than deviations from, betrayals of, or failures to live up to, the authentic founding principles of the United States which include liberty and equality' (28.002.h-3.4.B.i, x). The teacher is thus in a double bind: explicitly required to teach about white supremacy, but without teaching the concept of racial superiority or the ways in which some past and present white policy makers have intentionally shaped laws to favour some citizens over others while appearing or claiming to be equitable. Teachers are thus required to teach the history of race and racism in the US but forbidden to use the 'wrong' materials (for example, the 1619 Project) or come to the 'wrong' conclusions (suggesting racism might be systemic and contemporary).

At best, these sorts of laws are a mandate to teach issues of racism as strictly historical, rather than ongoing. At worst, it places teachers between a rock and a hard place, having to simultaneously teach about race and racism without making any sort of connection to students' contemporary experiences. Importantly, the Texas bill (HB 3979) explicitly provides protections for

---

[3] This bill was passed into law on 15 June 2021 with an effective date of 1 September 2021 (HB 3979, Texas, 2021).

students at the same time as it lays a trap for teachers: forbidding any actions that may 'result in the punishment of a student for discussing or have a chilling effect on student discussion of, the concepts described [above]' (28.002.h-5). Similar protections for teachers are noticeably absent, while the focus is on reprimanding teachers who raise these topics. This sort of space, where students can discuss challenging topics without fear of repercussion, is crucial but incomplete if those same protections are not also extended to teachers, especially given the importance of teachers in helping to ensure that student contributions are engaged in educative ways. Worse, the bill contains the same 'discomfort' clause mentioned previously, prohibiting teachers from teaching a concept that causes students to 'feel discomfort, guilt, anguish, or psychological distress' on account of their race or sex (28.002.h-3.4.B.vii). These clauses and lack of protections have led to teachers facing consequences including fines or termination for addressing controversial topics in the 'wrong' ways (Greene, 2021c; Marias, 2021).

Finally, some laws, such as the one proposed in Ohio, go beyond just limiting the discussion of controversial topics and forbid assignments or class activities that ask students 'to advocate for or against a specific topic or point of view' (HB 327 Sec. 3313.6027.B.1). Such assignments don't even have to be about divisive concepts; they are banned for all topics. This curtails opportunities for students to learn how to make an argument for a position or engage in discussion about opposed perspectives, regardless of the topic. Clearly, such skills are essential to living in a democracy, where citizens must weigh competing viewpoints and deliberate together.

Within the context of educating for democracy, divisive concepts might better be viewed as 'open' issues. Diana Hess, scholar of democratic discussion, distinguishes 'open' versus 'settled' issues. 'Open' issues are those where multiple reasonable positions can be taken, while 'settled' issues only have one reasonable position. Open issues, then, offer important opportunities for learning by introducing multiple perspectives and considering the merits of competing positions, while settled issues should be taught more directly and competing positions debunked, if mentioned at all (Hess, 2009; Hess and McAvoy, 2015).

Democracy flourishes with a diversity of views and beliefs, and democracy progresses when citizens wrestle with open controversies and solve public problems, including how to understand race and gender, and how to alleviate racism and sexism. Recent divisive concepts and related legislation rest on the premise that some interpretations of history (for example, the 1619 Project's centring of race in interpreting and understanding US history) are divisive to the point of danger (Sullivan, 2021). Engaging differing interpretations on open issues, accompanied by high-quality supporting evidence, offers students an opportunity to carefully consider and resolve competing perspectives. Even noxious historical concepts can and should be taught in schools – with appropriate context – to give students realistic, holistic and robust understandings of history. This is at the very heart of democracy. Banning evidence-based historical interpretation as 'too divisive' limits, rather than cultivates, students' civic skills.

These legislative efforts[4] are concerning because they work to intimidate, or even silence teachers who would otherwise take up contentious issues in their classrooms, including important elements of American history and life today, such as persistent racism and sexism. Perhaps most worrisome for the citizens being cultivated in our schools today, these laws create a legal basis for undermining crucial elements of teaching for democracy: open discussion, deliberation and dissent regarding unsettled political issues. The climate surrounding these bills, one that is breeding distrust of fellow citizens, especially teachers, exemplifies the need to better prepare our children not just for some future participation in an ideal democracy, but for the very sorts of contentious debates occurring right now in their struggling communities.

Civility and the fabric of democracy

In light of our deeply divided political communities, where fear and distrust undergird growing shouting matches at school meetings, we need civility – and we need to teach it – more than ever. Whereas civility is typically described as being polite and respectful, especially in our tone and the content of what we say, civility should be understood in a richer way as a form of responsiveness to others. When we act with civility, we acknowledge the dignity and humanity of our interlocutors, responding to them in ways that foreground our commitment to each other and to ongoing, just dialogue. Democracy depends upon this commitment to ongoing dialogue, for it is often necessary to solve shared problems. Keith and Danisch (2020) assert that democracy is undergirded not by abstract interaction or mere exchange of words and ideas, but by the relationships between members. They explain that 'many of the things associated with democracy – in particular, argument and deliberation – are constituted by specific kinds of relationships rather than (just) forms of speech'. This relationality is at the heart of Keith and Dansich's (2020) conception of 'civility'.

---

[4] It is worth briefly noting the legal landscape in the US is currently undergoing significant shifts, especially the conservative turn of the Supreme Court. The summer of 2022 – when this chapter was being reviewed and edited – saw a flurry of decisions curtailing abortion rights, rolling back the rights of arrestees, limiting the oversight powers of regulatory agencies, and allowing for public funding of private religious schools. Given this conservative shift, it seems more likely that the laws outlined in this section may survive judicial challenges.

Within this underlying social fabric, citizens are tied together in a sense of shared fate. This spirit of 'being in it together' recognises that our lives and outcomes in democracies are often intertwined, that we not only influence each other but also depend on each other (Ben-Porath, 2006). Moreover, democratic theorist Danielle Allen (2004, p xxi) suggests that the key to our relational ties as citizens is friendship, where friendship

> is not an emotion, but a practice, a set of hard-won, complicated habits that are used to bridge trouble, difficulty, and differences of personality, experience, and aspiration. ... Friendship begins in the recognition that friends have a *shared* life – not a 'common' nor an identical life – only one with common events, climates, built-environments, fixations of the imagination, and social structures.

The relational fabric is maintained through deliberation and collective decision-making, where we establish our trustworthiness with each other and forge friendships. These interactions, though, inevitably create shifting tensions between political friends. Keith and Danisch (2020) describe the fragility of the network and potential ways in which the social fabric may be 'threatened by plural opinions and beliefs that could tear it apart at any moment'. Perhaps this concern is also reflected by some, less nefarious, supporters of divisive concepts legislation, who seek to avoid discussions that might further separate our already struggling, polarised citizenry. We propose, however, that it may be better to understand tension as a potential source of strength, rather than just as a threat. Like the sail of a ship, tension arising from dialogue and deliberation can propel us forward. It can goad new ideas and potential solutions that otherwise might not have arisen. Tears in the fabric occur not because of the tension itself, but because of fraying connections between members, nodes in the network, indicating disruptions of dialogue, distrust of others, and more. With strong relational connections between members, tension can be productive.

Wholeness and dissent in democracy and in classrooms

Good political dissent sparks conversation and brings forward new ideas about how to best understand our world and live together in it, thereby keeping democracy attuned to the needs and experiences of its citizens. It entails critiquing the status quo, raising consciousness about problematic views or practices, and putting forward alternatives, sometimes building movements around those new ideas or invoking democratic structures to pursue change. In this way, it improves our civic inquiry because it breaks up group thinking and pushes citizens to more actively reflect on their experiences, allegiances and opinions so that the decision-making is more informed and just. When dissent clears the way for more informed decision-making, produces better solutions, and foregrounds the common good or justice for certain populations who are being harmed in some way, dissent can lead to more just and better living, thereby working to patch and enhance the social fabric (Stitzlein, 2014).

While some proponents of bills that ban the teaching of divisive concepts might seek a democracy where the citizenry is united as one, instead we follow Allen (2004) in celebrating, striving for 'wholeness'. To complement the social fabric metaphor, wholeness conveys a cohesive community that is tied together in relationships, commitments to democratic principles and shared fate. 'Oneness', however, homogenises the individual nodes and may erase dissent to smooth over differences or competing views on significant political matters. Oneness, then, risks good civic reasoning and our ability to solve problems together well in a democracy, while wholeness encourages a commitment to hearing the voices of and ensuring the wellbeing of everyone, including (and often even foregrounding) those whose views and experiences differ from the norm.

Good dissent brings forward new ideas and encourages productive discussion among members. While we strive for good dissent, teachers must be prepared to address an array of forms of dissent in the classroom. Dissent in the classroom won't always be well crafted or carefully framed to cultivate further discussion. But the classroom is a learning environment, and the instructor's role is to draw out the good, create learning opportunities and nurture effort.

A crucial skill for teachers in cultivating good dissent is effective framing and platforming, which should identify and draw out student responses in such a way that promotes robust inquiry, thoughtful discussion and learning. Improper framing when engaging harmful statements, absurd opinions, or takes on settled issues can give them inappropriate credence that ultimately harms our ability to deliberate. To borrow Hess's (2009) terminology, debating the basic facts of settled issues does little to effectively develop students' abilities to dissent well; rather, teachers should be careful to (re)focus class discussions on open issues. Harmful claims about particular people or populations may warrant an outright public rebuttal from the teacher or a redirecting comment where a deeper conversation happens one on one after class. It can even be as simple as revealing the implications of a claim on a classmate or other citizen and asking the utterer a key civic question posed by Allen (2004, p 140): 'would I treat a friend this way?' The focus should be on ongoing inquiry, educative conversations and supporting the relational fabric in the classroom.

This sort of framing and acknowledgement of open vs. settled issues are the key to fostering discussions of controversial or divisive issues. The history of all nations and cultures is full of facts and events that rightly make us uncomfortable. Turning away from or hiding these issues limits students' historical understanding and ability to understand contemporary issues, which emerge from that historical context. While teachers ought to certainly exercise their professional judgement about the developmental maturity of their students in presenting information, we ought to teach settled history.

Take, for example, the perpetually thorny issue of racism in the US. It is not possible to honestly and fully teach the history of the US (or even the historical context of many works of American literature) without encountering horrific instances of historical or contemporary racism. While some textbooks try to sanitise and obscure this history (Goldstein, 2020), any sober look at the historical record is clear. As teachers, we ought to present these settled histories and reserve discussion and deliberation for related issues that remain open and unsettled. For example, how to grapple with the historical legacies of discrimination is still very much an open question (Coates, 2014), worthy of discussion in our schools. It is not appropriate, however, to frame discussion in ways that students are invited to argue for historical atrocities or the limitations of others' rights on the basis of protected categories such as race. While there is room for tension, deliberation and constructive dissent around open issues, fostering it around settled questions is likely to misrepresent historical fact and harm classroom relationships.

Finally, even good dissent can be inhibited in the classroom because it may seem to transgress against ingrained power structures. If the teacher believes dissent is a challenge to their authority, they are unlikely to seize upon a teachable moment that can cultivate students' understanding of dissent. This does more to strain social relationships and weaken the connections between members than thoughtful engagement with such dissent. This requires a degree of epistemic humility from instructors (Keith and Danisch, 2020), who should be open to new interpretations and seek to cultivate the same openness in students. Of course, facilitating discussion and deliberation that strives for wholeness and attends to dissent is a difficult skill developed through practice and refined through self-reflection.

Improving education for democracy

Within a climate of growing distrust that risks fraying the social fabric and as new policies constrain how teachers talk about matters at the heart of some of our most longstanding injustices, how should we proceed to shore up democracy? Pushing back against efforts to curb discussions of politically controversial open issues, we must create and preserve educative spaces where competing views are discussed and analysed. We must model constructive dialogue, where students learn both how to dissent and how to respond to dissent. We should use classroom communities to build tolerance and trust between citizens, where relationships are nurtured with civility. In this final section, we offer a few suggestions for how teachers and schools might do so.

We must not shy away from contentious topics, both historical and contemporary. Rather, we must focus on cultivating spaces where students may dive deeply into these issues, thoughtfully consider them and engage in disagreement. Teachers should focus primarily on deliberative discussions, which seem to bridge partisan divides more effectively than debates (McAvoy and McAvoy, 2021). For example, structured academic controversies provide a useful guide in facilitating these discussions. Initial stages involve discussing in pairs and small groups with carefully defined roles, followed by a more open small group or whole-class discussions. Crucially, this practice seems to improve student perspective-taking (Conklin et al, 2021), which can improve student capacity for dissent and deliberation and bolster the classroom social fabric.

This process of navigating and building upon spaces of disagreement can be understood through a framework pioneered by 20th-century organiser Saul Alinsky, who practised cycles of polarisation and depolarisation within communities. Alinsky carefully cultivated relationships with opponents as well as allies, in an intentional effort to avoid alienating community members. After a particular issue was decided, Alinsky maintained those relationships, understanding that former opponents may be crucial allies on the next community issue (Keith and Danisch, 2020). This cycle of polarisation and depolarisation, where tensions are heightened and then dispelled through collaboration on other issues of shared interest, offers a more robust understanding of the type of relationship building that is necessary within classrooms. The instructor can cultivate, maintain and strengthen relationships by skilfully managing tensions within the social fabric classroom. Rather than merely positive relationship building, teachers can create a more robust and resilient social fabric through a facilitated process of tension and resolution. This creates a more fully educative space: one more attached and intertwined, and therefore more resistant to severance.

This goes beyond limited conceptions of safe spaces as conflict-free. Rather, it positions tension and resolution, polarisation and depolarisation, as critical to community building. Of course, conflict inevitably occurs within any community, but it is up to the instructor to facilitate these conflicts in appropriate, productive ways. It means creating a safe, but not always comfortable, environment for students. Students' expression of self, including protected categories such as race, gender and ability, must be fiercely protected. Attacks or disparagement based on these sorts of prejudices limit students' community membership and participation and have no place in a truly educative space. Students must be safe to be themselves, but not safe from discomfort and disagreement.

It is possible to build such an educative space and resilient community by offering exemplars and through habit formation. One approach employs the 'contact hypothesis' in social psychology, where dissenting people are introduced in the classroom. This contact serves not to other the dissenter as some sort of mere outsider or stranger, but, when paired with skills of listening generously, enables students to better understand the competing values held by the dissenter (Conklin et al, 2021). This is not an activity bent on reaching consensus or changing political stances, but rather is concerned with how we view other people – especially dissenters – and respond with civility. Engagement with such dissent can build tolerance and introspection, where students reflect on how their own dissenting views may be interpreted by others and where they come to value how dissenting views may improve the quality of decisions they reach about shared social problems.[5]

Given the continued and even increasing segregation of schools by race, class and even political ideology, at the same time as heightening political tensions, teachers should consider the contact hypothesis in structuring their classroom discussions. Through carefully and intentionally introducing competing views for consideration, paired with practices that cultivate generous listening, students can learn to respond with open-mindedness rather than overreaction or outright dismissal. This practice would be a crucial counter to increasing political hyperpolarisation and echo chambers, which are eroding trust in those with differing political opinions (Pew Research Center, 2016; Talisse, 2019). The classroom environment can offer an educative space, where students can be exposed to differing opinions, consider them in a structured way, and see the shared humanity even in disagreement. In an increasingly polarised environment, teachers have an opportunity to practise Alinsky's depolarisation, which can serve as a much-needed positive model that students can take with them beyond the classroom.

Students should also examine and discuss historical examples of dissent. These examples should be rich and should prompt reflection on contemporary social mores. In a history course, for example, Dr Martin Luther King Jr's opposition to the Vietnam War poses a powerful example for students to consider. His dissent can be read today to pose provocative challenges to contemporary social practices, especially in the post-9/11 era where displays of militarism and patriotism have become normalised

---

[5] Notably, challenging stereotypes and becoming more open-minded through classroom experiences that invoke the contact hypothesis requires fulfilling criteria laid out by founding theorist, Gordon Allport (1954). Those criteria are aligned with the spirit of shared fate, wholeness, civic friendship, and civility as a commitment to relationships that we have employed here.

within the US. Alternatively, in a literature course, instructors can showcase differing interpretations of a poem, short story, or book, allowing students to deeply explore each interpretation, then piece together their own analysis. Scaffolding skills are learned by examining the competing interpretations of others, students can then be encouraged to develop and share their own views in class. This provides an opportunity to learn how to take a stand, while also engaging with competing positions.

Practices of dissent and engagement should be nurtured as habits, understood in the sense promoted by educational philosopher John Dewey as dispositions to act in certain ways. To cultivate such habits, students need practise engaging in real dissent and democratic decision-making, which has significance to their lives and the potential for tangible impact. Within the confines of the classroom, these deliberations might take up the nature of a reward day, the format of an assessment, or the inclusion of a poem in the class curriculum. But this can expand to actionable local issues with consequences that will directly impact those students. Examples include determining the legitimacy of a rule placed on students, or deciding how to solve a problem facing the community, such as graffiti on school property. These actionable topics increase student buy-in and often have no clear or definitive solutions. The capacity for different visions, disagreement and creative recombination offer students opportunities to experience and practise deliberation, disagreement and civility. Crucially, students are then put into a position where they live the consequences of their collective deliberations, helping students to appreciate the value and impact of democratic decision-making. Through repeated practice, students are incentivised to develop habits that enable robust deliberation and effective dissent.

Conclusion

More and more, teachers are afraid to discuss contentious issues in their classrooms. Some leaders on both the Right and the Left have called for schools to be spaces free from politics or discussions of divisive matters. Recent Republican legislation across the US is further exacerbating the fears of teachers. Avoiding confrontations or silencing dissent, as such legislation seems to do, only further harms democracy and fails to prepare good citizens equipped with political knowledge and skills for navigating partisan divides. Rather than promoting 'safe' or politically neutral spaces, we need educative spaces that model civility as students engage in careful and constructive conflict.

Moreover, in those classrooms, students should be empowered to make real decisions with real consequences, where consensus may be hard to come by. Such practice can aid students in seeing that their decisions, even if contrary to the views of dissenters in the classroom and elsewhere, are often improved because of including conflicting perspectives and nurturing relationships with each other. This chapter has described a few ways in which students can learn to navigate controversial issues and bridge hyperpartisanship, including engaging dissenting people and views in the classroom, listening generously, and cultivating habits of dissent and civility. Together, these approaches and others can better prepare our students not only for participation in future democracy, but also may help them overcome current problems of political division, incivility and ineffective civic reasoning.

Acknowledgement

Funding for this project was provided by the Institute for Humane Studies.

References

Allen, D.S. (2004) *Talking to Strangers: Anxieties of Citizenship since Brown v. Board of Education*, Chicago, IL: The University of Chicago Press.

Allport, G.W. (1954) *The Nature of Prejudice*, Oxford: Addison-Wesley.

American Historical Association (2021) 'Joint statement on legislative efforts to restrict education about racism in American history': www.historians.org/divisive-concepts-statement

Ben-Porath, S. (2006) *Citizenship under Fire: Democratic Education in Times of Conflict*, Princeton, NJ: Princeton University Press.

Berkshire, J. (2021) 'Culture war in the K-12 classroom', *The Nation*, 21 June: www.thenation.com/article/society/culture-war-classroom-teachers/

Butcher, J. and Gonzalez, M. (2020) 'Critical race theory, the new intolerance, and its grip on America', The Heritage Foundation, 7 December: www.heritage.org/civil-rights/report/critical-race-theory-the-new-intolerance-and-its-grip-america

Coates, T. (2014) 'The case for reparations', *The Atlantic*, 15 June: www.theatlantic.com/magazine/archive/2014/06/the-case-for-reparations/361631/

Conklin, H.G., Lo, J.C., McAvoy, P., Monte-Sano, C.B., Howard, T. and Hess, D.E. (2021) 'Pedagogical practices and how teachers learn', in C.D. Lee, G. White and D. Dong (eds) *Educating for Civic Reasoning and Discourse*, Washington, DC: National Academy of Education, pp 353–96.

Delgado, R. and Stefancic, J. (2012) *Critical Race Theory: An Introduction*, New York: New York University Press.

Edelman, A. (2022) 'Iowa bill would require cameras in public school classrooms,' NBC News, February 3: www.nbcnews.com/politics/politics-news/iowa-bill-require-cameras-public-school-classrooms-rcna14789

Greene, P. (2021a) 'State task forces want to root out indoctrination in schools. How's that going?', Forbes, 17 September: www.forbes.com/sites/petergreene/2021/09/17/state-task-forces-want-to-root-out-indoctrination-in-schools-hows-that-going/

Greene, P. (2021b) 'New Hampshire and Moms for Liberty put bounty on teachers' heads', *Forbes*, 12 November: www.forbes.com/sites/peter greene/2021/11/12/new-hampshire-and-moms-for-liberty-put-bounty-on-teachers-heads/

Greene, P. (2021c) 'Arizona GOP hopes to clamp down on teachers', *Forbes*, 6 May: www.forbes.com/sites/petergreene/2021/05/06/arizona-gop-hopes-to-clamp-down-on-teachers/

Goldstein, D. (2020) 'Two states. Eight textbooks. Two American stories', *The New York Times*, 12 January: www.nytimes.com/interactive/2020/01/12/us/texas-vs-california-history-textbooks.html

H 6070, 2021 Regular Session (Rhode Island, 2021): https://legiscan.com/RI/bill/H6070/2021

HB 327, 2021 134th General Assembly, 2021 Reg. Sess. (Ohio, 2021): https://legiscan.com/OH/text/HB327/id/2404404

HB 3979, 2021 87th Legislature, 2021 Reg. Sess. (Texas, 2021): https://legiscan.com/TX/text/HB3979/2021

Heim, J., Natanson, H. and Jackman, T. (2021) 'Residents left fuming, fearful after contentious Loudoun County school board meeting', *The Washington Post*, 23 June: www.washingtonpost.com/local/education/loudoun-schools-transgender-critical-race-theory/2021/06/23/1691dfc2-d453-11eb-ae54-515e2f63d37d_story.html

Hess, D.E. (2009) *Controversy in the Classroom: The Democratic Power of Discussion*, New York: Routledge.

Hess, D.E. and McAvoy, P. (2015) *The Political Classroom: Evidence and Ethics in Democratic Education*, New York: Routledge.

HF 802, 2021 Reg. Sess. (Iowa 2021): www.legis.iowa.gov/docs/publications/LGR/89/HF802.pdf

Keith, W.M. and Danisch, R. (2020) *Beyond Civility: The Competing Obligations of Citizenship*, Philadelphia, PA: University of Pennsylvania Press.

Levine, P. (2016) 'The question each citizen must ask', *Educational Leadership*, 73(6): 31–4.

Marias, B. (2021) 'Sullivan County school board approves teacher termination charges, supporters outraged', *WJHL*, 8 June: www.wjhl.com/news/local/sullivan-county-teacher-facing-termination-at-school-board-meeting-tuesday-supporters-to-gather/

McAvoy, P. and McAvoy, G.E. (2021) 'Can debate and deliberation reduce partisan divisions? Evidence from a study of high school students', *Peabody Journal of Education*, 96(3): 275–84.

NC Family Policy Council (2021) 'Lt. Governor announces task force to protect students from indoctrination': www.ncfamily.org/lt-gov-announces-task-force-to-protect-students-from-indoctrination/

Pew Research Center (2016) *Partisanship and Political Animosity in 2016*: www.pewresearch.org/politics/2016/06/22/partisanship-and-political-animosity-in-2016

Pulliam, T. (2021) 'Lt. Governor Mark Robinson launches new website to report "indoctrination" in North Carolina public schools', WTVD, 17 March: https://abc11.com/mark-robinson-lt-governor-indoctrination-in-schools/10423650/

SB 803, 2021 58th Legislature, 2021 Reg. Sess. (Oklahoma 2021): http://webserver1.lsb.state.ok.us/cf_pdf/2021-22%20int/sb/SB803%20int.pdf

Stitzlein, S. (2014) *Teaching for Dissent: Political Activism and Citizenship Education*, New York: Routledge.

Stitzlein, S. (2021) 'Defining and implementing civic reasoning and discourse: Philosophical and moral foundations for research and practice', in C.D. Lee, G. White and D. Dong (eds) *Educating for Civic Reasoning and Discourse*, National Academy of Education: https://3e0hjncy0c1gzjht1dopq44b-wpengine.netdna-ssl.com/wp-content/uploads/2021/03/Chapter-1.pdf

Sullivan, A. (2021) 'Threat of "critical race theory" in Iowa schools is a specter of Republican lawmakers' imagination', *The Gazette*, 3 June: www.thegazette.com/opinion/threat-of-critical-race-theory-in-iowa-schools-is-a-specter-of-republicans-lawmakers-imagination/

Talisse, R. (2019) *Overdoing Democracy: Why We Must Put Politics in its Place*, New York: Oxford University Press.

4

The contested scope of academic freedom

Dina Kiwan

Introduction

Academic freedom has increasingly become a focus for heated debate, which is typically polarised and vitriolic, with a highly charged commentary of academic freedom being under attack. There is a presumed irreconcilability of the principles of academic freedom on the one hand, and diversity and inclusion on the other. Traditional libertarian approaches typically place a primacy on protecting free speech, in contrast to approaches expressing concerns that unfettered free speech can be utilised by those traditionally holding power in ways that harm traditionally marginalised communities. These disputes in turn impact on assumptions about what kind of political education is feasible in today's society.

In addition to dominant media and political discourses that academic freedom is increasingly under threat globally, data from the Academic Freedom Index report a widespread decline based on a number of empirical measures in countries in Asia, Latin America and Eastern Europe, as well as in the UK and the US. The most significant declines are reported to be in Hong Kong, Brazil, Turkey, Thailand, India and Russia, associated with significant declines in measures of democracy (Kinzelbach et al, 2022). However, it is argued that discourses claiming that academic freedom is under greater threat in contemporary times compared to the past are ahistorical, not recognising the ongoing debates on academic freedom and the related concept of free speech over several decades.

In the UK context in 2021, a Department for Education report on higher education and academic freedom set out the 'case for change' (DfE, 2021). The report argues that although UK universities have historically provided a space for academic freedom and freedom of speech, there is 'growing concern within government of a chilling effect on university campuses', citing a 2019 Policy Exchange report based on a survey of students (DfE, 2021, p 9). While noting that academic freedom is not absolute and, in order to be operationalised, will necessarily have boundaries, a concern is expressed about individuals' need – or perceived need – to self-censor 'unpopular' views. The politics of knowledge production is not acknowledged, whereby the traditionally powerful in society have typically controlled the production of knowledge.

This chapter critically examines debates pertaining to academic freedom in universities and schools in the UK in order to address the research questions of whether and how principles of academic freedom may be incompatible with principles of diversity and freedom, and the ways in which these may be reconciled. First, a brief history of academic freedom is discussed in order to critically interrogate the construct of academic freedom and contextualise it in relation to the sociopolitical context of the UK. The methodology of the critical policy analysis of two key Department for Education policy documents, *Higher Education: Free Speech and Academic Freedom* (DfE, 2021) and *Guidance: Political Impartiality in Schools* (DfE, 2022), is detailed before presenting key thematic findings. The conclusion presents potential ways forward, in the UK, the US and other countries caught up with similar controversies, to move beyond a polarised exchange of the presumed irreconcilability of the principles of academic freedom on the one hand, and diversity and inclusion on the other.

Brief history of academic freedom

The construct of academic freedom can be traced as far back as Ancient Greece, yet it is within the institutional framework of the university that modern constructions of academic freedom are situated. The Latin word *universitas* refers to 'a number of persons associated into one body, a society, company, community, guild, corporation, etc' (Lewis and Short, ([1879]1966). The earliest degree-granting university in the world is the University of Al Quaraouiyine in Morocco, founded in 859 AD by an Arab Muslim woman, Fatima al-Fihri. Al-Azhar University in Egypt is the second oldest university founded as a 'madrasa' (college of law) in 970 AD. It gained official university status in 1961, and now also offers secular programmes.

During the Islamic Golden Age – the medieval period from the 8th to 15th centuries – scholars from around the world were brought together to translate classical knowledge into Arabic. These universities enjoyed institutional and professional autonomy, and professors joined guilds, which gave them the freedom to teach and pronounce opinions. While scholars enjoyed a certain level of de facto academic freedom, this was not codified in law. The work of hundreds of scholars and scientists in this period is said to have had a significant influence on the emergence of science and higher education institutions in medieval Europe.

These universities in Europe were autonomous institutions of power, with their members setting their own rules, yet academic inquiry was limited within the 'truth' of Christianity (Stone, 2015). The Church directly censored universities until the 18th century. However, with the rise of science came conflicts with religious authority, and this religious constraint on academic inquiry, also evident in the American context, continued into the 19th century (Stone, 2015). The transformation of modern higher education has been strongly influenced by the Humboldtian university, with the idea that the university is premised on upholding academic freedom. Academic freedom entailed both the freedom to teach and the freedom to learn (Dea, 2018).

With the emergence of the modern nation-state in the 18th and 19th centuries, it became the nation-state that was the main restriction to academic freedom, which continues to the present day. For example, the Third Reich erased academic freedom, with 45 per cent of German professors removed from their positions by 1939. The quest for non-interference from an authoritarian state influenced conceptions of academic freedom in the 1930s, when in the Soviet Union, for example, science was under strict state control. The role of the state in relation to academic freedom was also exemplified in the US context of McCarthyism in the 1950s and 1960s. While the Humboldtian conception of academic freedom distinguished between freedom within and outside the university, the American conception drew on the American conception of freedom of speech and was codified in law in the American Association of University Professors, 1915 *Declaration of Principles on Academic Freedom and Academic Tenure*. Principles of academic freedom in the American context entail freedom to teach, freedom to research and the freedom of responsibly exercised 'extramural speech'.

Academic freedom in the UK has historically been taken for granted, especially at the oldest elite universities of Oxford and Cambridge. The illusion of a tradition of academic freedom can arguably be attributed to the historical privileges of Oxbridge academics, rather than constructed in terms of de jure academic freedom. It was not incorporated into law until the 1988 Education Reform Act, which inserted a clause protecting academic freedom, which is reflected in the statutes of most UK universities. While academic freedom is no longer taken for granted, in their report for the University and College Union (UCU), Karran and Mallinson (2017, p 2) describe academic freedom as 'a neglected right in the UK'.

At the international level, the two UN Human Rights Covenants do not explicitly state a protection for academic freedom in 'hard international law', although a range of articles – for example, Article 19 (right to freedom of opinion and expression) in the International Covenant on Civil and Political Rights, and Article 13 (right to education) and Article 15(2) (right to freedom indispensable for scientific research) in the International Covenant on Economic, Social and Cultural Rights – can be drawn upon and have substantial legal weight. Through the European Court of Human Rights, cases relating to free speech in an academic context have resulted in judgements.

In order to contextualise academic freedom in the UK, it should be remembered that the UK does not have a written constitution with a form of protection for freedom of speech. Historically, academic freedom as de facto rather than de jure has taken precedence. The UCU statement on academic freedom (UCU, 2009) invokes the 1988 Education Reform Act as having established the legal rights of academic freedom in the UK 'to question and test received wisdom and to put forward new ideas and controversial or unpopular opinions without placing themselves in jeopardy of losing their jobs or the privileges they have' (cited in UCU, 2009). It also draws on the 1997 UNESCO recommendation on the status of higher education teaching personnel.

In 2017–18, the Joint Committee on Human Rights conducted a parliamentary inquiry into freedom of speech in universities. Its report published in 2018 challenged media discourses of wide censorship of debate in universities. However, in 2019 and 2020, Policy Exchange published two reports on academic freedom claiming concerns for academic freedom and free speech in universities, advocating for a newly created governmental role to protect free speech, and also to amend the Education Act to require student unions to legally allow unimpeded free speech (Wonkhe, 2021). Building on these reports, the Department for Education's 2021 report made a case for strengthening freedom of speech and academic freedom in higher education in England, stating that 'there is a growing body of evidence citing a "chilling effect" on staff, students ... who may feel unable to express their cultural, religious or political views without fear of repercussion' (DfE, 2021, p 7). Gaps in the current legislative framework are noted, namely the operationalisation of enforcement. Appointing a 'Free Speech and Academic Freedom Champion' to the Office for Students (OfS) is proposed, along with the proposal to empower the OfS, the higher education regulator in England, to impose sanctions. These proposals now form part of the Higher Education (Freedom of Speech) Bill going through Parliament. There has been widespread public criticism of the Bill, with academics, students and the UCU describing it as 'a serious threat to freedom of speech and academic freedom', and a disproportionate response to perceived 'threats' (Tidman, 2021).

Methodology

As noted in the introduction, the guiding research questions entailed:

1. Do principles of academic freedom sit in tension with principles of diversity and inclusion?
2. In what ways do they sit in tension?
3. If so, how might these principles be reconciled?

The data analytic approach entailed a critical policy analysis of the following: *Higher Education: Free Speech and Academic Freedom* (DfE, 2021) and *Guidance: Political Impartiality in Schools* (DfE, 2022). The approach draws on key features of a grounded theory approach (Glaser and Strauss, 1967), where it is postulated that theory emerges from the data through a systematic approach to coding. While entailing an inductive approach to generating theory, the distinction between theory generation and theory verification is not clear-cut, and deduction is necessarily involved as theory generation requires progressive verification as well (Punch, 1998). The first stage entailed applying codes or categories to the policy documents, in an iterative fashion, with constant reference across and within the policy documents.

Three key themes that emerged from the analysis are examined. First, contestations between 'safety' and 'freedom' in relation to theories advanced by philosophers of education (Callan, 2016; Ben-Porath, 2017). They argue that the principles of justice and inclusion and the principles of academic freedom are complementary rather than contradictory, in that inclusivity should be conceived as a threshold condition for academic freedom (Callan, 2016; Ben-Porath, 2017). The emphasis on being 'dignity safe' (as distinct from 'intellectual safety') is thus presented as a prerequisite condition for inclusion in the university context and for the practice of academic freedom (Callan, 2016). This normative proposition aims to bridge between, on the one hand, traditional libertarian approaches placing a primacy on protecting free speech, which dismiss a perceived 'oversensitivity' of those engaged in topics of race, gender and other social justice areas, or historically vulnerable groups, in what is disparagingly labelled 'identity politics', and, on the other, those working from marginalised communities in Western democratic societies who have raised concerns that unfettered free speech can be utilised by those traditionally holding power in ways that harm traditionally marginalised communities.

A second theme is analysed in relation to notions of 'received wisdom' versus 'new ideas'. These themes contest different constructions of knowledge. For example, traditional models of knowledge see knowledge as objectively externalised, and hence understood as scientific, literal and non-metaphorical, separate and unrelated to the human mind. In contrast, Humboldtian models conceive of knowledge as co-constructed and it is viewed more subjectively, as a product of interpretation and negotiation, and influenced by geographical and temporal context.

Third, there is an emerging theme pertaining to the role of education, in particular higher education, conceived as playing a critical role in the promotion of democratic societies (for example, Dewey, 1916; Wright Mills, 1959). This relates to theorisations that emphasise the importance of informed and critical citizens in relation to the emergence of the modern nation-state, and now evident in discourses on global citizenship (Kiwan and Evans, 2015). In some discourses on the 'civic university', a liberal education is seen as central in the production of 'a particular kind of critical citizen', while other discourses call for a more radical 'transformation of higher education itself' (Biesta, 2007, p 470). It has been argued that higher education is one of the few remaining public spaces where 'unpopular' ideas can be explored and students can learn how to challenge authority (Giroux, 2002).

Challenges faced in universities and schools
Political impartiality in schools

Historically, citizenship had been taught implicitly in the school curriculum largely through traditional school subjects such as geography, history and religion. From the 1930s, a more direct explicit approach was generally advocated with the introduction of a 'civics' curriculum, which entailed teaching about British institutions and outlining rights and duties, rather than teaching citizenship in context (Kiwan, 2008). Post-1945 and through the 1960s, social studies and citizenship had a relatively low status; however, by the 1970s, a programme for political education was accepted, given its links to the lowering of the voting age to age 18 (Davies, 1999). However, with the Conservatives coming to power in 1979, this did not come to fruition.

With the 1988 Education Reform Act, citizenship was proposed as a cross-curricular theme, but as it was non-statutory, it was squeezed out. A historical shift occurred with the 1998 policy review of citizenship, with recommendations for citizenship education to be a statutory entitlement, and stand as a discrete subject. However, with the statutory introduction of citizenship education in schools in England in 2002, at the time when (New) Labour was in government, there was public debate and expressed concern that such a curriculum would politicise schools. Revisions to the citizenship curriculum were made statutory in 2007, where issues of identity and diversity were incorporated into the conceptual framework (Ajegbo et al, 2007). Despite a review of citizenship after the 2010 general election by the Conservative–Liberal Democrat coalition government, it remained as statutory in the curriculum but with changes in focus and scope, including, for example, the inclusion of financial education, traditional civics and options to include diversity and inclusion from 2014 (Moorse, 2015). The roll-out of citizenship education in schools has faced a number of barriers, including funding, teacher training, adequate curriculum time and senior management commitment in schools. Despite this, a 2021 survey indicates that approximately three quarters of parents believe that it is important for their children to learn about politics at school (Weinberg, 2021). This relates to the importance of a learning space for the development of informed and critical thinking skills and the preparation to contribute as active citizens and, as a consequence, to support democracy more broadly at a societal level.

In 2022, government guidance on political impartiality in schools was published, with the foreword by Nadhim Zahawi, then Secretary State for Education, stating that there has been much discussion of political impartiality, often in the context of 'specific political issues and movements' (DfE, 2022, p 2), and that the aim of the guidance is to provide support for teachers in navigating 'these complex issues'. Through a number of scenarios, the guidance aims to distinguish between, on the one hand, 'received wisdom'/ 'shared principles' equated with being non-political, and, on the other, political issues with different or 'partisan' perspectives. 'Received wisdom' is constructed as indisputable fact or 'shared values' that must be 'actively promoted' by teachers, as evident in the tradition of 'teaching British values', present in schools over the previous two decades; examples of these values are given as 'democracy', 'the rule of law', 'individual liberty' and 'mutual respect and tolerance of those with different faiths and beliefs' (DfE, 2022, p 5). There is a legal requirement that 'forbid(s) the promotion of partisan political views' (DfE, 2022, p 6). Partisan is then defined as 'one-sided' and political views are 'those expressed with a political purpose', such as 'to change the law or change government policy' (DfE, 2022, p 6).

That this distinction is theoretically and practically problematic becomes evident in the scenarios given in the document. Scenario A states that climate change is a fact and so does not constitute a political issue, whereas policy proposals to address climate change would constitute a political issue. A central problem with this kind of binary approach to categorising knowledge in the world – fact vs. opinion – is that it is ahistorical and does not take into account how what we now hold to be fact and the 'truth' changes over time. Indeed, climate change was at one time considered a partisan view, and through a process of research and expressing unpopular minority views, the notion of climate change has largely been accepted as scientific fact and to be 'true'. This problematic binary approach is particularly evident in the domain of the social sciences and humanities, where knowledge is often understood through an interpretivist rather than positivist paradigm, but is also problematic in science, where values and evidence/fact are intricately interlinked. Not only is this binary approach to knowledge ahistorical, but it also assumes universal knowledge. The declared shared principles elevated to the status of truth do not necessarily hold across different groups within British society, let alone globally. Not only is this polarisation of fact/opinion potentially arbitrary in practice, but it is also difficult pedagogically to justify.

The advocacy of such a pedagogical approach does a disservice to students' learning about the nature of knowledge production and the politics of knowledge. This is evident in the example in Scenario G, where an example is given in relation to choosing teaching resources that are deemed 'neutral' in relation to the Israeli–Palestinian conflict. What would be more advantageous for students to learn is that all knowledge, especially what is presented as 'fact', is socially constructed from the positionality of the author, who is positioned in space/geography and time, and that historical sources are not objective. That is, that the author cannot be neutral, but necessarily comes from their own context and position. Similarly, Scenario I condemns the use of resources from the Black Lives Matter movement, describing their material as representing '*views* which go beyond the *shared principle* that racism is unacceptable' (DfE, 2022, p 13). Such guidance proposing a clear distinction between a view and a shared principle is unlikely to clarify for teachers what is expected in relation to teaching on political contentious or controversial issues. In addition, teachers express a concern that this guidance will adversely affect minority students by removing a safe space to talk about sensitive issues around race, empire and sexuality. The guidance has been compared to Section 28 regulations in the late 1980s and 1990s that similarly said that while homosexuality can be talked about, it must not be 'promoted'. What happened was that the topic typically was avoided, and the concern is that the guidance on political impartiality will have a similarly 'chilling' effect in the classroom (Adams, 2022). Teachers and teaching unions have been critical of the guidance, seeing it as a 'war on woke' – essentially the pitting of academic freedom against diversity and inclusion.

The Higher Education: Free Speech and Academic Freedom *report*

In the *Charter on Academic Freedom* (UCU, nd), academic freedom is defined as the legal right as established in the 1988 Education Reform Act 'to question and test **received wisdom** and to put forward **new ideas** and controversial or unpopular opinions'. This is explained with reference to the process of the production of new knowledge, in that it paves the way to conducting **new research** against **existing orthodoxies**. Similarly, the report *Higher Education: Free Speech and Academic Freedom* (DfE, 2021, p 4) refers to the process by which 'new ideas' challenging 'consensus' go on to become 'accepted wisdom'. This also resonates with the arguments put forward in the preceding section on political impartiality in schools – that knowledge is constructed over time, and challenging the positivism of the objective indisputable 'truth' of accepted knowledge. It is this process of knowledge production that enables critical thinking and the development of democracy. Dominant discourses in media and politics arguing that academic freedom is under threat are predominantly coming from those holding traditional views – on race, empire, gender and many other societal issues. That is, their views have historically been in the mainstream – 'received wisdom' – and, increasingly, 'new ideas' have been challenging this orthodoxy. The above words cited in the Charter have been emboldened to highlight the critical concepts of 'received wisdom' and 'new ideas' in the conceptualisation of academic freedom. It is this concept – the protection of those with less power in society or with new ideas that therefore need protection – that is central to the understanding of academic freedom. This is why complaints of academic freedom under threat due to challenges against received wisdom are often perceived to be disingenuous and as 'weaponising' academic freedom. The spirit of academic freedoms was historically developed so that those expressing new ideas are afforded the necessary protections by academic freedom laws.

In the Foreword by the then Secretary of State for Education, Gavin Williamson refers to several cases where students or academics were in the news for expressing views deemed to be discriminatory with respect to race, sexuality and transgender, and suffering consequences of being disinvited to talks, visits or courses. This 'chilling effect' (DfE, 2021, p 9) is presented as the contextual backdrop to plans to strengthen protections for free speech and academic freedom in universities, and the establishment of a Free Speech Champion in the Office for Students.

Academic freedom is described as being 'concerned with the ability of academics to question and test perceived wisdom and to put forward new ideas and controversial or unpopular opinions without placing themselves in jeopardy of losing their jobs or privileges' (DfE, 2021, p 10). Yet the examples given, rather than being examples of new ideas, are actually a return to older discredited discriminatory ideas that undermine the referenced 'shared principles' of equality, tolerance and mutual respect of difference, as referenced in the government guidance on political impartiality in schools.

There is acknowledgement that academic freedom cannot, in practice, be absolute. There are forms of speech that can be in breach of criminal law, including speech that causes fear or incites violence, speech that can incite hatred on the grounds or race, religion or sexual orientation, speech that constitutes a terrorism-related offence, or speech causing harm or distress (DfE, 2021, pp 15–16). Yet contradicting these boundaries of academic freedom and free speech, the Foreword by the Secretary of State for Education dismisses notions of 'emotional safety', admonishing those who 'prioritise' it over free speech and describing it as intolerance.

The approach to academic freedom has been overwhelmingly within a national frame, despite the intense globalisation of higher education. The temporal and geographical positionality of knowledge has been noted, which also requires challenging the Western hegemony of knowledge and its production, calling for the need to situate knowledge sociopolitically and historically. Higher education has typically constructed the university's mission within a national frame, and the developing of informed, critical citizens and the promotion of democratic societies (Dewey, 1916; Wright Mills, 1959), in the context of the emergence of the modern nation-state.

With increased globalisation, there is an increase in the emergence of branch universities transnationally. Increasingly, universities are opening campuses abroad driven by financial interests, and concerns relating to improving rankings through internationalisation. These developments illustrate shifts in the conception of higher education as a public good to a neoliberal conception of education as a private good. This will necessarily have implications for the conception and practice of academic freedom that is not considered within the narrow national frame of the document.

Conclusions and recommendations

This critical policy analysis of the state of academic freedom in schools and universities illustrates the contestations around both the scope of academic freedom and associated pedagogical approaches. Both of the policy documents analysed reflect the three highlighted themes contesting, first, the boundaries between safety and freedom, second, received wisdom and new ideas, and, third, the role of educational institutions and underpinning models of education.

With regards to the first theme, while there are principles in law to protect against hate speech or distress by race, religion and sexuality, the government policy documents take a dismissive tone, arguing that 'emotional safety' must not be prioritised over academic freedom. The prefix of the word 'emotional' before safety suggests that the safety is imagined or perceived and perhaps is not 'real'; rather it is framed as a flawed character trait of being 'oversensitive'. Phipps (2015), writing about sexism and violence in the neoliberal university context, draws out parallels between 'lad culture' and practices of evaluation in higher educational institutions. Phipps (2015) notes that 'to offend with impunity is a function and exercise of privilege'. That language entails violence is dismissed as 'banter', and as such has been invisible in higher education institutions between staff, staff and students, and between students. Phipps (2015) further argues that such acts can be described as 'strategic misogyny', which functions to 'preserve masculine power and space'. The production of knowledge is necessarily restricted in racist, sexist contexts, and contexts of other forms of exclusion and violence. Ben-Porath (2017) and Callan (2016) argue that taking emotional safety – or what they refer to as being 'dignity safe' – is a necessary part of academic freedom. They argue for taking seriously the dangerous implications of speech against traditionally vulnerable or marginalised groups in society. Rather than a polarisation of academic freedom versus diversity and inclusion, the principles of justice and inclusion and the principles of academic freedom are complementary rather than contradictory, in that inclusivity should be conceived as a threshold condition for academic freedom.

Second, both policy documents (DfE, 2021, 2022) make attempts to distinguish between received wisdom/shared principles/values, on the one hand, and political issues with different partisan positions on the other. In the guidance relating to political impartiality in schools, teachers are told that they must actively promote the former, but must be neutral on the latter. Through the analysis of the scenarios provided, it becomes clear that this is not a clear distinction in practice, and is pedagogically flawed, in that it ignores the geographical and temporal situatedness of knowledge. In addition, it provides an inaccurate understanding of the process of knowledge production, and how what are now assumed to be shared principles or received wisdom were at one time politically contested. Educators have pointed to the anomaly that academic freedom and freedom of speech are being curtailed in the school domain yet championed in higher education. Halima Begum, chief executive of the Runnymede Trust, argues that teachers need support to talk about race, rather than ambiguous restrictions be imposed. She cites startling statistics that fewer than 1 per cent of students in England study a book by a non-white author at GCSE, with a key barrier being teachers' lack of confidence in managing discussion on race in the classroom. Furthermore, a survey of history teachers in 2019 found that 78 per cent wanted training on teaching about migration and empire (Begum, 2022).

Third, explicit links are made to academic freedom and the upholding of democracy in the policy documents. In discourses on the 'civic university', a liberal education is seen as central in the production of 'a particular kind of critical citizen'. This role of higher education continues to be contested, ranging from the idea that universities must produce 'true' knowledge, to the idea that universities' central mission is constructed in terms of creating economic growth, to the idea that the university is a means for change in an increasingly globalised world facing numerous challenges (Bogelund, 2015). These different constructions of the role of the university are underpinned by different constructions of knowledge, and therefore different understandings of academic freedom.

Recommendations building on this analysis require a move away from the existing politically fuelled polarisation of debate in current policy documents and policy and media discourses. It is important to examine a range of structural constraints on academic freedom, which largely arise from market-driven models of education. This includes the casualisation of the workforce, where those on part-time contracts feel unable to challenge the status quo. In addition, the marketisation of higher education results in competition, where marketing and communication of the university brand take precedence over individual academic autonomy in teaching and research. 'Performativity' becomes the guiding rationale where productivity is the new moral framework for the contemporary academic way of being, illustrated in the pressure to publish, secure grants and recruit more students, for the benefit of the university's ranking and economic prospects (Ball, 2012). Furthermore, with the marketisation of higher education and the introduction of fees, the construction of the student has changed significantly to a marketised understanding of the student as a 'client' or 'customer', where the 'customer is always right'. The construction of student as 'client/customer' therefore impacts on the academic freedom of the professor, reflected in their power to potentially censor and control the curriculum. In addition, the Research Excellence Framework (REF) and impact case studies also reflect the state's marketisation of higher education, where knowledge equates to capital, and individual academics are conceptualised as 'units of resources' (Ball, 2012). As a consequence, this agenda determines what research is considered important, and has the temporal bias towards measurable short-term impact. It also encourages a faster rate of publication, and it has been argued that the system results in mediocre research. Furthermore, 'REF panels give extraordinary gatekeeping power to a disproportionately older, male, white – and overwhelmingly Russell Group and former 1994 Group – academic elite' (Sayer, 2014).

Moving forward, it is important that political education in schools does not result in teachers avoiding engagement with controversial topics and political issues, as occurred in the 1980s and 1990s in England, relating to Section 28 and the directive of prohibiting the 'promotion' of homosexuality. The development of critical thinking based a range of sources of evidence must be championed in both primary and secondary schools, in order to prepare students for higher education in navigating the contested terrain of free speech and academic freedom. This requires a co-construction between students and teachers of a framework for civil debates and exploration of new ideas balanced by safeguards for dignity-safe learning.

References

Adams, R. (2022) 'Curbing political topics in English schools will harm minority students say critics', *The Guardian*, 18 February: www.theguardian.com/education/2022/feb/18/curbing-political-topics-in-english-schools-will-harm-minority-students-say-critics

Ajegbo, H., Kiwan, D. and Sharma, S. (2007) *Curriculum Review: Diversity and Citizenship* (Ajegbo Report), London: DfES.

Ball, S.J. (2012) 'Performativity, commodification and commitment: an I-spy guide to the neoliberal university', *British Journal of Educational Studies*, 60(1): 17–28.

Begum, H. (2022) 'The government wants open debate in universities, why stifle it in schools', *The Guardian*, 18 February: www.theguardian.com/commentisfree/2022/feb/18/tories-debate-universities-schools-government-impartial-teaching

Ben-Porath, S. (2017) *Free Speech on Campus*, Philadelphia: University of Pennsylvania Press.

Biesta, G. (2007) 'Towards the knowledge democracy? Knowledge production and the civic role of the university', *Studies in Philosophy and Education*, 26(5): 467–79.

Bogelund, P. (2015) 'How supervisors perceive PhD supervision – and how they practice it', *International Journal of Doctoral Studies*, 10: 39–55.

Callan, E. (2016) 'Education in safe and unsafe spaces', *Philosophical Inquiry in Education*, 24(1): 64–78.

Davies, I. (1999) 'What has happened in the teaching of politics in schools in England in the last three decades, and why?', *Oxford Review of Education*, 25(1/2): 125–40.

Dea, S. (2018) 'A brief history of academic freedom', University Affairs: www.universityaffairs.ca/opinion/dispatches-academic-freedom/a-brief-history-of-academic-freedom/

DfE (Department for Education) (2021) *Higher Education: Free Speech and Academic Freedom*: www.gov.uk/government/publications/higher-education-free-speech-and-academic-freedom

DfE (2022) *Guidance: Political Impartiality in Schools*: www.gov.uk/government/publications/political-impartiality-in-schools/political-impartiality-in-schools

Dewey, J. (1916) *Democracy and Education: An Introduction to the Philosophy of Education*, New York: Macmillan.

Giroux, H. (2002) 'Neoliberalism, corporate culture, and the promise of higher education: the university as a democratic public sphere', *Harvard Educational Review*, 72(4): 425–64.

Glaser, B. and Strauss, A. (1967) *The Discovery of Grounded Theory*, Chicago: Aldine.

Karran, T. and Mallinson, L. (2017) *Academic Freedom in the UK: Legal and Normative Protection in a Comparative Context*, Report for the University and College Union: www.ucu.org.uk/academic-freedom-in-2017

Kinzelbach, K., Lindberg, S.I., Pelke, L. and Spannagel, J. (2022) *Academic Freedom Index: Update 2022*: www.pol.phil.fau.eu/files/2022/03/afi-update-2022.pdf

Kiwan, D. (2008) *Education for Inclusive Citizenship*, London: Routledge.

Kiwan, D. and Evans, M. (2015) *Global Citizenship Education: Topics and Learning Objectives by Age*, Paris: UNESCO.

Lewis, C.T. and Short, C. ([1879] 1966) *A Latin Dictionary*, Oxford: Clarendon Press.

Moorse, L. (2015) 'Citizenship in the national curriculum', in L. Gearon (ed) *Learning to Teach Citizenship in the Secondary School: A Companion To School Experience*, New York: Routledge.

Phipps, A. (2015) 'Sexism and violence in the neoliberal university', Sexual Harassment in Higher Education conference, Goldsmiths, University of London, 2 December: https://genderate.wordpress.com/2015/12/02/sexism-and-violence/

Punch, M. (1998) 'Politics and ethics in qualitative research', in N.K. Denzin and Y.S. Lincoln (eds) *The Landscape of Qualitative Research*, Thousand Oaks, CA: Sage Publications, pp 156–84.

Sayer, D. (2014) 'Five reasons why the REF is not fit for purpose', *The Guardian*, 15 December: www.theguardian.com/higher-education-network/2014/dec/15/research-excellence-framework-five-reasons-not-fit-for-purpose cited in Stanonis, A.J. (2016) 'No time for muses: the research excellence framework and the pursuit of mediocrity', in C. Hudson and J. Williams (eds) *Why Academic Freedom Matters: A Response to Current Challenges*, London: Civitas.

Stone, G.R. (2015) 'A brief history of academic freedom', in A. Bilgrami and J.R. Cole (eds) *Who's Afraid of Academic Freedom?*, New York: Columbia University Press, Ch 1.

Tidman, Z. (2021) 'Government "exaggerating threat to freedom of speech to push through new laws", says university union', *Independent*, 14 May: www.independent.co.uk/news/education/education-news/free-speech-university-laws-ucu-b1846076.html

UCU (University and College Union) (nd) *Charter on Academic Freedom*: www.ucu.org.uk/media/4160/Scottish-Charter-on-Academic-Freedom/pdf/Academic_Freedom_charter.pdf

Weinberg, J. (2021) *The Missing Link: An Updated Evaluation of the Provision, Practice and Politics of Democratic Education in English Secondary Schools*, Project Report for the All-Party Parliamentary Group on Political Literacy, London: https://bit.ly/3wvlXMm

Wonkhe (2021) 'This is not the first government crack down on free speech in universities': https://wonkhe.com/blogs/this-is-not-the-first-government-crack-down-on-free-speech-in-universities/

Wright Mills, C. (1959) *The Sociological Imagination*, Oxford: Oxford University Press.

5

Rethinking citizenship education for political literacy

Tony Breslin

Political literacy sits at the heart of the definition of 'citizenship education' offered by Professor Bernard Crick in the landmark report, *Education for Citizenship and the Teaching of Democracy in Schools* (QCA, 1998). The 'Crick Report', as it came to be called, was clear about the task to hand: 'We aim at no less than a change in the political culture of this country both nationally and locally: for people to think of themselves as active citizens, willing, able and equipped to have an influence in public life' (QCA, 1998, p 7). When David Blunkett became Secretary of State for Education in the UK in 1997, one of his first acts was to commission Crick, his former politics tutor, to bring together an advisory group that would inform its content.[1]

In terms of both citizenship *and* citizenship education, the Blunkett-Crick nexus was to produce two further reports, *Citizenship for 16–19 Year Olds in Education And Training* (FEFC, 2000),[2] and, during Blunkett's subsequent tenure as Home Secretary, *The New and the Old* (Home Office, 2003), a document focused on the still controversial terrain that sits between *citizenship education* for children and young people in schools, colleges and similar settings, and *citizenship* (not least in the legal sense) for newcomers to Britain and for some long-settled migrants.

The growing concern about the settlement, integration and (legal) citizenship of both newcomers and the members of settled communities that intensified after the bombings in New York in 2001 (9/11) and London four years later spawned a broader literature concerned with community life and questions of national identity. Here, the former area is the main concern of, for instance, *Our Shared Future* (2007), produced by the Commission on Integration and Cohesion led by Darra Singh, while the latter is the focus of, for example, *Citizenship: Our Common Bond* (Goldsmith, 2008), part of a broader literature that emerged from the Ministry of Justice as a strand

---

[1] Crick's development of citizenship education within a statutory framework led directly to focused research on the impact of such education. See Chapter 10 for lessons from the research.

[2] I was a member of the advisory group that produced this report.

of the wider 'Governance of Britain' initiative launched following Gordon Brown's becoming prime minister in June 2007, which brought with it a new focus on 'Britishness' (Breslin, 2007a). This agenda found its resonance in educational settings in the 'British values' debate and the role of schools in promoting these, a debate that gained renewed momentum in the second decade of the 21st century, as these morphed into *fundamental* British values and a new requirement on schools to promote these and to evidence such values in teaching programmes (DfE, 2014).

By 2010, schools in England would not only have a new curriculum subject to embed but also a formal statutory duty to promote community cohesion (Rowe et al, 2011, 2012) and a key and contentious role in the implementation of the still-controversial Prevent strategy, a part of the UK's counterterrorism response in light of events in New York, London and elsewhere.

Meanwhile, these schools, or at least those in the secondary phase, were still grappling with the practicalities of introducing a new national curriculum subject, *citizenship*, which had been one of the key outcomes from Crick's endeavours in that first report (QCA, 1998), experimenting with teaching and curricular models, and working out how citizenship might sit alongside areas of related provision, most notably personal, social and health education (PSHE).

Clearly, there was a risk that the focus on the development of political literacy, so central to Crick's original analysis and emphasised in the report's title, through the 'teaching of democracy in schools' would become marginalised in a subject now tasked with a multitude of additional and post-Crick concerns, not always ones that sat easily with Crick's original aims. Furthermore, as we shall see, there was a risk that citizenship itself, where it had been 'parked' within programmes created to deliver PSHE and designed to attend to the spiritual, moral, social and cultural development of children and young people during the statutory schooling years (RSA, 2014), would get marginalised in that mix. In short, there was a risk of 'politics' getting lost within citizenship, and citizenship itself getting lost within PSHE.

Citizenship education: matters of definition and operationalisation

Outlining and understanding the richness of the educational and broader policy landscape with which citizenship educators and school leaders have had to contend over the past quarter of a century is vital if we are to understand the state of teaching about politics in our schools.

Crick had opted for the formation of a stand-alone membership association after rebuffs from both the Politics Association (PA) and the Association for the Teaching of the Social Sciences (ATSS), both of whom opted to remain focused on the (slightly) more rarefied subjects of A-level politics and sociology respectively.[3] It may be telling that during the very period when proponents of citizenship education have been struggling to establish the subject in English schools, and colleagues across a range of other national settings have been focused on equivalent enterprises, both the ATSS and the PA have ceased to exist. Their shared reluctance to embrace the emergence of citizenship is worthy of further exploration in the context of the debate here.

At the heart of the trepidation about citizenship education among those longer established in the teaching of politics and sociology (subjects that, in the UK, were predominantly taught at A-level following their exclusion from the national curriculum introduced in English schools in the late 1980s) lay a range of issues:

1. The belief that attempts to teach at least a form of 'politics' during statutory schooling involved too great a 'watering down' of a complex subject (and academic discipline) better suited to older, or especially able, learners.
2. The belief that citizenship was not a 'real' subject (in the way that both politics and sociology, as established and discrete academic disciplines, were), but a composite of different subjects or disciplines that hung together, at best, precariously.
3. The view that, as one experienced and nationally profiled progressive state school head put it to me at a seminar convened by what was then the National Union of Teachers, in the months leading up to the introduction of citizenship to the statutory national curriculum in England, 'you can't teach citizenship in 45-minute lessons, you'll bore the kids to death'; my response, 'Well, that's never stopped us with maths, English, physics, geography', brought a wry laugh but it hides a truth: we often strangle innovation by posing questions and making assumptions about the innovation in question that we never make of the established order, in this case those established curriculum subjects that have dominated state and independent schooling in the English-speaking world since the inception of such schooling itself.
4. The related view that citizenship could either be incorporated into non-specialist and tutor-led teaching programmes as a part of a revised PSHE offer, or delivered in a cross-curricular manner, with minor adaptions to the teaching of other subjects.
5. The absence, at launch in 2002, of a skilled teaching community trained and ready to deliver the new subject and, as importantly, to champion it in the staffroom and the senior leadership team, especially given the

---

[3] In the latter case, in spite of my efforts as chair of ATSS at that time to swing the Association behind Crick's initiative.

reluctance of some who might have done so: the sociologists, the political scientists, the historians and so on.
6. The broader idea, in spite of Crick's title extension, 'and the teaching of democracy in schools', that citizenship was to be 'caught' not 'taught'.
7. The concern (from the political Right) that teaching citizenship to younger children amounted to the promotion of 'leftwing' ideas in the classroom and staffroom (and, therefore, as a conservative press might have put it, 'the dangerous leftwing indoctrination of our children').
8. The alternative view (from the political Left) that the citizenship programme, as proposed or in its likely interpretation, amounts to the promotion of an essentially conformist agenda around compliance and cohesion and being a 'good' (and, therefore, well-behaved) citizen.

In fairness, Crick had anticipated all or most of this:

- Establishing the Association for Citizenship Teaching (ACT).
- Persuading the Department for Education to fund the Citizenship Education Longitudinal Study (led for over a decade with distinction by David Kerr[4] at the National Foundation for Educational Research), which produced a battery of instructive reports (NFER, 2002–2010).
- Publishing the new curriculum in 2000, two years ahead of its launch so as to facilitate a preparation period.
- Persuading those agencies and influencers concerned with teacher education to launch a range of Postgraduate Certificate in Education (PGCE; initial teacher training) courses in citizenship education.
- Rolling out a nationally profiled continuing professional development programme (delivered in partnership with ACT) for existing teachers interested in becoming a part of the vanguard for the new subject.
- Commissioning a teachers' manual, *Making Sense of Citizenship* (Huddleston and Kerr, 2006), two complementary copies of which were sent to every English secondary school from an initial DfE-funded original print run in the region of 60,000 copies.

Nevertheless, these philosophical, practical and political concerns constituted a challenging terrain for the emerging subject of citizenship. I have argued that citizenship, in being constituted as a subject of the secondary national curriculum (having previously been designated as one of five overarching but non-statutory 'cross-curricular themes'), needed to move from being 'less than a subject' to being 'more than a subject' and that in teaching citizenship:

---

[4] See Chapter 10.

> Schools are dealing with something that, like Management Sciences or Integrated Humanities, does not have the academic heritage of those subjects that have long dominated our school curriculum … [Citizenship] has much to learn from other areas that have struggled with the concept of subject identity in the past: PSHE, Careers Education and Guidance, and the wider vocational field. (Breslin, 2004)

Moreover, I have further argued that to succeed, citizenship education was more likely to thrive in the context of a 'citizenship-rich' school (Breslin and Dufour, 2006; Breslin, 2007b, 2008, 2010). To summarise, the citizenship-rich school has the following qualities:

1. Citizenship education is clearly identified in the curriculum model, on the timetable, in assessment frameworks, in continuing professional development provision and in the school's improvement and development plans.
2. It enables young people to develop their citizenship knowledge through a skills-based and learner-centred pedagogy.
3. Citizenship learning, thus, takes place not only within designated timetable space – vital though this is – but through a range of opportunities and activities, on and off the school site, that are valued by students, teachers and the wider community.
4. The school encourages and facilitates the active and effective participation of all – students, teachers, parents, the wider community – in its day-to-day activities.
5. The school models the principles it teaches in citizenship in the way it operates as an institution and a community and proclaims this outlook in its documentation.

Thus, the citizenship-rich school was proposed as, quite literally, a different type of school, one that was both different as a community and in the community, and one that, because of its nature, fostered the three pillars of Crick's framework: social and moral responsibility, community involvement and, of course, political literacy.

The visibility of citizenship education

As Barry Dufour and I have long argued, the debate is not about *whether* citizenship is taught in a subject-specific way *or* a cross-curricular manner, it is the need to do both *alongside* each other, such that cross-curricular work delivered, for instance, through a discussion of the suffragettes in history or the process of electing class representatives for a school council needs to have the anchorage point of specialist teaching in dedicated citizenship lessons (Breslin and Dufour, 2006).

Thus, in an approach that we described as 'core-plus', we recommended not a *general* cross-curricular approach but one in which specified modules in particular and pre-identified 'carrier' subjects (such as the study of inequality in an English text) or projects (such as a year-group wide community volunteering programme) enable the practical enactment and the reiteration of themes initially explored in citizenship.

Furthermore, when these take place within the context of the citizenship-rich school, the multiple democratic practices of the school as an institution help to reinforce the lessons delivered within and beyond the core citizenship programme. Thus, citizenship is not just subject-specific *and* cross-curricular; it is also actively and deliberately taught *and* caught, term after term, day in and day out. And this process, rich in pupil engagement, drawing on the knowledge base of citizenship education while constantly enabling its practice in the life of the school, provides the engine for the development of political literacy, rather than simply a knowledge of politics, vital though that is.

The proposal, therefore, isn't just for *active* citizenship but for *effective* citizenship, enabling young people to drive social change in their communities as a result of their grasp of the politics of those communities, an approach demonstrated by Carrie Supple at the Citizenship Foundation through the Youth Act! programme that she and the team around her had developed. Indeed, a BBC *Newsnight* film to mark the tenth anniversary of Blair's election used a Youth Act! project based at a school in northeast London to epitomise the kind of community activism that the period, and in no small part citizenship education, had helped to spawn.

Sadly, months of negotiation with government departments did not secure the funding to facilitate a national roll-out of the Youth Act! initiative. Such a roll-out would have given tremendous visibility, not just to the impact of citizenship education in the classroom, but to the impact of deliberately seeking to develop political literacy among groups of young people who might have struggled in those classrooms, who may never have stood for election to the growing number of school councils, another significant legacy of Crick (Whitty and Wisby, 2007), but who ached to play their part in the transformation of their communities.

Political literacy: a loss of focus?

Long before the publication of the 1998 Crick Report, Crick was a defining figure in the emergence of thinking about political education in schools and other settings. His text, *In Defence of Politics* (Crick, 1962), became established as a keynote text for postgraduates, undergraduates and those aspiring to study politics in further or higher education, and he was a leading mover and founding member of the Politics Association (a membership association established to support those teaching politics in schools) and the Political Studies Association, which, at the time of its establishment, had a similar remit in universities but now also supports those in secondary and further education.

However, Bernard Crick's original advisory committee drew its members from across the political landscape, and included some who had reservations about the teaching of 'politics' as such. It was both all-party and, determinedly, *no* party. In this context, a language centred around 'citizenship' rather than 'politics', one that gave less attention to human rights focused approaches than some might have liked, and one that was essentially neutral on all matters European, had obvious attractions. Crick, in short, was willing and sufficiently *politically* savvy to produce a report that those of a conservative mindset could support, even if it did not go as far as some progressives might have preferred. His job was to let the 'citizenship cat out of the bag', secure in the knowledge that his critics might struggle, at risk of mixing metaphors, 'to put the toothpaste back in the tube'. And the citizenship focus also sat easily with the communitarianism that was seen as key to the wider Blair project.

Nonetheless, more than two decades after the publication of the first national curriculum citizenship programmes of study for those teaching in English schools, concern about the political literacy of those exiting the UK's schooling systems are as high as ever, and trust in formal politics as low as it could be, not just in the UK but in a range of national settings. In their different ways, the disturbances in the so-called 'northern towns' investigated by Ted Cantle (2001), the national disturbances of summer 2011 that started in Tottenham (a disadvantaged area in northeast London, and the site of an early example of the kind of youth activism enabled through the Youth Act! project) and spread across the towns and cities of the UK, the rise of the far Right in Britain and elsewhere, the rise in popularity and subsequent election of Donald Trump in the US, the Brexit vote in the UK, and the election of Jeremy Corbyn to lead the Labour Party in Britain in its wake all point to a disaffection with the political mainstream, at least sometimes borne of a lack of political knowledge and understanding – an understanding that Crick might have hoped his citizenship curriculum, infused with the aspiration to build political literacy, would address. Indeed, where political literacy has grown strongly during this period, it has done so autonomously in movements and around causes rather than through parties and parliaments: Black Lives Matter, Pride, Me Too, Extinction Rebellion and the wider environmental movement. And sometimes schools have felt implored to stand against such movements – where, for instance, young people have taken 'strike' action to participate in environmental campaigns or to protest against some aspect of school life, such as at the Pimlico Academy in Central London in 2021.

As it is, the majority of English schools do not teach citizenship as a *discrete* subject in an identifiable form in spite of its statutory status, other than where the 'C' of citizenship is inserted into the 'PSHE' of personal, social and health education to form PSCHE, or even PSCHEE, where a concern for economics and personal finance education is also cast towards this particular social curriculum catch-all, which is usually taught by non-specialists alongside a range of vital but essentially pastorally focused endeavours. In short, too often, citizenship has become the latest guest in the great PSHE sleepover. And, needless to say, there is little place at such a 'sleepover' for politics to get its voice heard, or for political literacy to be developed.

Teaching politics in a new political environment

In the build-up to the 2010 UK general election, those of us active in the citizenship education community were focused on two things:

1. Completing a body of work undertaken in partnership with England's Qualifications and Curriculum Development Agency (QCDA, formerly QCA) in preparation for the expected passing of a new Education Act that would see the introduction of citizenship to the national curriculum taught in primary (or elementary) schools, an achievement long lobbied for by the citizenship education community and seen by many as the completion of Crick's mission.
2. Building bridges with Conservative shadow ministers and their advisers in anticipation of political change.

The attempts at bridge building were sadly unsuccessful. Removing the duty on schools to promote community cohesion and abolishing a range of educational agencies (those devoted to development rather than compliance), including the QCDA (which had, under the leadership of Mick Waters, been a strong advocate of citizenship education), as part of a so-called 'bonfire of the quangos', were among the first actions of the Conservative-led coalition government. An even bigger setback for the citizenship education community was the loss of the envisaged Education Bill in the run-up to the election as a result of something called the 'mop up', a process whereby the legislative timetable is collapsed ahead of an election, so as to ease the lawmaking load. Many had seen the presumed introduction of citizenship in the primary phase as both a 'done deal' and a re-energising moment. It would not be given another chance under the Conservatives, who instead proposed a narrower statutory curriculum focused on traditional 'academic' subjects, and a focus on the 'mastery' of the knowledge within these subjects.

Against this background, maybe, just maybe, it is time for us to consider calling the subject 'politics' rather than 'citizenship'. And, other than this contextual reality, what of the rationale for such a reconsideration? Perhaps the following three points are pertinent:

1. The English education system, in common with most in the English-speaking world, has a predilection with academic disciplines as the building blocks for secondary or high school curricula, according the highest status to subjects (or disciplines) with the longest heritage, not always on a particularly logical basis, such that, for instance, Latin is typically thought of as being of a higher status than the 'newer' subject sociology.
2. Concurrently and consequently, the English system reduces those programmes that are not rooted either in single subject disciplines or are based on some combination or integration of those disciplines to a lower status (PSHE, integrated humanities, combined science, business studies, media studies, film studies), a fate that is inevitably accorded to citizenship education.
3. The preference for long-established academic subjects transfers into a preference for summative, 'high stakes' terminal examinations and a disdain for project-based study and courses in the domain of professional and vocational education.

In this context, politics is both a single academic discipline and a long-established one. Moreover, it might be that some of those who once baulked at calling for politics in the curriculum now recognise the need that Crick was seeking to address a quarter of a century ago, given enduring levels of political disinterest and alienation. And the need might not be for every child to study politics on a full-time, full year, year-on-year basis throughout the secondary or high school phase, but rather as part of a modular programme that might give specialist time to a range of disciplines pertinent across the citizenship and PSHE domains, as I have argued at some length and with illustrative models elsewhere, notably as part of a wider investigation into the social curriculum and the social, moral, spiritual and cultural development of children and young people in schools (RSA, 2014; Breslin, 2014a).

Candidates for inclusion in such a programme might, in addition to politics, include law, economics, sociology and psychology as well as modules focused on aspects of personal development and wellbeing. Moreover, this kind of modular specialism might be delivered by specialist teachers currently concentrated on the delivery of advanced pre-university courses in the upper and non-statutory years, who would now have a chance to showcase their subjects and interests to those in the mainstream school.

In short, if we want young people to learn about politics, we might just have to teach courses called 'politics', just as if we want them to understand the nature of economics or personal finance, we might need them to follow courses called 'economics'. Lord Hodgson of Astley Abbotts, the chair of a

House of Lords Select Committee on Citizenship and Civic Engagement (2018), acknowledges as much and calls for a renewed emphasis on citizenship education: 'Individuals do not learn about the government and political institutions by osmosis. They need to be taught and taught well. The neglect of citizenship education in recent years is to be much regretted.'

Giving a renewed prominence to the teaching of politics need not mean a ditching of the term 'citizenship'. The overarching title for such a programme might be citizenship and, if we extend this thinking to PSHE, it might be something like citizenship and personal development, but at its core would sit branded, specialist inputs on politics, law, economics and so on. And if we continue to develop schools that are 'citizenship-rich', we might create environments in which young people gain a range of opportunities to practise politics for real, turning the political knowledge of the specialist-delivered modules into political literacy and social action informed by this – producing citizens that are not just active but *effective* in their endeavours.

But I hear a lingering objection, in part from some of my friends and colleagues in the citizenship education community, including some of my former colleagues at the Citizenship Foundation, namely to teach a discrete and dismembered politics in this way is to return to the 'old civics', akin to the British constitution course that some of us undertook in our school days, a triumph of 'dry' political knowledge over the wider project of developing political literacy, which was Crick's aspiration. There is something in this, but it may be that in seeking to engage, excite and innovate, aspects of political real estate – the political knowledge required to be politically literate – were overly ignored. Political literacy is not achieved through simply accumulating a body of knowledge about how local, national and international politics works, but, arguably, it cannot be fully developed *without* such knowledge.

And this may lead us to another weakness in the citizenship education project to date: the extent to which we have failed to offer a sufficient number of children experience in the development of what I tend to call the 'utilitarian skills' of citizenship: researching, debating, public speaking, voting.[5] True, student voice has flourished over the past quarter of a century, with school councils and the like now part of the ordinary furniture of everyday schooling, but it may be that in too many settings the increasing number of conduits for the channelling and expression of student voice have been populated by a narrow cohort of already engaged and assertive young people, while these processes (and the personal development opportunities they offer) pass the majority of their peers by, virtually unnoticed (Breslin,

---

[5] For an exploration of what universities can do to advance such practical political skills, see Chapter 9.

2010). The participation gaps in most societies closely mirror socioeconomic gaps, which are, in turn, patterned by matters of ethnicity and disability.

If this has happened, we may as citizenship educators – and (rightfully) as champions of student voice – have contributed to the 'overvoicing' of a minority of young people, later to progress to political careers via degrees in philosophy, politics and economics (PPE) and apprenticeships served in think tanks and what I have previously termed the 'spad-ocracy' (Breslin, 2014b), ahead of a career in politics. Arguably, this professionalisation of the political process has closed out traditional routes into national politics through the Chambers of Commerce, trade unions and local government, and created an arena in which politicians have never been younger or better educated, and never so cut off from, and despised by, those they serve. That was never what any of us intended.

Opportunities and grounds for optimism

It is an irony, that as citizenship entered the English national curriculum as a foundation subject in September 2002, the school inspectorate in England (Ofsted) introduced a new framework for the inspection of schools. In so doing, it removed the mainstay of the predecessor framework, especially in the secondary phase, the inspection of individual subjects, replacing this with a focus on pupil outcomes, particularly examination results, especially in a narrow range of longer established subjects.

This approach was subsequently reinforced with the introduction of the so-called 'English Baccalaureate' (EBacc) in 2010, a framework that focused schools on particular outcomes for pupils at 16 across five subjects or clusters of subjects (DfE, 2019). There was no place for citizenship or the social sciences more broadly and, therefore, no place for politics either. Moreover, and mirroring this change, educational advisory services based in local authorities pivoted away from 'support and development' across the multiple subjects of the curriculum towards 'school improvement', a concept that was increasingly defined through success across a narrow range of core subjects, literacy and numeracy in the primary years and those within the EBacc in the secondary phase.

Thus, citizenship was seeking to establish itself as a subject – a new *kind* of subject no less – just as – for those outside the core – a post-subject terrain was emerging. In truth, whatever the merits of the changes to the Ofsted framework at that time, advocates of citizenship education had lost a lever to compel schools to take this new subject seriously, whatever their ambivalence about such a lever, and the exclusion of citizenship education from the EBacc a decade later removed an incentive for schools to place citizenship at the core of the upper secondary curriculum and to adopt the new, and initially popular, public examinations in the subject at 16. And the marginalisation of citizenship as a subject in the conventional sense disproportionately impacted on teaching and learning specifically in the sphere of politics: Why? Because, although politics offered a body of subject knowledge for formal assessment that could be assessed in the examination hall, the broader range of reforms – most notably those introduced between 2010 and 2015 by the Conservative–Liberal Democrat coalition government – steered the focus away from subjects outside the EBacc core and, therefore, away from citizenship and its constituent elements, including politics, as a result.

However, there may yet be opportunities to re-energise the citizenship education project and to do so within a framework that places 'teaching about democracy' at its heart. In this, three developments are preeminent:

1. The lockdowns of the COVID period have created both a pause and a system shock that are together causing a reconsideration about the nature and form of schooling in terms of both process and purpose (Breslin, 2021, 2023).
2. The evident failure of educational systems not just in the UK but in the US and elsewhere to educate young people about politics means that the very concerns that exercised Bernard Crick, not just in his series of reports but across a working lifetime, remain as prevalent today as ever.
3. The return, in England, to an inspection model (Ofsted, 2019) that, again, places curriculum and subject knowledge at its heart, while also placing a stronger focus on the personal development of young people (including their development as citizens) may just open the door to curricular models in which the lost subjects of the social curriculum, including politics specifically and citizenship more broadly, have a chance to flourish.

We owe it to all those who have long campaigned for a curriculum that has as a core purpose not just the *teaching* of children and young people but their *development* as citizens and, of course, we owe it to the legacy of the late Professor Sir Bernard Crick to do so. There are multiple lessons and many gains of the past 25 years that we can trace to Crick, especially the development of a cadre of schools that are much more citizenship-rich, much more open and often less hierarchical, and a cadre of professionals, many now at senior positions in schools and in the educational infrastructure, committed to these principles. We also have a growing number of young people politicised through the enduring campaigns for greater equality and for a greener world that have characterised this period. It is time to harness the energy of these teachers and students, and the educational institutions in which they are located, to achieve the aspirations that Crick and many others have set out, not just in the various landmark reports cited here, but across their multiple professional careers.

References

Breslin, T. (2004) 'New subject: new "type" of subject', *Teaching Citizenship* (Issue 8), London: Association for Citizenship Teaching.

Breslin, T. (2007a) 'Citizenship education and identity formation', in N. Johnson, *Britishness: Towards a Progressive Citizenship*, London: the Smith Institute/Commission for Racial Equality.

Breslin, T. (2007b) 'Developing citizens: developing citizenship-rich schools', in *Secondary Headship*, London: Optimus Publishing.

Breslin, T. (2008) 'From citizenship education to citizenship-rich schools', *Governors' News*, London: National Governors' Association.

Breslin, T. (2010) 'The state and civil society: issues of relevance and problems of access', *Social Science Teacher*, 39(3), London: Association for the Teaching of the Social Sciences.

Breslin, T. (2014a) 'Schools with soul', *Governance Matters*, Birmingham: National Governors' Association.

Breslin, T. (2014b) 'How the Labour Party can reverse the rise of the spadocracy, *The Guardian*, 14 June.

Breslin, T. (2021) *Lessons from Lockdown: The Educational Legacy of COVID-19*, London: Routledge.

Breslin, T. (2023) *Bubble Schools and the Long Road from Lockdown: The Educational Legacy of COVID-19*, London: Routledge.

Breslin, T. and Dufour, B. (eds) (2006) *Developing Citizens: A Comprehensive Introduction to Effective Citizenship Education in the Secondary School*, London: Hodder Murray.

Cantle, T. (2001) *Community Cohesion: A Report of the Independent Review Team*, London: Home Office.

Commission on Integration and Cohesion (2007) *Our Shared Future*, London: Department for Communities and Local Government.

Crick, B. (1962) *In Defence of Politics*, London: Bloomsbury.

DfE (Department for Education) (2014) *Promoting Fundamental British Values through SMSC*, London: DfE.

DfE (2019) *Guidance: English Baccalaureate (EBacc)*, London: DfE.

Further Education Funding Council (FEFC) (2000) *Citizenship for 16–19 Year Olds in Education and Training*, Report of the Advisory Group to the Secretary of State for Education and Employment, Coventry: FEFC.

Goldsmith, P. (2008) *Citizenship: Our Common Bond*, London: Ministry of Justice.

Home Office (2003) *The New and the Old: The Report of the "Life in the United Kingdom" Advisory Group,* Croydon: Home Office Social Policy Unit.

House of Lords Select Committee on Citizenship and Civic Engagement (2018) *The Ties that Bind: Citizenship and Civic Engagement in the 21st Century*, Report of Session 2017–19, HL Paper 118, London: House of Lords.

Huddleston, T. and Kerr, D. (eds) (2006) *Making Sense of Citizenship: A Continuing Professional Development Handbook*, London: Hodder Murray.

NFER (2001–2010) *Citizenship Education Longitudinal Study*, Slough: National Foundation for Educational Research.

Ofsted (2019) *Framework for the Inspection of Schools*, Manchester: Office for Standards in Education.

QCA (1998) *Education for Citizenship and the Teaching of Democracy of Schools: Final Report of the Advisory Group on Citizenship*, the Crick Report, London: Qualifications and Curriculum Authority.

Rowe, D. and Horsley, N. with Thorpe, T. and Breslin, T. (2011) *School Leaders, Community Cohesion and the Big Society: Perspective Report*, Reading: Confederation of British Teaching Education Trust.

Rowe, D. and Horsley, N. with Thorpe, T. and Breslin, T. (2012) 'Benefit or burden? How English schools responded to the duty to promote community cohesion', *Journal of Social Science Education*, 11(4): 87–106.

RSA (2014) *Schools with Soul: A New Approach to Spiritual, Moral, Social and Cultural Education*, London: Royal Society for the Arts.

Whitty, G. and Kisby, E. (2007) *Real Decision Making? School Councils in Action*, London: UCL Institute of Education.

PART II

What could be done differently

6

Populism, classrooms and shared authority

Kathleen M. Sellers and Kathleen Knight Abowitz

On a summer afternoon, twenty-two years ago, I joined my mother, a veteran schoolteacher, in a crowd of several thousand people to listen to a campaign speech by a U.S. Presidential candidate. I was 13 years old, about to begin 8th grade and start my tenure as Student Council President at my elementary school. At the time, I didn't have particularly strong political leanings, but I was excited to be part of the political process. After the candidate gave his speech, I left my mom's side to run to the front of the crowd, joining a line of people gathered along a metal barrier, hoping to shake the candidate's hand. I was the first person in the line, and next to me clustered a group of young people, a dozen or so of us, all about the same age. Clearly, none of us were old enough to vote, but how exciting, how affirming, that we had all found our way to the front of the crowd! For a few moments, I felt a valued part of this ritual. Our excitement grew as the candidate descended the stairs from the stage. In front of him, along the length of the metal barricade, stood a line of citizens, all of us eager to meet him. I watched his eyes skim the crowd, beginning with us young people, then darting to my left, toward the adults. My heart sank, as he pivoted to the side and began walking briskly toward the first adult in line, who he greeted with a smile and handshake, before moving on to the other adults. The group of us young people stood utterly ignored. This was a moment I would not soon forget.

However personally disappointing to the young Kathleen Sellers, the cordial political tenor of that rally two decades ago bears little resemblance to the polarised and even violent energy present in American politics today. We live in a 'populist moment' (Mouffe, 2018, p 1), a time of frequent uprisings and movements of the people, the *demos*, making demands of political leaders. Edda Sant (2021, p 75) has suggested that populist political action is 'an alert to a crisis, and an anticipation of times of change'. We are living through this liminal moment, when our democratic norms are changing, and the very notion of democracy feels more tenuous (Lee et al, 2021). As those in education are well aware, teachers have been drawn into this political fray, in ways that fundamentally undermine their classroom authority and question the legitimacy of public education itself (Stitzlein, 2017; Sant, 2021).

In response to this democratic and educational crisis, the National Academy of Education (NAEd) published *Educating for Civic Reasoning & Discourse*, a multi-authored report investigating current understandings of democracy, citizenship and civics education (Lee et al, 2021). At the heart of this report is the essential civic question: 'What should we do?' (Levine, 2016; Dishon and Ben-Porath, 2018; Stitzlein, 2021). This question is directed not at teachers, but at students, who through civic education should develop civic competences that enable them to answer this question well. From this question stems recommendations for pedagogical and policy actions. Yet, underlying this question, but unaddressed in the report, is the notion of student authority. In this chapter, we seek to answer the question: Who is authorised to ask and answer questions regarding 'what should we do' as a public, as a democratic people? We approach this question from the perspective of classroom teachers, those figures perhaps best positioned in America 'to advocate for a strong civics education' (Lee et al, 2021, p 4). We agree with Sant (2021, p 124) that civic 'education needs to acclimatise to the current circumstances of conflict and uncertainty rather than pretending that it is business as usual', and we draw on the work of Paulo Freire (1993, 2001) and Mary Parker Follett (1924, 1970, 1995; Metcalf and Urwick, 1941) to argue that embedded in the ethos of populist activity is one important remedy for what ails our democracy and civic education: shared authority.

We will make this argument in four parts. First, we briefly review relevant literature on populism, notions of democratic citizenship and civics education, critical pedagogy, and authority. Then, we present an argument regarding our central claim, that students-as-citizens have the authority to ask and answer the essential civic question 'What should we do?', but are not permitted to exercise this authority in traditional 'banking classrooms'. We will then explore this argument through two diverse theoretical perspectives. The first of these are Freirean critiques of banking education as well as his recommendations for problem-posing education (1993). The second comes from the organisational power theories of Mary Parker Follett, a pioneer in theorising control in organisations as more humanely based in social processes rather than subordination (Metcalf and Urwick, 1941). Our last section provides practical examples of how educators are creating innovative ways to share classroom authority in civics, maths and science classrooms, exploring possibilities of pedagogical power-sharing in this populist moment.

Populism and the democratic authority of (future?) citizens

Populism is a political phenomenon with deep roots in Western legal and cultural history (Kaltwasser et al, 2017). The term 'populist' emerged in the late 19th century in the US when a diverse group of farmers, angry about elected officials' neglect of their collective economic interests, launched a third political party, the People's Party, at a national convention in Cincinnati, Ohio. Members of this political party came to be known as 'Populists' and their ideas came to be realised decades later in US progressive-era New Deal policies (Frank, 2020). As of late, populist political activity has been documented on every inhabited continent and expresses itself both on the political Left and Right (Kaltwasser et al, 2017; Sant, 2021). For example, in the 2016 US presidential election, candidate Donald Trump would be an expression of Right populism, while candidate Bernie Sanders would be an expression of Left populism.

Populism, as a political phenomenon, has been defined variously as a 'thin-centred ideology' (Mudde, 2004; Taggart, 2018), a political strategy (Akkerman, 2003), a cultural phenomenon (Ostiguy et al, 2020), a social movement (Aslanidis, 2020; Singer, 2021), or a discursive strategy (Laclau, 2005; Mårdh and Tryggvason, 2017; Mouffe, 2018). Edda Sant (2021, p 47) explains that while political scientists may disagree on the particulars, 'there is a general agreement that populism is a "vague" term referring to political practices that polarise society into two distinct groups, the elite and the people, where "the people" underpin the ultimate source of the general will'. Because of its commitment to the will of the people, the *demos*, populism has often been linked with democracy (Boyte, 2007; Baker, 2019). For the purposes of this discussion, we employ Sant's (2021) definition of populism and add to it the additional understanding, which is widely acknowledged in the literature: populists can be good at naming serious political problems (Baker, 2019), albeit less adept at the complex resolution of said problems through political processes. Because populism hinges on the people's belief that their collective will is the ultimate source of political legitimacy, populist mobilisation can often serve as a litmus test of democratic crisis, when the legitimacy of those 'elite' in power is fundamentally questioned (Sant, 2021).

In a democracy, it is the responsibility of citizens to contribute to the common good of associated life. While the notion of citizenship is often defined in narrow, legalistic terms, we agree with Sarah Stitzlein (2021, p 25), writing in the NAEd report, that citizens are better defined 'in terms of what they do ... Citizens ... [are] people who engage in activities of citizenship', even if they 'are not granted citizenship in terms of formal legal or informal membership status'.

The membership status attached to most meanings of citizenship is also strongly attached to legal ages of adulthood. People who are not old enough to vote are often, in practice, excluded from the formal category of citizenship, a reality that has implications for classroom instruction and school culture writ large. We see this, for example, in the same NAEd report, when Lee et al (2021, p 3, emphasis added) claim that civic skills 'are essential to cultivate as students prepare for their *future roles* as adults, citizens, and being full members of their varied communities'. This claim is consistent with contemporary discourse on democratic education and reveals how Americans are regularly socialised, and what most civic educators are expected to understand about their students: young people are not *full* members of their varied communities but *future* adults and citizens (DeCesare, 2021, 2022). Such a narrow understanding seems to imply that the *real* mark of citizenship is limited to some unspecified marker of adulthood, perhaps voting, in which case one becomes a real citizen at the moment they reach the age of enfranchisement, a strictly legal definition and a literal marker of one, albeit important, civic action. This is a paradox we mean to trouble.

To challenge these dominant meanings of 'citizenship' for students, teachers and their broader communities, we need to make two things clear. First, while we agree that students, like all citizens, are in an ongoing process of learning civic competences, it is also true that students are able to contribute to civic life in distinct and meaningful ways. This has implications for civic education, because it indicates that students and teachers alike, by virtue of their mutual citizenship, have responsibility to exercise shared authority. Second, shared, or democratic authority, is expressed through a process of co-creation enacted by students with teachers. Paulo Freire (2001) explains that

> democratic authority carries the conviction that true discipline does not exist in the muteness of those who have been silenced but in the stirrings of those who have been challenged, in the doubt of those who have been prodded, and in the hopes of those who have been awakened ... I will know better and more authentically what I know the more efficaciously I build up my autonomy vis-à-vis the autonomy of others. (pp 86–7)

Freire's notions of autonomy are not individualistic; his conception of education views autonomy as 'a condition arising from the ethical and responsible engagement with decision-making' (Weiner, 2003, p 90). Freirean ideas of democratic authority are fluid and dynamic, created through student engagement in practices that are meaningful for civic learning and decision-making. Put more simply, teachers express democratic authority by engaging in problem-posing education (that is, critical pedagogy) with their students, and students express their democratic authority by the same process. Sant (2021) reinforces this claim when she writes:

Teachers' authority should not only be dependent on how much they know. Social respect can also be a consequence of whether teachers facilitate educational experiences that allow (or at least do not prevent) learners from understanding themselves better, feeling more comfortable in their skins and making meaningful political contributions. (p 135)

Sant's choice to ground authority in both knowledge and experience is, she explains, a response to contemporary populist actions, some of which call into question truth claims made by 'elite' figures, including teachers. As Sant suggests, while traditional forms of teacher authority in the classroom are based on knowledge expertise (and not, coincidentally, notions of banking education), rethinking classroom authority and student voice within and beyond the classroom ought to be a fundamental realisation for educators in the present global populist moment.[1]

Classroom authority: 'coactive', not coercive

Theorists of power and control in organisations provide frames for building new habits and knowledge related to classroom authority. Writing in the early 20th century, Mary Parker Follett (1995, p 154) asserted that 'authority is a self-generating process'. This process is carried out by people employing their knowledge, experience and skill to meet the responsibilities inherent to specific roles. Such authority, if it is to be employed successfully, can never be coercive, or 'power-over'. Rather, it must be what she called 'coactive' or 'power-with' (Follett, 1924, p 200). Accordingly, legitimate authority could only be exercised through collective problem-solving,[2] a characterisation consistent with Freire's (1993, 2001) notion of critical pedagogy. And also like Freire (2001), Follett (1918, 1924, 1995) understood that the fruit of such authority is freedom *for* action that has civic impact. Writing specifically about the student–teacher relationship, Follett (1970, p 137) explained: 'The greatest service the teacher can render the student is to increase his freedom – his free range of activity and thought and his power of control.' For this reason, teachers need 'faith in our students' (Follett, 1970, p 139) that they have the capacity to fulfil their role as citizens. Classroom

---

[1] For details of how Sant applies this approach to the teaching of national identity in political education, see Chapter 7.
[2] Follett (1924, 1995) identifies three ways of dealing with difference: domination (coercive 'power-over'), compromise (both sides lose some and express some 'power-over') and integration ('coactive power-with'). Follett believed that only integration, which required co-active problem-solving, could offer an effective way to deal with difference.

authority, as a relational and dynamic process, involves an ongoing practice of 'self-fashioning' for both teacher and students, whereby teacher–student and students–teachers balance each other's contributions to the learning process and, in so doing, shape each other's identities and actions as (civic) agents (Bingham 2009, p 144).

This brings us back to our initial query: Who is authorised to ask and answer questions regarding 'what should we do?' Let us remember that the NAEd report makes the claim, and rightly so, that we need students *capable* of answering the fundamental civic question. Underlying this is the unstated but critical assumption that students have the *authority* to answer the question. Follett (1995) reminds us that authority is inherent to roles; that is, how people leverage their knowledge, skills and experience to responsibly meet the demands (and duties) of their roles. This is a dynamic process and, to be effective, must be enacted with others. Let us remember, also, that citizenship is about civic action, not only a legal status or age, and despite adults (including teachers) being socialised to the contrary, students are citizens by this definition. Accordingly, in so much as students are citizens, they absolutely have authority to ask and answer civic questions. And, for students to learn the civic competences necessary to ask and answer civic questions well, they must be allowed to exercise this authority in (and beyond) classrooms. Herein lies the rub for pedagogy and curriculum in schools.

Traditional banking methods of education (Freire, 1993) are coercive; such practices deny students the freedom to function as civic agents (Freire, 2001). Indeed, banking logics conceive of students as passive recipients of their teachers' knowledge (Freire, 1993). Follett (1924) calls this type of student–teacher relationship coercive, because it relies on an unequal power relationship to achieve its aims. In banking education, the teacher has 'power-over' the student, not 'power-with' (Follett, 1924). Likewise, traditional conceptions of the role of students, as future citizens (DeCesare, 2021, 2022; Lee et al, 2021), imagine students as receiving knowledge about citizenship rather than engaging in citizenship activities. *Future* citizen is not a role with the authority to ask or answer the civic question.

We suggest that this banking mode of civic education is typical of most classrooms, and most adults inside and outside classrooms are socialised to imagine students as future, not current, citizens. This has the double effect of dominating and constructing non-citizens, that is, people without agency and authority to ask and respond to the essential civic question of 'what should we do?' If teachers do not have 'faith in our students' (Follett, 1970, p 139) to ask and respond to this question, then students habituate themselves to oppressive (Freire, 1993) and coercive (Follett, 1995) modes of learning and, by extension, oppressive and coercive modes of political life. It's little wonder, then, that for more than two decades, the majority of American students have failed to demonstrate proficiency in a national assessment of civic competency (Campbell, 2019). American students are demonstrating exactly what they've been authorised to learn: non-citizenship.

Banking education is enabled, however, not simply by the traditional relations of 'power-over' in classrooms, but also by our conceptions of what types of curriculum are most essential for creating good citizens. As the previous mention of national (and international) assessments of civic competency reminds us, much curriculum oriented towards civics learning emphasises knowledge and skills related to history and government. Too often, our interests in creating better citizens get translated into more standardised and fixed content rather than the engaged inquiry and practice across the curriculum. As Stitzlein (2021, p 29) notes: 'citizenship education should not be boiled down to a fixed body of static knowledge to convey to children. Instead, knowledge should be taught as part of active inquiry into authentic controversies in our democracy and struggles to live well together within it'.[3]

Freire's conception of 'problem-posing' education was meant to dismantle banking relations in education by shifting the focus of learners and teachers to shared problems – the means to knowledge construction – that would motivate shared inquiry and shifting power relations. Freire (1993, pp 60–1) writes that 'liberating education consists in acts of cognition, not transferals of information', and that education based in authentic dialogical relations between teachers and students must be based in 'the capacity of cognitive actors to cooperate in perceiving the same cognizable object'. This, in turn, is a holistic form of authority, much akin to Follett's notion of 'power-with'; that working towards a shared focus of inquiry, individuals coactively exercise free will on common ends in group process. Parker explains the implications of Follett's theory:

> As a social process, self-control allowed the exercising of free will. The individual was not to be dominated by others because "A" did not control "B," nor did "B" control "A." Instead, they inter-mingled and exchanged views and ideas in a continuing social process in order to produce the collective thought and the collective will (Follett, 1918). The group-oriented process of shared self-control therefore constituted the major aspect of the Follett behavioral model of control. (Parker, 1984, p 740)

The group-oriented process of shared control provides a focus on how power-with enables a shifting of classroom authority relations. This

---

[3] See Chapter 3 for a detailed examination of the problems associated with the teaching of controversial political issues and 'divisive concepts'.

major shift is from a vertical, teacher to student transmission of content, to more horizontal group processes in which teacher and students are oriented around learning that is activated around problems, experiments, or creative endeavours.

These processes help create the 'we' of teachers and students in classrooms and, importantly, elevate students into more agentic roles in (and beyond) classrooms. The more horizontal authority relations of the classroom are needed to socialise and model for students what it means to work together on shared problems outside school boundaries. To achieve this reorientation, we suggest a fundamental change: teachers need to engage students as citizens, a role vested with authority to ask and answer the essential civic question. This requires adults – families and teachers, school administrators and community leaders – who are willing and able to honour students' role as citizen (and its inherent authority) and share civic authority with them, as they strive together to respond to the essential civic question.

As we approach this civic problem, we take lessons from populist movements, whose activity is sparked by a democratic will. At its heart, populism is concerned with the authority of the people, the *demos*. If the people's will is not expressed through the actions of those elites in office, then their authority is perceived as illegitimate (Aslanidis, 2020; Sant, 2021). Here, we could say that populist movements often express a form of coactive leadership (Follett, 1924), in which the will of some body of people seeks to be integrated, or coherent with that of their leaders. Thus, when the people's problems are not adequately addressed, if democracy is to persist in a manner they perceive as legitimate, populists feel they must resist the coercive power-over (Follett, 1924) of the elites by posing their problems to those in power, a process at which populists are quite skilled (Baker, 2019) and which is often very emotional (Mudde, 2004; Sant, 2021; Zembylas, 2020). By joining together into a civically active 'we', populists assert their authority, the same authority to which any citizen is entitled (and expected to express) in a democracy. Whether the particular wishes of any populist movement *ought* to shift policy or decision-making is not the point here. Rather, the point is that becoming part of the 'we' of the civic question, 'what ought we to do', is something going on all around us in this populist moment of diverse resistances to leadership or authorities understood to be coercive.

For classroom teachers, trusted with civic education, our populist moment amplifies two important truths. First, the authority of citizens – and this includes youth and adults – is crucial to democratic life. Second, problem-posing is a critical educational and civic activity. We suggest that these features of democratic life, citizen authority and problem-posing, can and should work together to enhance the types and varieties of education created in classrooms. This coheres with Freire's (1993) notion of critical pedagogy, which understands students and teachers to be in an equitable and dynamic relationship. And critical praxis is predicated on students and teachers, together, responding to some problem posed in their environment. In this respect, critical pedagogy is also a form of civic pedagogy (Freire, 2001), because both occur as a response to real-life problem-posing. Such education meets more than a pedagogical need; it is responsive to any human need that might surface in daily life (Follett, 1970). Further, the collective response of students and teachers together must be productive, not 'a mere shibboleth of empty words' (Follett, 1924, p xiii). We next provide examples illustrating some pedagogical formations that meet this standard.

Teacher engagements in sharing power and authority

For teachers trying to sort out how to facilitate education for civic life, a first step is recognising the role their students possess as present citizens, and then honouring that role by co-developing the authority inherent to it. They must also create opportunities to problem-pose and problem-solve in ways responsive to the needs of the students, their communities and the lived experiences of democratic life. Teachers must figure out these tasks and new arrangements within the parameters of their content areas, school cultures, broader community and, too often, inhospitable political contexts.

Below, we provide three examples of pedagogy that work to shift classroom authority relations, elevate and empower student voice, and form collective organisational structures that facilitate shared inquiry and expertise. Only one of the three content areas of the examples described here is traditionally conceived as *civics* content; we purposefully position the work of elevating student authority and voice as a challenge for *all* content areas and grade levels in a school.

Public sensemaking in high school mathematics

Lo and Ruef (2020, p 17) describe public sensemaking classrooms as places where teachers are 'widening the ways that students can perform competence – when there are more ways to be "good at math," more students will be competent'. Public sensemaking instruction (Ruef, 2016) includes pedagogy that cultivates respect and acknowledgement of one another's perspectives, 'welcoming mistakes and productive struggle as aspects of learning; and taking risks' by sharing one's thinking through presentations, critiques, revisions, and refining work (Lo and Ruef, 2020, p 18). Mathematics classes should, in this view, enable students to become 'collaborative and critical problem solvers prepared to leverage productive change in the world' (p 17). Students become 'active partners in creating learning opportunities for each other', and agency is no longer the sole province of the teacher, but distributed through the network of students, who take on different roles in equitable teaching and learning practices in the classroom (p 16).

Lo and Ruef's study explores mathematical interactions around different kinds of 'interactive positioning', in groupwork problem-solving. One can be positioned as an expert, novice or facilitator; ideally, students and teachers shift their positions depending on the problem, the content knowledge required, and one's level of relative expertise or experience with that particular problem.

> Ideally, in an equitable classroom, positions are impermanent as an equitable classroom culture would produce relatively frequent shifts in positioning. This is because each student brings a different level of prior knowledge or expertise to the task at hand. A student who recalls a strategy used in a similar problem may be viewed as an expert on one task and a novice on another where the student has less mathematical insight. (Lo and Ruef, 2020, p 19)

Lo and Ruef (2020) sought to understand the ways that students are negotiating different positions in their interactive maths groups in a public sensemaking classroom in an urban high school. The pedagogical design allows students and teachers to collectively mediate authority in groups and between groups, enabling students to distribute agency and authority within groups as situations and individual personalities demand. 'Teaching and learning become more equitable when students do not permanently position each other. Temporary positioning, fluid across activities, creates space for students to fluctuate between expert, facilitator, contributor, novice and [other] positions' (Lo and Ruef, 2020, p 29). This process of repositioning teacher and student expertise in collaborative maths groupwork exemplifies Follett's (1995) notion of authority as 'coactive'. Public sensemaking in mathematics pedagogy also highlights the notion of authority as constructed, produced and achieved over time through risk-taking; the enactment of learning as a co-active, social endeavour rather than an individual one; and the important civic proposition that expertise is not the sole property of the professional in the room.

Expressing civic agency through science education collaboration

In 'Adaptations to a secondary school-based citizen science project to engage students in monitoring well water for arsenic during the COVID-19 pandemic', Anna Farrell et al. (2021, p 1) illustrate how students, teachers, and scientists collaborated to promote 'positive long-term health impacts on the students and their communities', through scientific inquiry and data literacy in and beyond classrooms. The All About Arsenic project (www.allaboutarsenic.org), which Farrell et al's article explores, engaged middle and high school students in Maine and New Hampshire, the two US states with the highest reliance on private wells for drinking water, as citizen scientists. This presented students with a real problem that they could address through scientific inquiry and civic action, in and beyond the classroom. With the support and guidance of scientists and 16 science teachers during the 2019–20 school year, students collected 518 'well water samples for arsenic analysis' (p 1), analysed data and organised it into graphs and maps that were pertinent to their local context, and shared their findings and resources for mitigating arsenic contamination in public forums. From these samples, 82 wells were identified as having elevated levels of arsenic, and the owners of the wells were immediately contacted and provided with resources to address this issue. This is just part of the way that this project commits all participants to translating 'data to action' in the students' community. Additionally, students and teachers worked co-actively to design and implement community outreach, resulting in such varied actions as virtual meetings between students and their state representatives to discuss students' research findings, students writing to their local elected officials and newspapers to inform the public about this community health issue, and developing longer term plans for 'student participation in a town-wide effort to get all wells tested' (Farrell et al, 2021, p 9). This variety of civic actions reflects the project's broader structure as a framework, rather than a strict lesson or unit plan. 'Each teacher involved in the project embeds this citizen science initiative into their curriculum in different ways' (Farrell et al, 2021, p 3), allowing the integration of civic and science learning at different grade levels and in different subject areas, including chemistry and biology. Sharing authority with students as citizens provides many possibilities for curriculum and teaching innovations.

Controversial issues discussions

Diana Hess (2009) demonstrates the democratic power of dialogue by profiling several case studies of teachers who adeptly use controversial issues discussions in their pedagogy. Controversial issues discussions are designed to give students practice in inclusive deliberation, critical reasoning and explorations of and tolerance for political and other forms of difference. Such discussions are based on contemporary questions that have controversial and conflictual elements. Controversial issues discussion is

> teaching *for* and *with* discussion, [wherein] the teachers direct the full resources of their pedagogical content knowledge to the lesson planning

process, and they devote a generous amount of classroom time to teaching students how to prepare for discussions, how to participate in them, and how to debrief them. (Hess, 2009, p 56)

One example is a classroom town hall meeting model developed by Ann Twain, a middle school social studies teacher, for her interdisciplinary US history, civics and world geography class (Hess, 2009, p 56). Ms Twain's students participated in eight town hall meetings across the school year, weaving in service learning programming across the curriculum as well. Ms Twain chose topics that were presently being discussed or deliberated at local, state or national levels. One example of a successful topic was an upcoming ballot initiative that would ban local and state government affirmative action programmes based on race and gender. Students created, and then assumed, the roles of those participating in the town hall discussion – each role was a person with a particular point of view or position in this controversial issue. Students worked through extensive background materials prior to the meeting, to make sure that the deliberation was productive and based on good evidence, sources and testimonial. Students shared power with teachers throughout the process, from creating the initial guidelines for the discussion activity to doing preparation work to actually being at the centre of the discussion. Teachers, like Ms Twain, who successfully practised this pedagogy, viewed discussions as a 'forum for their students', not another soapbox for teacher authority (Hess, 2009, p 75). Likewise, Ms Twain's students deliberated with each other at their town hall meetings, rather than centring on the teacher's power.

There is no one way to renegotiate authority relations between students and teachers, yet all three examples show how pedagogical innovation can provide structures for students to address complex problems and issues that matter. In the maths class, students experiment with different positionalities as they work through maths problems. When they have expertise, they facilitate, but when they are novices or struggle with a skill, they play other roles. In science class, students are active participants in water sampling, testing and communicating with community members regarding water safety. In a controversial issue discussion, students are active participants in staging, conducting and evaluating vital exchanges of information and argument in regards to substantive, controversial issues of the day relevant to the school curriculum and the real world. These examples demonstrate the variety of pedagogical approaches for students to contribute as citizens in the present moment and not at some abstract point in the future.

Becoming the 'we' of democracy

We began this chapter with a personal example of civic engagement outside the classroom. In a moment of heightened political emotion, a young citizen and her peers were ignored by a political candidate, who devoted his time and energy, instead, to engagement with adults of apparent voting age. She read this action then, and we read the action together now, as a failure to acknowledge the citizenship of young people. Such failures communicate to young people that their contributions today do not matter to civic life. Similar actions take place in American classrooms every day, and they have serious consequences for the kinds of citizens we shape in schools.

We have argued that students-as-citizens have the authority to ask and answer the essential civic question 'What should we do?', and as such, it is incumbent upon educators to employ problem-posing education that allows space for students across the curriculum and grade levels to co-actively solve problems relevant to their daily lives. The examples of controversial issues discussions (Hess, 2009), the All About Arsenic project (Farrell et al, 2021) and public sensemaking in mathematics (Lo and Ruef, 2020) illustrate what this can look like in context. These examples underscore that the teacher needs to be prepared to engage with their students and co-actively plan and implement responses to the essential civic question. Only then will the teacher render the student the greatest service possible, 'to increase his freedom – his free range of activity and thought and his power of control' (Follett, 1970, p 137). Indeed, in our populist moment: 'The test of the teacher-student relation is: Is the teacher's work such, are his ideas and aims such, that the student can *carry on*, can *take over* just where the teacher leaves off' (Follett, 1970, p 139).

The education of citizens requires that we reconceive the fundamental notions of authority in classrooms, and who has the right and responsibility to ask and answer civic questions in our society. We can tinker with civics education curriculum and assessment questions, yet still miss analysing a foundational question about how students understand themselves to be citizens, as part of the 'we' of democracy. The expansion and increase of populist expression, whether coming from the Left or the Right, signifies that more and more of us feel disenfranchised. Banking pedagogy sets up that dynamic. However, by taking our cues from populist expression, we might pursue a more co-active, authoritative civic education.

References

Akkerman, T. (2003) 'Populism and democracy: Challenge or pathology?', *Acta Politica*, 38(2): 147–59.

All About Arsenic (2022) 'Data to action: a secondary school-based citizen science project to address arsenic contamination of well water': www.allaboutarsenic.org

Aslanidis, P. (2020) 'Major directions in populism studies: Is there room for culture', *The Open Journal of Sociopolitical Studies*, 13(1): 59–82.

Baker, P.C. (2019) '"We the people": the battle to define populism', *The Guardian*, 10 January: www.theguardian.com/news/2019/jan/10/we-the-people-the-battle-to-define-populism

Bingham, C. (2009) *Authority is Relational: Rethinking Educational Empowerment*, Albany, NY: State University of New York Press.

Boyte, H.C. (2007) 'Populism and John Dewey: Convergences and Contradictions', University of Michigan Dewey Lecture, Ann Arbor, MI: University of Michigan.

Campbell, D.E. (2019) 'What social scientists have learned about civic education: a review of the literature', *Peabody Journal of Education*, 94(1): 32–47.

DeCesare, A. (2021) 'What about "current" citizens? Challenging the future- and school-orientation of democratic education', paper presented at the annual meeting of the Ohio Valley Philosophy of Education Society, Nashville.

DeCesare, A. (2022) 'The future is now: rethinking the role for children in democracy,' *Philosophy of Education*, forthcoming.

Dishon, G. and Ben-Porath, S. (2018) 'Don't@ me: rethinking digital civility online and in school', *Learning, Media and Technology*, 43(4): 434–50.

Farrell, A., Buckman, K., Hall, S.R., Muñoz, I., Bieluch, K., Zoellick, B. and Disney, J. (2021) 'Adaptations to a secondary school-based citizen science project to engage students in monitoring well water for arsenic during the COVID-19 pandemic', *The Journal of STEM Outreach*, 4(2): 1–4.

Follett, M.P. (1918) *The New State: Group Organization the Solution of Popular Government*, New York: Longmans, Green and Co.

Follett, M.P. (1924) *Creative Experience*, New York: Longmans, Green and Co.

Follett, M.P. (1970) 'The teacher-student relation', *Administrative Science Quarterly*, 15(2): 137–48.

Follett, M.P. (1995) 'The basis of authority', in P. Graham (ed) *Mary Parker Follett: Prophet of Management*, Boston, MA: Harvard Business School Press, pp 141–54.

Frank, T. (2020) *The People, NO: A Brief History of Populism*, New York: Metropolitan Books.

Freire, P. (1993) *Pedagogy of the Oppressed*, new rev. 20th anniversary edn, trans. M.B. Ramos, New York: Continuum.

Freire, P. (2001) *Pedagogy of Freedom: Ethics, Democracy, and Civic Courage*, trans. P. Clarke, Lanham, MD: Rowman & Littlefield.

Hess, D.E. (2009) *Controversy in the Classroom: The Democratic Power of Discussion*, New York: Routledge.

Kaltwasser, R.C., Taggart, P., Espejo, P. and Ostiguy, P. (eds) (2017) *The Oxford Handbook of Populism*, Oxford: Oxford University Press.

Laclau, E. (2005) *On Populist Reason*, London: Verso.

Lee, C.D., White, G. and Dong, D. (eds) (2021) *Educating for Civic Reasoning and Discourse*, Washington, DC: National Academy of Education: https://naeducation.org/wp-content/uploads/2021/04/NAEd-Educating-for-Civic-Reasoning-and-Discourse.pdf

Levine, P. (2016) 'The question each citizen must ask', *Educational Leadership*, 73(6): 31–4.

Lo, M. and Ruef, J. (2020) 'Student or teacher? A look at how students facilitate public sensemaking during collaborative groupwork', *Journal of Urban Mathematics*, 13(1): 15–33.

Mårdh, A. and Tryggvason, A. (2017) 'Democratic education in the mode of populism', *Studies in Philosophy of Education*, 36(6): 603–13.

Metcalf, H. and Urwick, L. (eds) (1941) *Dynamic Administration: The Collected Papers of Mary Parker Follett*, London: Pitman.

Mouffe, C. (2018) *For a Left Populism*, New York: Verso.

Mudde, C. (2004) 'The populist zeitgeist', *Government and Opposition*, 39(4): 541–63.

Ostiguy, P., Panizza, F. and Moffitt, B. (eds) (2020) *Populism in Global Perspective: A Performative and Discursive Approach*, New York: Routledge.

Parker, L. (1984) 'Control in organizational life: the contribution of Mary Parker Follett', *The Academy of Management Review*, 9(4): 736–45.

Ruef, J. (2016) 'Building powerful voices: co-constructing public sensemaking', unpublished doctoral dissertation, Stanford University.

Sant, E. (2021) *Political Education in Times of Populism: Towards a Radical Democratic Education*, Cham: Palgrave Macmillan.

Singer, J. (2021) 'Power to the people? Populism and the politics of school choice in the United States,' *Journal of School Choice*, 15(1): 88–112.

Stitzlein, S.M. (2017) *American Public Education and the Responsibility of its Citizens: Supporting Democracy in the Age of Accountability*, Oxford: Oxford University Press.

Stitzlein, S.M. (2021) 'Defining and implementing civic reasoning and discourse: philosophical and moral foundations for research and practice', in C. Lee, G. White and D. Dong (eds) *Educating for Civic Reasoning and Discourse*, Washington, DC: National Academy of Education, pp 23–52.

Taggart, P. (2018) 'Populism and "unpolitics"', in G. Fitzi, J. Mackert and B. Turner (eds) *Populism and the Crisis of Democracy*, New York: Routledge, pp 79–87.

Weiner, E. (2003) 'Secretary Paulo Freire and the democratization of power: toward a theory of transformational leadership', *Educational Philosophy and Theory*, 35(1): 89–106.

Zembylas, M. (2020) 'The affective modes of right-wing populism: Trump pedagogy and lessons for democratic education', *Studies in Philosophy and Education*, 39: 151–66.

7

Different approaches to teaching civic and national identity

Edda Sant

Introduction

Mass schooling was first introduced in the 19th century for different reasons, including the expectation that it would fulfil two important political purposes. On the one hand, teachers were to educate citizens to become autonomous, independent thinkers (Biesta, 2006). Political education was expected to help learners to find their singular political perspectives. On the other, schooling was to contribute to cohesive and peaceful intra-state societies (Durkheim, 1956). Aligned with processes of nation-state building, schools were seen as key settings where children and young people could 'acquire' the national identity associated with their legal citizenship status (Sant et al, 2016).

As time went by, globalisation fostered the migration of political sovereignty from nation-states to international organisations (Brown, 2014). Political education began a process of decentring, where multiple political identities (national, European, global) were co-taught and/or recognised (Veugelers, 2020). However, in the past two decades, we have seen a range of nationalistic movements resulting in unexpected political processes, such as Brexit in the UK, the Catalan movement for independence (Spain), or the election of Donald Trump as US president. Processes associated with globalisation, including the rise of cultural diversity, the 2008 financial crisis, the commodification of democratic politics (Mouffe, 2018), or even a global pandemic, have invigorated nationalist discourses. We live in times of complexity (Sassen, 2013). Globalisation is very much alive but coexists, and sometimes competes, with re-energised forms of nationalism (Sellar et al, 2022).

Such complexity has further problematised the role and purpose of political education (Veugelers, 2020). In contexts relevant to the focus of this book (mainly liberal democracies influenced by Anglo-American political culture), where there has been an increase of political polarisation, cultural diversity, increasing inequalities and growing support for nationalist discourses, policy makers have reinforced the teaching of national identities as a way to secure social cohesion. Certainly, many have seen these renationalisation trends in political education as a push towards more essentialist, assimilationist, and/or acritical approaches (see, for example, Jerome and Clemitshaw, 2012; Lander, 2016). Yet, others have also raised the issue that without nation-states, many of us are likely to lose what is left of our political rights and sovereignty (Mouffe, 1993). For one reason or another, national identities have regained their status as necessary allies of state structures (Sellar et al, 2022) and the debate about whether political education should encourage the teaching of national identities has been reinvigorated (see, for example, Peterson, 2013; Chong et al., 2016; Sant and Hanley, 2018).

This chapter will examine the teaching of national identities within political education. First, it will begin by conceptualising the notion of national identity in relation to existing theory and research. Second, it will discuss the challenges and possibilities of teaching national identities in the context of political education. Third, the chapter will consider three different approaches to the teaching of national identities: partisan, deliberative and agonistic approaches. The chapter will conclude by emphasising that, while agonistic approaches are well placed to expand partisan and deliberative approaches as we respond to our current challenges, they are not 'miracle cures', and they need to be considered within a more holistic social strategy.

Political, national and civic identities

This chapter takes as its starting point the poststructuralist understanding that identities are processes of identification with communities (Laclau and Zac, 1994). In the context of late modernity, political communities have four attributes that are particularly relevant for us here:

1. Political communities cannot be all-encompassing (Butler, 2000) – they need to be built in opposition to something or someone (Laclau, 2007). We identify with a community only insofar as this community feels different from others.
2. Political communities are 'constructed'. All political communities, perhaps other than 'primordial villages of face-to-face contact' are imagined. They are not driven by any primordial or rotted connection and cannot be distinguished by their 'falsity/genuineness' (Anderson, 1996, p 6).
3. The 'meaning' attributed to political communities is contingent. Political communities are open to change and there cannot be a consensus (within or outside the margins of the community) of what a political community looks like.
4. Our identification with political communities operates at the emotional level. Processes of identification are not driven by any rational calculation,

but by our need to belong to something larger, and our feelings that we will enhance ourselves in togetherness with others (Sant, 2021a).

Nationhood is one of these political communities. Nations are imagined, antagonistic and susceptible to the influence of different understandings. Among these understandings, social scientists usually differentiate two types of nationhood (Sant and Hanley, 2018). Ethnic/cultural conceptualisations see the national community in relation to ethnic, linguistic, religious, or cultural factors. Ethno-nationalist discourses emphasise this type of perspective on the nation. In contrast, the civic nation is 'a political structure, the state, which can be summarised as the set of institutions, rights, and rules that preside over the political life of the community' (Bruter, 2004, p 190). Civic nationalism is framed by this political understanding.

Regardless of its nature (ethnic or civic), national identities can provide transcendence to state structures, operating as the 'soul' from which state sovereignty emerges and perdures (Sellar et al, 2022). National identities can contribute towards intra-group solidarity and social cohesion (Conover, 1995). National identities mobilise passions and facilitate political engagement (Mouffe, 2018). Yet, these potentialities have a cost. National identities are historically constructed through relationships of power and they tend to naturalise distinctions between the national 'we' and the external 'other', foster stereotypes, exclusions and the imposition of dominant values (see, for example, Ahmed, 2014).

Perhaps because of this, national identities are extremely complex and controversial. In the past few decades, processes of deterritorialisation have led to more complex relationships between the state and the nation (Appadurai, 2006). Groups of people often self-defined as 'nations' are spread across state boundaries (such as Turkish people) and others attempt to build state structures (for example Catalonia, Spain; Scotland, UK). Meanwhile, deterritorialisation has also contributed to a new political divide between 'globalists' and 'nationalists' that challenges traditional Left-Right spectrums (Friedman, 2007). National identities drive passions among both, those who support and those who oppose them (Sant, 2021b).

Political education and the teaching of national identities

Not without controversy, the teaching of national identities has become a major issue in the educational agenda of policy makers worldwide (Chong et al., 2016). For example, in England, in the context of the counterterrorist agenda, all teachers, regardless of their specialism, are expected to promote fundamental British values – defined as democracy, the rule of law, individual liberty and mutual respect and tolerance of those with different faiths and beliefs (Department for Education, 2013). In Hong Kong, the introduction in 2012 of a new *Moral and National Education Curriculum Guide* resulted in the clear opposition of different parent and student groups, who considered the guidelines to be an example of Chinese nationalism (see Chong et al, 2019). In Colombia, since the 2016 Colombian peace agreement (which ended five decades of conflict between the government and FARC), there have been attempts to re-emphasise the national sense of belonging as a way of strengthening peaceful coexistence (Sant and González Valencia, 2018).

However, the teaching of national identities is currently susceptible to numerous debates, within and outside the Anglosphere. On the side of those who advocate the need for a political education that embraces national identities, the teaching of national identities is often seen as a question of responsibility and an instrument for social cohesion. Regardless of whether they are explicitly discussed, schools are permeable to controversies related to national identities and teachers of politics have a responsibility to address them (Hand and Pearce, 2009). Indeed, when in the context of Catalan nationalism, the Catalan Ombudsman found out that teachers had given up discussing questions related to nationhood, concerns arose about students' rights to access a plurality of views and be informed (Sindic, 2018). Further, in situations of cultural, economic and political fragmentation, political education is expected to facilitate new generations in embracing a minimal universalism or common values and a sense of belonging, which guarantee political trust and engagement, social stability and, ultimately, nation-state survival (Olssen, 2004). For instance, in Colombia, the teaching of national identities is justified in terms of its contribution to a more peaceful and harmonious society (Colombia Ministerio de Educación, 2018). In England, the promotion of fundamental British values is part of the Prevent agenda to combat initial 'symptoms' of radicalisation (Arthur, 2015).

On the other side, the teaching of national identities is seen to be problematic in two different ways. First, there is the question of whether teaching national identities can be compatible with political autonomy. Traditional forms of teaching national identities could be 'an instrument through which the state can potentially coerce citizens into uncritical acceptance and support' (Peterson, 2013, p 14). In Hong Kong, for instance, many saw the 2012 *Moral and National Education Curriculum Guidance* as an example of an authoritarian regime (Li, 2018). Meanwhile, teaching national identities is often conceived as a way to reinforce the dominant political, economic and cultural values (Christou, 2007; Sant et al, 2015). As such, it can lead to processes of assimilation and/or exclusion. As Lander (2016, p 276) explained in the case of the promotion of British values, the same nationalist discourse that targets social cohesion 'serves to exclude the very members of its society that are constructed as the terrorist "Other"'.

The debates and questions surrounding the teaching of national identities are numerous and complex, yet three questions are particularly important for political educators: Can the teaching of national identities contribute to some minimal common ground to facilitate social cohesion and engagement? Can this be done in such a way that it does not undermine political autonomy or reinforce existing exclusions? If so, how?

Three approaches to the teaching of national identities

My argument in this chapter is that responses to these questions are to some extent dependent on the educational practices recommended by academics, policy makers and teacher educators, and enacted by teachers. And that while there isn't a perfect pedagogy for the teaching of national identities, we can examine our contexts and find ways to better balance this political education dilemma. While I will draw on a range of worldwide examples for illustrative purposes, my analysis will not seek a universal recipe to approach the teaching of national identities. Rather, my aim is to critically examine how political education can respond to the challenges currently faced by liberal democracies influenced by Anglo-American political culture.

Theory and research identify at least three different pedagogical approaches to the teaching of national identities: a partisan approach, a deliberative approach, and an agonistic approach (Sant, 2021a). Each of these approaches are examined in turn, considering the three questions outlined above.

Partisan approaches

We will begin with the pedagogical approach to the teaching of national identities that consists in openly promoting (nationalist) or rejecting (anti-nationalist) the identification with such identities. The partisan/nationalistic approach underpins many political education policies and practices in contemporary democracies. On some occasions, nationalist approaches emphasise ethnic or/and cultural constructions of the nation. Practices such as flag-waving exist in a range of countries, from Japan to Chile (Ho, 2016; Flández and Margarita, 2019). On other occasions, nationalist approaches focus on civic understandings of the nation. In the case of the promotion of fundamental British values, Arthur (2015) emphasises the civic or political nature of the construction of Britishness emerging from the policy. Very often, both constructions are integrated within policies. For instance, according to the aforementioned Hong Kong *Moral and National Education Curriculum Guidance*, young Hong Kongers were expected to learn about 'the etiquette of raising the national flag' (Curriculum Development Council, 2012, p 30), as well as 'to recognise and realise the importance of the rule of law, human rights, democracy, equality, freedom, and justice to society' (p 55).

While rarely found within existing policies, partisan/anti-nationalist approaches are relatively popular within some sectors of the academic and teaching community. From this perspective, the nation is an ideological construct designed to distribute dominant discourses (Hobsbawm and Ranger, 2012). National identities are seen as undermining political autonomy and inclusion, and teaching 'anti-nationalism' is seen as a 'solution' to this problem. The role of teachers is to foster critical reflection on the construction of nationhood and its structures of domination (Christou, 2007), so young people can be independent from the ideological mechanisms through which nationhood operates (see, for example, Jerome and Clemitshaw, 2012).

While there are many ethical, practical and ideological differences between nationalistic and anti-nationalistic approaches, both partisan strategies fail to address the desirable aims of political education. None of these approaches is helpful in generating a common identity or a set of common values. Despite teachers' attempts to promote or challenge national identities, my own empirical research suggests that children and young people will only incorporate these perspectives if they are meaningful with the rest of their life experiences (Sant, 2021b). This is because these two approaches fail to recognise the complex discursive practices that underpin processes of identification and the competing passions that national identities mobilise. The mere mention of 'nation' (or Britain, Spain or the US), no matter if this is followed by ethnic, cultural, or civic attributes, generates as much love as hate (Sant, 2021a). Young people do not 'acquire' a common identity via schooled partisan/non-partisan approaches unless they were already 'interested' in doing so. Instead, it is more likely that by promoting one view or another, young people who do not see themselves represented in the schooled perspective might disconnect or reject such a view (Johansson, 2013).

Both nationalistic and anti-nationalistic approaches somehow undermine political autonomy. The way the nation should be approached (either positively or negatively) is already decided beforehand, limiting the possibilities for young people to find their unique singularities. Aligned with these two points, both partisan approaches foster exclusions. This is obviously problematic when, in situations of cultural diversity, the nation is defined in relation to some ethnic or cultural attributes and others are 'racialised'. But the dilemma is not resolved when the nation is constructed in 'civic' terms either. Political autonomy then becomes a 'national quality', 'value' or 'virtue', which is inherently underpinned by individualist conceptions that crash against more communitarian values (Panjwani, 2016). As a result, 'the discourse of civic nationalism which purports to accommodate plurality' becomes contradictory (Lander, 2016, p 276). It becomes apparent that no construction of nationhood, not even the civic one, can be all-encompassing.

Similarly, and against their intentions, anti-nationalist approaches are at risk of undermining political autonomy and fostering exclusions. For anti-nationalists, the nation is always an ideological construct designed to cover structures of domination. No matter if nationalistic demands are open to change and to different meanings and purposes (some of which could be legitimate), the anti-nationalist approach condemns any construction of the nation. This is just not an option, from this approach. Young people who feel emotionally attached to the construction of nationhood are implicitly or explicitly excluded from such teaching practices (Sant, 2021b).

Deliberative approaches

A second approach to address the teaching of national identities is the deliberative method. This perspective frequently draws on epistemic assumptions for which

> the central aim of education is to equip pupils with a capacity for and inclination to rational thought and action, teachers have an obligation to endorse views for which the relevant evidence and argument is decisive, regardless of whether there are people who sincerely hold contrary views. (Hand, 2014, p 79)

Very often this approach is framed by the work of Habermas (1973), who emphasises argumentative reasoning as the process of reaching consensus in situations in which participants interact as equals, and listen to the arguments of others. Teachers should teach controversies, issues where multiple views fulfil the academic standard of reasonableness (Hess and McAvoy, 2014). The teaching of national identities is one of these controversial issues (Hand and Pearce, 2009). In this respect, it is recommended that teachers should approach nationhood as a controversy – students should engage in the reading and evaluation of evidence via a process of deliberation that often results in some consensual classroom decisions (Sant et al, 2022).

Deliberative approaches are highly embedded within existing academic discourse and educational policy, as they are often seen as a non-partisan way to overcome existing political polarisation (see, for example, Sibbett, 2016; Arneback and Englund, 2020). The teaching of controversial issues is recommended in numerous policies from a range of policy makers, including UNESCO (2016), the Council of Europe (2016) or the Curriculum Development Council (2012) in Hong Kong. While there is little evidence that these policies identify national identities as one of the controversies over which deliberation is needed, this appears to be the assumption within a range of academic texts (see, for example, Hess and Ganzler, 2007; Hand and Pearce, 2009).

However, these approaches are not necessarily helpful to address all the potentialities and challenges associated with the teaching of national identities. First, deliberative approaches privilege rationality and dismiss the embodied and affective nature of politics (Backer, 2017; Lo, 2017). These approaches fail to acknowledge that the teaching of national identities is a *political* education issue and, as such, it necessarily involves cognitive *and* affective domains (Peterson, 2013). As discussed earlier, national identities are not a consequence of any rational calculation and therefore cannot be tackled at the cognitive level. Empirical research with young extreme right supporters suggests that educational practices that fail to engage with affective registers are unlikely to succeed (Miller-Idriss and Pilkington, 2017). Deliberative approaches are unlikely to generate emotional attachments that are needed for any political identification and, ultimately, for social cohesion.

Second, these approaches are ultimately driven by an interest in generating political autonomy. However, the question of nationhood is examined only in reference to views that fulfil the academic standard of reasonableness. In doing so, these approaches do not consider the relationship between power and knowledge (Foucault, 1980). The debate on nationhood is only presented in relation to academic evidence, without acknowledging that, when referring to question of nationhood, the divide is not 'between knowledge and ignorance' but between 'one worldview and another' (Runciman, 2016). Consequently, autonomy is only confined within the 'pre-existing order of modern reason' (Biesta, 2006, p 7), excluding all other possible ways of being and knowing.

Third, deliberative approaches target inclusivity as an aim, yet these approaches are at risk of fostering alienation (Sibbett, 2016). Deliberation and consensus are seen as the primary forms of democratic engagement. There is no room for other forms of participation, potentially resulting in the oppression, marginalisation and discrimination of social groups who are seen as incoherent, incapable or invisible (Postero and Elinoff, 2019, p 16).

Agonistic approaches

The third pedagogical approach is underpinned by theories of agonistic democracy (Mouffe, 2013). According to these theories, all forms of knowledge are socially constructed, and emotions are a legitimate and necessary way to engage with politics (Ruitenberg, 2009). Conflicts can never be entirely resolved, yet we might find ways to transform moral arguments where the other is seen as an 'enemy to be destroyed' to political arguments where the other is seen as an 'adversary whose existence is legitimate and must be tolerated. We will fight against his ideas but we will not question his right to defend them' (Mouffe, 1993, p 4).

There are still relatively little policy, practice and research that directly engage with agonistic approaches (Sant, 2019; Koutsouris et al, 2021), and even less that do so to tackle the teaching of national identities (Sant, 2021a). Furthermore, agonistic approaches are not unified in a particular teaching practice but rather in a constellation of strategies and ways of relating to others that, when grouped together, can facilitate or at least not undermine the desirable aims for political education (cohesion, non-coercion, inclusion).

In a nutshell, these practices fall into three large categories:

1. *Pedagogies of articulation* (Sant, 2021a) *or simplification* (Tryggvason and Mårdh, 2019) refer to situations in which educators request learners to take a stance about a political question. This is somehow similar to deliberative approaches where nationhood is tackled as a controversy. Yet, while deliberative approaches only focus on the cognitive domain of political education, pedagogies of articulation are open to more experiential accounts, facilitating engagement with young people's affective registers. For instance, in my own research (Sant et al., 2021), we asked learners in Manchester, England to openly and immediately show agree/disagree cards in response to several controversial statements related to globalisation. Similarly, Cento Bull et al. (2019, p 622) report a video game in the exhibition 'War Makes Sense' in the Ruhr Museum in Germany, 'in which visitors have to engage with multiple sociopolitical perspectives through roleplaying and have to make decisions about a number of historical and memory dilemmas'.

2. In *pedagogies of differences* (Sant, 2021a) *or orientation* (Tryggvason and Mårdh, 2019), educators facilitate the 'demystification' of 'the object of emotion by showing its history of production' (Tryggvason and Mårdh, 2019, p 240). Pedagogies of differences use similar strategies to those enacted by anti-nationalist/partisan approaches. Yet, in contrast with these approaches, any other social concept (such as cosmopolitanism, social class, gender) is 'treated' as a construct and therefore susceptible to an investigation. In the context of Cyprus, for instance, Zembylas (2011, p 64) explains how 'conflicting narratives as well as new formations of "we" ... need to be constantly interrogated rather than taken for granted'. Backer (2017), drawing on the work of bell hooks, emphasises that in response to openly racist comments, educators should stop the class and focus on a deep examination of 'race' through discussion.

3. *Pedagogies of equivalences* (Sant, 2021a) *or circulation* (Tryggvason and Mårdh, 2019) are designed to facilitate young people's political actions. For instance, Knight Abowitz and Mamlok (2020) report an example in the US where young people, after a mass shooting in a school, mobilised in favour of gun control, supported by curricular activities aimed to enhance their political and digital literacies. In Colombia, Caballero Dávila (2017)

explains how a group of teachers supported young people in creating a memory wall where different narratives on Colombian recent history were presented, shared and supported to the wider audience.

Grouped together, this constellation of agonistic approaches can enhance some of the potentialities of teaching national identities while tackling some of their major challenges. Indeed, my argument is that, by directly engaging with emotions, normalising political disagreement and demonstrating the contingency of all political alliances, these approaches offer a good chance of overcoming some of the limitations of majoritarian partisan and deliberative approaches. Agonistic approaches can help to respond to our current contexts of fragmentation without directly contributing to the problems that political education aims to address; that is, cohesion, polarisation, exclusion and disengagement (Ruitenberg, 2009; Zembylas, 2011; Tryggvason and Mårdh, 2019; Sant et al, 2021; Sant, 2021a).

However, as previously mentioned, no approach to the teaching of national identities is perfect. These practices cannot be seen as universal recipes. As Tryggvason and Mårdh (2019) well expose, the role of teacher is to consider the situated teaching–learning experience and to prioritise the type of pedagogy that could be more aligned with democratic practices. For instance, following Knight Abowitz and Mamlok's example (2020), if students would oppose gun control, teachers could prioritise the use of pedagogies of difference to 'demystify' guns. In other situations, for instance when a classroom action is needed, it might be important to facilitate students' engagement in a process of consensus-reaching (Lo, 2017). On such occasions, teachers can prioritise deliberative approaches. Only teachers can make final decisions in response to their context, their student body and their own politico-educational possibilities (Sant, 2021a).

Furthermore, the question arises of whether we, as educators, teachers and more broadly as a society, are prepared to engage with disagreement, political emotions and to open ourselves to young people finding and expressing their singularities. Research suggests that teachers are trained to deal with academic knowledge, but they are rarely comfortable when dealing with conflict and disagreement (Bickmore and Parker, 2014; Sant et al, 2021). Teachers, like everyone else, can struggle to channel their political emotions in a 'positive' way (Tryggvason, 2017). Agonistic approaches will probably not be able to be implanted into school contexts if they are not previously (or simultaneously) tackled at teacher education level. Even if that is the case, national identities are historically constructed through complex relationships of power (Ahmed, 2014), and these constructions cannot be altered only by the work of teachers, who are also part of a 'result' of such historical processes. Also, if we are indeed committed to facilitating young people in finding their own viewpoints, nothing guarantees that these viewpoints will indeed benefit more inclusive social arrangements (Tryggvason and Mårdh, 2019; Sant, 2021a). Agonistic approaches do not promise a resolution to all political education dilemmas, but they offer a way to teach national identities that respond to our current challenges facilitating political engagement and cohesion, without directly undermining inclusion and autonomy.

Conclusion

This chapter has discussed the teaching of national identities in the context of political education in contemporary democracies. After defining national identities as social and historical constructs that are antagonistic, emotionally driven and contingent, the chapter has questioned whether teaching national identities could potentially favour political engagement and social cohesion without undermining social inclusion and political autonomy.

Three approaches to the teaching of national identities (partisan, deliberative and agonistic) have been examined. Partisan approaches, regardless of whether they defend ethnic or civic constructions of nationhood or anti-nationalist discourses, limit the possibilities of young people in finding their own singularities and are unlikely to generate common ground across those differently positioned in relation to nationalist discourses. Instead, if teachers approach national identities in a partisan matter, a range of students will likely disconnect or reject the school discourse. Meanwhile, deliberative approaches, where the nation is investigated in relation to 'reasonable' evidence and discussed in processes of deliberation, are not always helpful to address national identities in school contexts. This is because these approaches fail to engage with the emotional register of identities and end up constraining political engagement only based on narrow conceptions of reason while excluding everything and everyone else.

Agonistic approaches include a constellation of teaching strategies and ways of engaging in the classroom that aim to tackle political emotions, normalise political disagreement and facilitate political engagement. Agonistic approaches can complement and expand some of our existing deliberative and partisan practices and enhance some of the potentialities of teaching national identities, while tackling some of its main challenges. By facilitating open discussion (pedagogies of articulation) and supporting young people's political actions (pedagogies of equivalence) while deconstructing historical processes leading to national identities (pedagogies of difference), these pedagogies can simultaneously tackle political engagement and cohesion, inclusion and agency.

However, a final note is necessary to emphasise that agonistic pedagogies cannot be seen as a 'miracle cure' for all our social problems. In many contemporary democracies, cultural, political, and social polarisation is lived in many contexts including schools. Like it or not, schools are entirely permeable to controversies related to the nation. As political educators, we have a responsibility to tackle these issues, but we need to acknowledge that we are also impacted by their challenges. A more holistic educational and social change is needed if we wish to prepare teachers and more broadly, all of us as a society, to respond to our current nationalist debates in more democratic ways.

References

Ahmed, S. (2014) *Cultural Politics of Emotion*, 2nd edn, Edinburgh: Edinburgh University Press.

Anderson, B. (1996) *Imagined Communities*, London: Verso.

Appadurai, A. (2006) *Fear of Small Numbers: An Essay on the Geography of Anger*, Durham, NC: Duke University Press.

Arneback, E. and Englund, T. (2020) 'Teachers' deliberation on communicative potentials in classrooms when students express racism', *Reflective Practice*, 21(1): 28–40.

Arthur, J. (2015) 'Extremism and neo-liberal education policy: a contextual critique of the Trojan horse affair in Birmingham schools', *British Journal of Educational Studies*, 63(3): 311–28.

Backer, D.I. (2017) 'The critique of deliberative discussion. A response to "education for deliberative democracy: a typology of classroom discussions"', *Democracy & Education*, 25(1): 1–6.

Bickmore, K. and Parker, C. (2014) 'Constructive conflict talk in classrooms: divergent approaches to addressing divergent perspectives', *Theory and Research in Social Education*, 42(3): 291–335.

Biesta, G. (2006) *Beyond Learning: Democratic Education for a Human Future*. Boulder: Paradigm.

Brown, W. (2014) *Walled States, Waning Sovereignty*, Brooklyn, NY: Princeton University Press.

Bruter, M. (2004) 'Civic and cultural components of a European identity: a pilot model of measurement of citizens' levels of European identity', in K. Herrmann, T. Risse and M. Brewer (eds) *Transnational Identities: Becoming European in the EU*, Lanham, MD: Rowman & Littlefield, pp 186–213.

Butler, J. (2000) 'Restaging the universal', in J. Butler, E. Laclau and S. Žižek (eds) *Contingency, Hegemony, Universality: Contemporary Dialogues on the Left*, London: Verso, pp 136–81.

Caballero Dávila, L.F. (2017) 'Hacia una pedagogía de la memoria, el desacuerdo y el acontecimiento: El caso de la galería de la memoria "somos protagonistas de la historia" del Colegio IED Tibabuyes Universal', *Revista Cambios y Permanencias*, 8(2): 1109–24.

Cento Bull, A., Hansen, H.L., Kansteiner, W. and Parish, N. (2019) 'War museums as agonistic spaces: possibilities, opportunities and constraints', *International Journal of Heritage Studies*, 25(6): 611–25.

Chong, E.K, Davies, I., Epstein, T., Peck, C., Peterson, A. et al (eds) (2016) *Education, Globalization and the Nation*, London: Palgrave.

Chong, E.K., Sant, E. and Davies, I. (2020) 'Civic education guidelines in Hong Kong 1985–2012: striving for normative stability in turbulent social and political contexts', *Theory & Research in Social Education*, 48(2): 285–306.

Christou, M. (2007) 'The language of patriotism: sacred history and dangerous memories', *British Journal of Sociology of Education*, 28(6): 709–22.

Colombia Ministerio de Educación (2018) Lineamientos curriculares: www.mineducacion.gov.co/1759/w3-article-339975.html

Conover, P.J. (1995) 'Citizen identities and conceptions of the self', *Journal of Political Philosophy*, 3(2): 133–65.

Council of Europe (CoE) (2016) *Teaching Controversial Issues*: https://rm.coe.int/16806948b6

Curriculum Development Council (2012) *Moral and National Education Curriculum Guide (Primary 1 to Secondary 6)*, Hong Kong: CDC.

Department for Education (DfE) (2013) *Teachers' Standards: Guidance for School Leaders, School Staff and Governing Bodies*: www.gov.uk/government/uploads/system/uploads/attachment_data/file/665520/Teachers__Standards.pdf

Durkheim, E. (1956) *Education and Sociology*, trans. S.D. Fox, Glencoe: Free Press.

Flández, V. and Margarita, E. (2019) 'Construcción del estado-nación, producción de identidad nacional y expresión de valores en el ciclo ritual de la escuela pública', *Revista Paideia Surcolombiana*, 24: 52–66.

Foucault, M. (1980) *Power/knowledge: Selected Interviews and Other Writings 1972–1977*, New York: Pantheon Books.

Friedman, J. (2007) 'Cosmopolitan elites, organic intellectuals and the reconfiguration of the state', in A. Kouvouama, G. Abdoulaye, A. Piriou and C. Wagner (eds) *Figures croisées d'intellectuels: trajectoires, modes d'action, productions*, Paris: Kharthala, pp 431–54.

Habermas, J. (1973) 'A postscript to knowledge and human interests', *Philosophy of the Social Sciences*, 3(2): 157–89.

Hand, M. (2014) 'Religion, reason and non-directive teaching: a reply to Trevor Cooling', *Journal of Beliefs & Values*, 35(1): 79–85.

Hand, M. and Pearce, J. (2009) 'Patriotism in British schools: principles, practices and press hysteria', *Educational Philosophy and Theory*, 41(4): 453–65.

Hess, D. and Ganzler, L. (2007) 'Patriotism and ideological diversity in the classroom', in J. Westheimer (ed), *Pledging Allegiance: The Politics of Patriotism in America's Schools*. New York: Teachers College Press, pp 131–8.

Hess, D.E. and McAvoy, P. (2014) *The Political Classroom: Evidence and Ethics in Democratic Education*, London: Routledge.

Ho, W.C. (2016) 'A comparative review of music education in mainland China and the United States: from nationalism to multiculturalism', *International Education Journal: Comparative Perspectives*, 15(2): 38–57.

Hobsbawm, E. and Ranger, T. (eds) (2012) *The Invention of Tradition*, Cambridge: Cambridge University Press.

Jerome, L. and Clemitshaw, G. (2012) 'Teaching (about) Britishness? An investigation into trainee teachers' understanding of Britishness in relation to citizenship and the discourse of civic nationalism', *The Curriculum Journal*, 23(1): 19–41.

Johansson, S. (2013) 'Innovative methods and models of collaboration in the field of pedagogical prevention of xenophobia, anti-semitism and right-wing extremism: chances and perspectives for a better cooperation between formal and non-formal education in Germany', *Social Theory, Empirics, Policy and Practice*, 7: 119–32.

Knight Abowitz, K. and Mamlok, D. (2020) '#NeverAgainMSD student activism: lessons for agonist political education in an age of democratic crisis', *Educational Theory*, 70(6): 731–48.

Koutsouris, G., Stentiford, L., Benham-Clarke, S. and Hall, D. (2021) 'Agonism in education: a systematic scoping review and discussion of its educational potential', *Educational Review*, 1–26.

Laclau, E. (2007) *On Populist Reason*, London: Verso.

Laclau, E. and Zac, L. (1994) 'Minding the gaps: the subjects of politics', in E. Laclau (ed) *The Making of Political Identities*, London: Verso, pp 11–39.

Lander, V. (2016) 'Introduction to fundamental British values', *Journal of Education for Teaching*, 42(3): 274–79.

Li, H. (2018) 'Chinese students' perceptions of the "good citizen": Obedience to an authoritarian regime', *Citizenship Teaching & Learning*, 13: 177–192. doi:10.1386/ctl.13.2.177_1

Lo, J.C. (2017) 'Empowering young people through conflict and conciliation: attending to the political and agonism in democratic education', *Democracy & Education*, 25(1): 2–12.

Miller-Idriss, C. and Pilkington, H. (2017) 'In search of the missing link: gender, education and the radical right', *Gender and Education*, 29(2): 133–46.

Mouffe, C. (1993) *On the Political*, London: Routledge.

Mouffe, C. (2013) *Agonistics*, London: Verso Books.

Mouffe, C. (2018) *For a Left Populism*, London: Verso Books.

Olssen, M. (2004) 'From the Crick report to the Parekh report: multiculturalism, cultural difference, and democracy – the re-visioning of citizenship education', *British Journal of Sociology of Education*, 25(2): 179–92.

Panjwani, F. (2016) 'Towards an overlapping consensus: Muslim teachers' views on fundamental British values', *Journal of Education for Teaching*, 42(3): 329–40.

Peterson, A. (2013) 'Civic patriotism as a legitimate aim of education for citizenship in England', *Citizenship Teaching & Learning*, 8(1): 5–20.

Postero, N. and Elinoff, E. (2019) 'Introduction: a return to politics', *Anthropological Theory*, 19(1): 3–28.

Ruitenberg, C.W. (2009) 'Educating political adversaries: Chantal Mouffe and radical democratic citizenship education', *Studies in Philosophy and Education*, 28(3): 269–81.

Runciman, D. (2016) 'How the education gap is tearing politics apart', *The Guardian*, 5 October: www.theguardian.com/politics/2016/oct/05/trump-brexit-education-gap-tearing-politics-apart

Sant, E. (2019) 'Democratic education: a theoretical review (2006–2017)', *Review of Educational Research*, 89(5): 655–96.

Sant, E. (2021a) *Political Education in Times of Populism: Towards a Radical Democratic Education*, Cham: Palgrave Macmillan.

Sant, E. (2021b) 'National myths and democratic history education: secondary students' discursive construction of Catalan nationhood', *Pedagogy, Culture & Society*, 29(2): 173–91.

Sant, E. and González Valencia, G. (2018) 'Global citizenship education in Latin America', in I. Davies, L.C. Ho, D. Kiwan et al (eds) *The Palgrave Handbook of Global Citizenship and Education*, London: Palgrave Macmillan, pp 67–82.

Sant, E. and Hanley, C. (2018) 'Political assumptions underlying pedagogies of national education: the case of student teachers teaching "British values" in England', *British Educational Research Journal*, 44(2): 319–37.

Sant, E., González-Monfort, N., Santisteban Fernández, A. and Oller Freixa, M. (2015) 'How do Catalan students narrate the history of Catalonia when they finish primary education?', *McGill Journal of Education/Revue des sciences de l'éducation de McGill*, 50(2–3): 341–62.

Sant, E., Davies, I. and Santisteban, A. (2016) 'Citizenship and identity: the self-image of secondary school students in England and Catalonia', *British Journal of Educational Studies*, 64(2): 235–60.

Sant, E., McDonnell, J., Pashby, K. and Menendez Alvarez-Hevia, D. (2021) 'Pedagogies of agonistic democracy and citizenship education', *Education, Citizenship and Social Justice*, 16(3): 227–44.

Sassen, S. (2013) 'Land grabs today: feeding the disassembling of national territory', *Globalizations*, 10(1): 25–46.

Sellar, S., Lingard, B. and Sant, E. (2022) 'In the name of the nation: PISA and federalism in Australia and Canada', in D. Trohler, N. Piattoeva and W.F. Pinar (eds) *World Yearbook of Education 2022: Education, Schooling and the Global Universalization of Nationalism*, London: Routledge, pp 153–68.

Sibbett, L.A. (2016) 'Toward a transformative criticality for democratic citizenship education', *Democracy & Education*, 24(2), 1: https://democracyeducationjournal.org/home/vol24/iss2/1

Sindic (2018) *El pluralisme a les escoles de Catalunya com a garantia del no-adoctrinament*, Barcelona: Sindic de Greuges de Catalunya: www.elllobregat.com/adjuntos/15506/Informe_noadoctrinament_cat_def.pdf

Tryggvason, Á. (2017) 'The political as presence: on agonism in citizenship education', *Philosophical Inquiry in Education*, 24(3): 252–65.

Tryggvason, Á. and Mårdh, A. (2019) 'Political emotions in environmental and sustainability education', in K. van Poeck, L. Östman and J. Öhman (eds) *Sustainable Development Teaching: Ethical and Political Challenges*, New York: Routledge, pp 234–42.

UNESCO (2016) *A Teacher's Guide on the Prevention of VIOLENT EXTREMISM*, Paris: UNESCO: https://en.unesco.org/sites/default/files/lala_0.pdf

Veugelers, W. (2020) 'How globalisation influences perspectives on citizenship education: from the social and political to the cultural and moral', *Compare: A Journal of Comparative and International Education*, 51(1): 1–16.

Zembylas, M. (2011) 'Ethnic division in Cyprus and a policy initiative on promoting peaceful coexistence: toward an agonistic democracy for citizenship education', *Education, Citizenship and Social Justice*, 6(1): 53–67.

8

Active learning of marginalised young people

Kalbir Shukra

Introduction

Throughout the 21st century, academics and politicians in the UK and Europe (Kitanova, 2020) have expressed concern about a lack of youth engagement in electoral politics. There has been some contention about whether the underlying issue is a deficit in young people or a narrow understanding of what counts as politics (Henn and Foard, 2014; O'Toole, 2015). From both perspectives, there is room to promote political participation among young people for the benefit of a healthier democracy, though the methods have been contested. Since 2002, citizenship education in schools has been established as a primary vehicle (QCA, 1998), the objective being to 'instil in students values which make it likely they will want to engage in British democracy' (Kisby and Sloam, 2014, p 53).[1]

Following the introduction of citizenship studies, the debate moved on to its effectiveness (Tonge et al, 2012; Pontes et al, 2017). Despite efforts to shift thinking away from a deficit in young people and in a lack of trust in formal politics or limited opportunities to participate (Henn and Foard, 2014), the argument that formal political education in schools is necessary persists (Mycock and Tonge, 2014). According to Matteo Bergamini (2014), for example, 'the introduction of a Politics GCSE for everyone would give young people the information they need and require to become active citizens of the future'.

The starting point for this chapter is an understanding that not only is the meaning of active citizenship contested, but 'minoritised' or 'marginalised' young people may experience additional barriers to meaningful political participation. This has been evident in relation to adult Black and minority ethnic political participation (Saggar, 1998; Shukra, 1998). Attempts to increase the political participation of ethnic minorities in Britain began

---

[1] See Chapters 5 and 10 for more on Crick and the development of citizenship education in England.

in the 1970s (Anwar, 1986; Fitzgerald, 1987) and reached a peak in the 1980s with the election of four 'Black' MPs (Shukra, 1990; Layton-Henry, 1992). Since the 1990s, ethnic minority representation in political parties, policy making, community organisations, campaigns and unions has grown (Solomos and Back, 1995; Saggar, 1998). With young Black and Asian people remaining marginalised, interventions to engage this group are of particular concern. Anxiety arising from the frustrations of young Black people were highlighted by young campaigners in the worldwide movement around the slogan Black Lives Matter (BLM). As the purpose of meaningful political engagement is to create a more just and equal society, the salient question is one of how the democratic participation of marginalised groups can be increased. Discussion on this is limited or diverted into matters of identity-based representation.

While Black and Asian parliamentary representation is more visible, this is not the limit of political participation. Wider politics can include involvement in social movements, civil society organisations and elections. We have seen this in efforts to address youth participation and promote anti-racism in political education that has largely come from young people and their advocates, in campaigns ranging from the public sector to unions and independent action. This chapter contextualises and explores a range of active learning opportunities in local authorities, community groups and youth projects working with schools. We argue that such projects can facilitate young people cultivating a positive political consciousness in a way that includes rather than marginalises. We also highlight a selection of initiatives that enable young people to develop forms of political representation that have successfully involved marginalised young people by supporting them to express their lived experience to grow their voice and a sense of agency, potentially making a wider difference. We see that in considering what works in engaging young people with youth democracy programmes, it is essential to focus less on changing young people and more on listening to them. Whether young people are involved in youth democracy projects or participate in politics outside a formal, adult sanctioned arena or social movement, it is vital to hear their grounded expressions and recognise informal as well as formal engagements as political.

Political learning opportunities for young people

Among established political studies scholars examining political education, age has been a key marker, but few have discussed age and 'race' together in depth. Political education through youth participation tends to receive generic consideration, with race inequality being a side issue, if considered at all. We can bridge that gap here by drawing on reflections from established research on how minority ethnic communities have organised, along with insights from successful London-based youth democracy programmes, some of which have had national and international connections.

Autonomous activists are not consistently recognised as conducting legitimate actions as part of a conscious citizenry. From 2010, for example, when we saw a strong youth response to the Conservative-led coalition government's austerity budget that included university occupations, demonstrations, school student walkouts and campaigns to defend youth projects, the headlines presented young people either positively as new civil rights activists or negatively as anarchists or criminals. Mahatma Gandhi, Martin Luther King Jr and Nelson Mandela are among those who were problematised in their time for challenging and using unorthodox methods before being canonised for their roles in social change, because what in some contexts is seen as criminal or riotous behaviour, in other contexts can be seen as liberatory and inspirational. From the perspective of participants, direct action can be framed as forms of resistance, rebellion or an assertion of citizenship. Riots in 1981, 1985, 2001 and 2011 can be seen as responses to policing, inequality, far right activity and/or austerity (Keith, 1993; Rebel History Calendar, 2021). Similarly, youth-led protests that turned into 'riots' were seen as acts of criminality by many, but could equally have been understood by others as forms of resistance. As Perez (2022) notes, Martin Luther King Jr said: 'In the final analysis, a riot is the language of the unheard.'

Certainly, the upsurge in interest in 2020 around the BLM movement and associated activism points to a generation deeply interested in the politics of discrimination, questions of identity, concerns about the environment and a sense of urgency around social change. Independent acts of youth-led political participation seem to unnerve the establishment. Indeed, the organisation of young people in support of Jeremy Corbyn, a mainstream older, white, male political leader, created the sense of a major challenge or potential 'youthquake' during the 2017 general election.

Acts of autonomous political activity of young people have been matched by facilitated youth work initiatives to increase young people's participation. Projects explicitly addressing youth participation grew significantly from 2000 but the work was conceived and understood in different ways. For some, youth participation was presented as an opportunity to offer training to young people. This was usually to shape young people into productive members of society, provide constructive leisure opportunities or help with managing behaviour. Youth work and social policy came together in this to encourage young people to 'engage as morally and socially responsible citizens' (Wood, 2010). In addition, there were distinctive approaches to youth participation that saw young people as 'consumers, as creators or simply as problematic' (Shukra et al, 2012). However, following the introduction of austerity measures, many youth work projects struggled to stay open, despite being National Youth Agency accredited. With a reduction in projects, youth workers became increasingly interested in collaborating with schools as anchor organisations through which they might deliver youth activities.

So, what is the state of facilitated political learning opportunities for young people from Black and minority ethnic backgrounds? There are at least three distinctive forms:

1. Involvement with political organisations that are community based and led by Black or minority ethnic adults. Although adult led, these can be of interest to young people because the issues taken up affect them or their community. Sometimes, the organisations actively seek out youth voice. Alternatively, the organisation may be one that is self-organised by Black or minority ethnic young people.
2. Intervention where mainstream youth-oriented organisations take account of Black and minority ethnic young people's concerns. This may be through project work or highlighting an issue.
3. Local authorities and service providers that take account of young people, including Black and minority ethnic young people. This is typically framed as attempts at 'community engagement' or engaging 'hard to reach' communities.

The following sections discuss these forms of political learning opportunities, with selected examples. We go on to provide a detailed case study of the Young Mayor Programme in the London Borough of Lewisham, which illustrates the way in which a programme that is supported by the full spectrum of agencies in the locality has attracted consistent engagement from marginalised young people.

Self-organised Black or minority ethnic political organisations

In adult politics, there has been much contention surrounding the opportunities afforded to Black and Asian people. This meant that organising for change often involved community-based politics as well as more formal party politics. Discrimination and exclusion in the 1950s and 1960s led to Asian and African-Caribbean communities setting up organisations to advocate for their networks, particularly around matters of housing, employment, policing and education (Sivanandan, 1982). During the 1970s and early 1980s, some of the equal rights campaigns took a more radical turn, seeking to bring minority ethnic groups together to grow a Black radical political consciousness to join with class-based organisations against the state. A more compromising approach was taken by organisations in the 1980s and 1990s, as they considered the potential value of working from within institutions. Many, as in the case of Labour Party Black Sections and the

Black Socialist Society, aiming to address minority representation in Labour Party electoral politics, continued to meet significant difficulties as well as successes in representation (Shukra, 1998). More recently, in the 2020s, a Young Black Leaders Summit, organised by Black Labour members, focused on how to revive the flagging fortunes of Black representation within Labour circles and to correct the underrepresentation of Black men.

Black-led professionalised organisations with expertise in campaigning for race equality have responded to young Black people's demands for social justice in the 2020s. For example, Operation Black Vote (OBV; nd) is an organisation set up outside political parties to lobby for political representation and mobilise and educate Black and Asian minority voters. It encourages local authorities and other institutions to be mindful of Black and minority ethnic representation, including in relation to young people. Its work raises awareness and political representation in democratic and civic society. With regard to the political education and representation of young people in politics and other state organisations, OBV organises mentoring, shadowing opportunities and events with high-profile figures such as Reverend Jesse Jackson and Diane Abbott, as well as activists, to raise awareness among young people of how they might make a difference (Back et al, 2023).

In the activist realm, the 2020s has seen an expansion of black self-organisation in the name of 'Black Lives Matter', as well as other forms of minority ethnic cultural expression and political autonomous organisation. There has also been a growth in opportunities to engage with umbrella organisations that lobby on issues emerging on the ground. The Windrush scandal and health disparities are examples of how casework stimulated campaigns. Growing numbers of Black and minority ethnic organisations seek to influence policy on race that can relate to young people and their communities, whether that is about the disproportionate stop and search of young Black people during the pandemic or strip searches of Black students, as exemplified in the case of 'Child Q'. The Runnymede Trust is a strong example of this sort of organisation, producing resources and reports in support of events and campaigns, mindful of a new generation of youth activism.[2]

Mainstream youth work

Outside school settings, youth work has sometimes been a vehicle for 'non-formal' and 'informal' political learning. The 1960 Albermarle Report called for young people to be included in political processes and the setting up of youth councils (Taylor, 2008), but it was from the 1990s that youth

---

[2] For more information on the Runnymede Trust, visit: www.runnymedetrust.org/

participation was mainstreamed and a variety of projects were established across the UK. They were developed to engage young people in decision-making and were particularly underpinned by New Labour's policies on 'active citizenship' (QCA, 1998), 'community cohesion' (Cantle, 2008) and consultation rights enshrined in the Children Act 2004 and the Education Act 2002.

Despite the closure of significant youth organisations and reduction in local authorities' spending on youth services in England between 2010/11 and 2019/20 (YMCA, 2020), there are funders and organisations that specialise in supporting marginalised groups, whether young women, LGBTQ+ young people, disabled young people, young people from particular faith backgrounds or Black/minority ethnic young people. Across the board, there is an expectation that young people are not left at the level of being service users but are also given a voice in the shape of the provision. The charity UK Youth (www.ukyouth.org) provides support to a network of thousands of youth organisations. In the wake of the George Floyd murder in the US, it set up a space specifically for young Black people in the form of the '#YoungAndBlack' campaign,[3] a network of young Black leaders and organisations. Its aim was to enable young Black people to explore Black gendered and Black LGBTQ+ identities through their experience of growing up and to provide a platform for young Black voices.

Political education in youth work and outside formal school structures and schools' councils has been arranged in different, sometimes competing ways. Some projects are modelled on the politics of identity while others emphasise deliberative democracy. There are also important examples that integrate both types to support youth representatives in campaigning or to influence policy development. Projects such as these broadly offer some form of political education to introduce young people to local authority strategy, service design and parliamentary processes. For example, the British Youth Council established a UK Youth Parliament to offer 11- to 18-year-olds from across the country, elected as local representatives, an opportunity to identify issues of relevance and debate them, including in televised parliamentary sittings: 'Members of Youth Parliament across the UK work to give young people a voice – listening to marginalised groups, organising events, making films, meeting MPs, lobbying for change, organising campaigns and appearing in the media, all to amplify the views of their peers' (British Youth Council, 2022).

Some local authorities across the UK also established political education projects such as Young Advisors and Youth Mayors. They represent the voice of young people in their locality, advising service providers seeking to include a youth perspective in strategy or delivery of services. In more

---

[3] For more information, see: www.iwill.org.uk/youngandblack-with-uk-youth

recent years, charities such as UK Youth and the National Council for Voluntary Organisations have brought together some of the local Young Advisor groups in a bid to turn them into trained 'social entrepreneurs' to be commissioned to 'deliver meaningful bespoke analysis to help shape your planning, marketing, communications, products, or service development', offering 'deliverables' such as reports, infographics, and presentations (Young Advisors, 2020). In doing so, Young Advisors groups enable participants to gain key skills, although they also run the risk of losing their focus as young citizens seeking to grow their political education through experiential, non-formal youth work and to benefit their peers. Charities under financial pressures in an extremely challenging climate have developed a way of turning Young Advisors into young researchers trained in a particular model as part of a mechanism to procure funded research and consultancy work.

Similar opportunities were created by other organisations, including organisations focused on faith perspectives. Specifically targeting over 20-year-olds and diverse faith communities, the 'ParliaMentors' programme set out to upskill potential leaders with cross-cultural principles and a capacity for interfaith advocacy. Central to its processes are mentoring, shadowing and training (Peacock, 2021). In delivering on the demand for more youth participation projects, youth work faces additional dilemmas: 'The paradox is that if we attempt to over-manage the acquisition of these qualities in young people through instructive citizenship education, we may in fact diminish their curiosity and capacity to negotiate their own social identities' (Wood, 2010, p 66). Historically, youth workers were concerned to support young people in a facilitative rather than a prescriptive way (Batsleer and Davies, 2010). A challenge for non-formal political education learning is to grow based on those principles.

Local authorities and service providers

A wide range of adult-led political learning opportunities have also been created for young people beyond youth services, through schools and local authorities and partnerships. Outside the formalised mentoring and training approach, there are few local authorities that take the risk of an informal education approach to youth participation and successfully engage marginalised groups.

One of the best known successful examples sits in the London Borough of Lewisham, which has the longest running Young Mayor Programme (YMP). It is a civic youth democracy programme that emerged from the Lewisham Youth Participation Project of the late 1990s.[4] Set up at the

---

[4] Lewisham Youth Participation Project was set up and led by youth workers Malcolm Ball and Dennis Hunter, who went on to help design and lead the Young Mayor Programme.

turn of the century, the YMP was based in the heart of the town hall until the building had to be turned into a COVID-19 testing centre. It hosts the election of a directly elected young mayor, mirroring new governance arrangements in the borough and an intention to involve young people as part of a programme of democratic engagement (Quirk, 2006). The annual elections allow young people in the borough to elect their young mayor, deputy young mayor, and Lewisham representatives to UK Youth Parliament. The election campaign process encourages candidates and their supporters to stay active by joining the Young Advisors Group. Representatives normally meet weekly and engage with peers, politicians and other adults on local, regional, national and international activities. These include campaigns, strategic conversations and project development.

Young advisers also take responsibility for consulting peers on how the young mayor should spend a budget of £25,000 each year, reporting back directly to the mayor and cabinet about their activities and proposals for the spend. This process allows young people to experience elections and campaigns as part of a real process of representing their peers and influencing decisions. That the programme is not about simulation but is about the lives and politics in the borough makes it an authentic experience in political education for everyone involved – whether voters, candidates or council officials.

Through more than a decade of participant observation during the annual election period, alongside interviews with the founders and participants of the programme, it has been possible to learn a great deal about the programme and participant perspectives. Initially, it was striking to find that most participants each year were Black or minority ethnic young people, with high proportions of young Black women involved, as few institutional initiatives had engaged young Black people at that time. Participants also include young people who were managing a wide range of disabilities. One of the strengths of the YMP has been its success in engaging young people of diverse educational, faith and ethnic backgrounds in a wide range of projects around civic political life locally, regionally and nationally. With the full-time staff and founding politicians and executives being white, it demonstrates that institutions can be inclusive of local communities if they choose to do so proactively. That said, the programme has also benefited significantly from the support of Black and minority ethnic youth workers and alumni. The programme received significant interest, and visitors from Norway to Japan asking how it works. Indeed, some of the visits resulted in international relations being developed between the Lewisham programme and youth projects across Europe with the support of EU funds.

Case study: Lewisham's Young Mayor Programme (YMP)

Lewisham's YMP owes much of its success and longevity to its foundations. It was collaboratively designed and set up with support from the highest levels of the local authority, including the mayor, the local authority's chief executive and service directors. The two senior youth workers that helped to configure it insisted that operations should be underpinned by an informal, inclusive and collaborative 'ethos and culture' that promoted trust and dialogue between young people, the adult advisers and politicians.

The purpose of the programme for these youth workers, who went on to become the first 'adult advisers to the young mayor', was 'social and political education' and 'building a social movement'. Although the project was best known for its annual elections, they saw it as about more than teaching young people to vote. It gave young people an opportunity to view the civic arena as their space – a place where they could meet and speak out. In that sense, the project has been distinctive, although other youth mayor and adviser programmes have developed around the country. Rather than offering formal political education training opportunities, the YMP was organised to provide active and experiential learning spaces in which everyone was encouraged to share their opinions and represent their peers' views. As participants went to school and/or lived in the borough, they were expected to be in conversation with their peers, making them more accountable than adult politicians tend to be.

At the centre of the original ethos was an everyday practice of involving young people as they presented, encouraging them to reflect on and represent their lived experience rather than trying to mould them into professional politicians. There was no sense in which participants were expected to dress more formally or speak differently, except to appeal to their peers creatively – indeed it was 'keeping it real' that enabled young people to win the votes and respect of their peers. The distinctiveness of this approach was notable even in the individualistic and informal way that young participants tended to dress and speak in the most formal of settings. Rather than reading from scripts prepared for them and rehearsed with adults, they were encouraged to relax and respond based on their opinions, which took shape through discussions with other young people and in dialogue with decision-makers and service providers. This was not always easy – it would take time for young people to feel comfortable with other young people who they did not know in the grand setting of a town hall.

This was particularly important for the adult advisers to bear in mind, as the borough features in official tables of multiple deprivation and the hope was to engage some of the most disenfranchised young people. One way in which young Black people came to be comfortable in being involved was through recognising their creative self-organisation. Grime and spoken word were two such formats. Grime has been a significant youth music scene in Lewisham since the early 2000s and adult advisers had supported youth music projects in previous youth work roles. Lewisham grime, an autonomous music scene, expressed a lived appreciation of poverty and life in the neighbourhood. It was music by young Black men and a space where Black masculinity was performed and celebrated, while sharing a more complex persona privately (Boakye, 2017). It was through grime, rap and spoken word poetry that some of the connections between election candidates and the youth electorate were made. Like grime, spoken word poetry was performed to express insights from the lived experience of the poet but, unlike grime, it promoted a feminist critique of the world.

During election campaigns, these creative ways of communicating were used by some of the young election candidates. Diverse ways of speaking, accents and expressions allowed for a trustworthiness that facilitated conversations with the most alienated of young people. It did not mean that discussions were not serious, nor that the YMP was universally supported. On the contrary, the struggle to engage young people was continuous but informality allowed young people to raise the most challenging of issues. They could feel comfortable speaking about experiences and issues that mattered, whether that was diminished opportunities, financial issues, violent crime, issues at school, policing or poverty.

Another aspect of the programme has been its collaborations with schools. All schools in the borough host YMP polling stations, so election day proves to be a significant annual event, polling over 50 per cent of the youth electorate. The process provides an opportunity to be involved in local democracy at work, transforming school-based political literacy and what candidates described as 'tokenism' in school councils. Candidates from the programme reported the greater scope they have to set agendas, be heard and 'make a difference' in the YMP, while also wondering what happens to the feedback provided.

Candidate responses to questions of why they were standing for election revealed a mix of two motivators: aspirations for personal development and altruism. Candidates generally recognise that they might gain something of personal value. They cited 'leadership experience', 'self-confidence', 'learning how to campaign' and to 'become more open-minded'. However, they also expected to achieve something for others. For example:

- I want to bring the youth of today closer to their dream jobs.
- To bring people together across Lewisham and allow them to feel safe and proud of the borough and encourage young people to get out there and make memories.
- To stop ... the abusive language towards the LGBT community.

- To improve Lewisham for young people and improve the welfare of people living in Lewisham.

Each year, candidate responses pointed to young people being keen to make positive changes that would enable their peers to feel safer and healthier and to be heard. They wanted to create work experience opportunities and wellbeing support structures.

In the context of the global BLM movement following the killing of George Floyd in May 2020, there was a marked rise in interest in Black and minority ethnic political activism, often associated with calls for social justice and a more representative educational curriculum. The potential and capacity of school student activism and sense of agency were evident in the South London school protests in the 1980s that resulted in some schools supporting Black history teaching, as well as in the 2022 protests, following the case of 'Child Q' in Hackney. Campaigns around 'decolonising the university' and Black history in schools gained a national hearing, pointing to the potential to turn school-based political literacy into a more vibrant and relevant political education that has equality principles at its core.

Against this backdrop, the YMP developed an international dialogue with its partners on the question of whether colonial statues should be replaced. Also, in recognition of the 40th anniversary of the 1981 Black People's Day of Action seeking justice for the 14 young Black people who died as a result of a house fire in New Cross that was widely believed to have been started by racists, the YMP developed school workshops about it with the local university and community members. Young people described how this history was new to them, noting that they had learned about African American history rather than about UK community history in school. There was an appetite for more content that might reflect local diasporic community histories.

That enthusiasm coincided with moves by the local authority to produce a school-based race equality charter, which enabled the YMP to work with schools, politicians, community members and young people to develop components that might contribute to a 'Curriculum for Lewisham'. Linked to this, curriculum workshops grew into a mechanism for the YMP to facilitate student debate on a school 'equality pledge'. Youth-led discussion on the pledge resulted in challenges to school policies on behaviour, dress codes and uniforms – mechanisms that can function to control through discipline and punishment. The aim of the Curriculum for Lewisham work was to encourage students to think about the communities they live in and their hopes, fears and expectations for the future. The purpose was not to create an alternative heritage for celebrating colonialism or memorialising the past, but to create opportunities to learn how people have organised and responded to discrimination. Enabling young people to consider their role in improving society for themselves and their communities constitutes a form of political education that goes beyond political literacy and takes account of Britain's colonial legacy and multiethnic present. This was also a national politics issue involving rallies, and a petition to teach Britain's colonial history in schools was debated by MPs: e-petition 324092 far exceeded the threshold needed for parliamentary debate, accumulating 268,772 signatures in total (Ayodele, 2021).

In response to their experience of the COVID-19 national lockdowns, young people worked with the adult advisers to develop a 'bank of things', which could provide young people with essentials they might not be able to afford. The young mayor budget in 2021/2 was used to co-produce the project with a local voluntary organisation. The bank of things was located in a high-street shop, and enabled more young people to join in the project and volunteer, challenging the idea that young people are not active citizens. Within the YMP, there was a growth in youth political literacy and engagement, a more relevant and exciting local politics, expanded youth leadership, increased youth voter registration, youth civic pride and identity, and expanded intercultural engagements.

Key to achieving this has been a mix of experiential learning opportunities, informal education, collaborative partnerships, and a personal, social and political youth work approach that centres the young person at its heart in critical dialogue with adults. Beyond understanding how the democratic system works, political education needs to be about growing a political consciousness and a sense of agency for social change. Formal political associations and parties usually have a pre-existing ideological agenda that participants align to. Youth participation projects aim to develop participant skills and knowledge in operating semi-professionally and focus on self-management or behavioural modification. Autonomous activist organisations might create an agenda and way of operating more collectively. The YMP has operated in a formal and relatively well-resourced framework but in a non-formal way, supporting young people to think of themselves as agents whose opinions count, even if they find themselves marginalised in other areas of their lives. They can develop personally in the process of pursuing issues they have identified and reflect on the limits and barriers they come across to recognise the value of their relative collective strength while building solidarities.

Conclusion

This chapter pointed to the need to nurture projects that use interactive informal political education that gives space to young citizens shaping agendas rather than projects that seek to mould young people. This involves embracing young people's ideas and expertise, acknowledging difference and self-expression, and respecting dissent. Such political participation and informal education opportunities offer a road to potentially decreasing alienation and strengthening democracy. The Young Mayor Programme was highlighted as an example of how it is possible to engage marginalised young people in electoral, deliberative and community politics, despite ongoing claims that young adults are not interested in politics or do not vote. It is no surprise then that some young mayors, along with the UK Youth Parliament, have campaigned for the voting age to be reduced to 16.

Proponents of compulsory formal school citizenship education have claimed that government support provided to deliver it has been severely limited, leaving it to schools, local authorities, youth organisations and academics to develop localised strategies to increase political participation and grow youth democracy projects. Such projects tend to take it for granted that electoral politics can secure a better society for all. However, it is not necessarily the case that positive experiences of voice and agency in a youth project automatically translate for everyone as a positive outlook on adult politics, where opportunities to make a difference may appear severely limited. While political education projects are important, political cynicism among younger adult politics may have less to do with a lack of political literacy and more to do with their reasonable expectations of adult politics not being met.

References

Anwar, M. (1986) *Race and Politics: Ethnic Minorities and the British Political System*, London: Tavistock

Ayodele, M. (2021) 'MPs to debate petition on teaching Britain's colonial past as part of the curriculum', Operation Black Vote: www.obv.org.uk/news-blogs/mps-debate-petition-teaching-britains-colonial-past-part-curriculum

Back, L., Keith, M., Shukra, K. and Solomos, J. (2023) *The Unfinished Politics of Race: Histories of Political Participation, Migration and Multiculturism*, Cambridge: Cambridge University Press.

Batsleer, J. and Davies, B. (2010) *What Is Youth Work?*, London: Sage.

Bergamini, M. (2014) 'Compulsory political education is a must if we are to stem the flow of disengagement from politics', Democratic Audit, 5 April: www.democraticaudit.com/2014/09/05/compulsory-political-education-is-a-must-if-we-are-to-stem-the-flow-of-disengagement-from-politics/

Boakye, J. (2017) *Hold Tight: Black Masculinity, Millennials and the Meaning of Grime*, London: Influx Press.

Cantle, T. (2008) *Community Cohesion: A New Framework for Race & Diversity*, Basingstoke: Palgrave Macmillan.

Fitzgerald, M. (1987) *Black People and Party Politics in Britain*, London: Runnymede Trust.

Henn, M. and Foard, N. (2014) 'Social differentiation in young people's political participation: the impact of social and educational factors on youth political engagement in Britain', *Journal of Youth Studies*, 17(3): 360–80.

Keith, M. (1993) *Race, Riots and Policing: Lore and Disorder in a Multi-Racist Society*, London: UCL Press.

Kisby, B. and Sloam, J. (2014) 'Promoting youth participation in democracy: the role of higher education', in A. Mycock and J. Tonge (eds) *Beyond the Youth Citizenship Commission: Young People and Politics*, London: Political Studies Association, pp 52–6.

Kitanova, M. (2020) 'Youth political participation in the EU: evidence from a cross-national analysis', *Journal of Youth Studies*, 23(7): 819–36.

Layton-Henry, Z. (1992) *The Politics of Immigration: Race and Race Relations in Postwar Britain*, Oxford: Blackwell.

Mycock, A. and Tonge, J. (2014) 'Some progress made, still much to do: youth political engagement since the Youth Citizenship Commission', *Beyond the Youth Citizenship Commission: Young People and Politics*, London: Political Studies Association, pp 8–13.

Operation Black Vote (OBV) (nd) 'What we do': www.obv.org.uk/what-we-do

O'Toole, T. (2015) 'Beyond crisis narratives: changing modes and repertoires of political participation among young people', in K. Kallio, S. Mills and T. Skelton (eds) *Politics, Citizenship and Rights*, Cham: Springer, pp 1–15.

Peacock, L. (2021) *Building Closer Communities: An Evaluation Report*, Coventry: The Centre for Trust, Peace and Social Relations, Coventry University.

Perez, J.A. (2020) 'Rioting by a different name: the voice of the unheard in the age of George Floyd, and the history of the laws, policies, and legislation of systemic racism', *Journal of Gender, Race & Justice*: www.bowdoin.edu/oid/pdf/rioting-by-a-different-name.pdf

Pontes, A.I., Henn, M. and Griffiths, M. (2017) 'Youth political (dis)engagement and the need for citizenship education: encouraging young people's civic and political participation through the curriculum', *Education, Citizenship and Social Justice*, 14(1): 3–21.

QCA (1998) *Education for Citizenship and the Teaching of Democracy in Schools: Final Report of the Advisory Group on Citizenship*, the 'Crick Report', 22 September, QCA.

Quirk, B. (2006) 'Innovation in local democracy: the London Borough of Lewisham', *Local Government Studies*, 32(3): 357–72.

Rebel History Calendar (2021) 'This week in UK history, 1981: uprisings and riots all over the country': https://pasttenseblog.wordpress.com/2021/07/03/this-week-in-uk-history-1981-uprisings-and-riots-all-over-the-country/

Saggar, S. (1998) *Race and British Electoral Politics*, London: UCL Press.

Shukra, K. (1990) 'Black sections in the Labour Party', in H. Goulbourne (ed) *Black Politics in Britain*, Farnham: Avebury, pp 165–89.

Shukra, K. (1998) *The Changing Pattern of Black Politics in Britain*, London: Pluto Press.

Shukra, K., Ball, M. and Brown, K. (2012) 'Participation and activism: young people shaping their worlds', *Youth & Policy*, 108: 36–54.

Sivanandan, A. (1982) *A Different Hunger: Writings on Black Resistance*, London: Pluto Press.

Solomos, J. and Back, L. (1995) *Race Politics and Social Change*, London: Routledge.

Taylor, T. (2008) 'Young people, politics and participation: a youth work perspective', *Youth & Policy*, 100: 253–63.

Tonge, J., Mycock, A. and Jeffery, B. (2012) 'Does citizenship education make young people better-engaged citizens?', *Political Studies*, 60(3): 578–602.

Wood, J. (2010) '"Preferred futures": active citizenship, government and young people's voices', *Youth & Policy*, 105: 50–70.

YMCA (2020) *Out of Service: A Report Examining Local Authority Expenditure on Youth Services in England & Wales*, London: YMCA: www.ymca.org.uk/wp-content/uploads/2020/01/YMCA-Out-of-Service-report.pdf

Young Advisors (2020) 'Commissioning us', https://youngadvisors.org.uk/commissioning/

9

Universities' role in teaching practical politics

Titus Alexander

Universities have a major responsibility for the state of the world. For over a century they educated the people who run most institutions, providing ideas and methods that guide society. Graduates contributed to dramatic improvements in life expectancy, health, leisure time, gender equality and other indicators of human development. But university-educated politicians and professionals also lead the organisations that produce global heating, loss of biodiversity, extreme inequality and numerous existential threats to humanity's future (Rees, 2003; Bostrom, 2014).[1] Universities share responsibility for these flaws.

Humanity's most serious problems today are political, not technical. They require political ability and persistence to solve. Yet most universities dare not teach practical politics. Scholars study problems, publish about what's wrong and even propose solutions. But few teach the political skills to apply their knowledge, so most research is wasted. However, universities do teach practical business, now their biggest subject area.[2]

This chapter aims to show why and how universities can make education for democracy and practical politics part of their core mission, to help citizens solve problems and create a better world for all, with examples to inspire and inform.

Why teach skills for democracy?

Universities have a self-interest in effective, inclusive democratic government. If they are seen as serving privileged minorities, they will lose public support.

---

[1] See also: The Future of Humanity Institute, University of Oxford: www.fhi.ox.ac.uk
[2] In 2016/17, 17 per cent of UK qualifications gained were in business and administrative studies, followed by medicine and social studies: www.hesa.ac.uk/news/11-01-2018/sfr 247-higher-education-student-statistics/qualifications. American business BAs rose from 14 per cent in 1970/1 to 19 per cent in 2018/19; MBAs rose from 11 per cent to 24 per cent: https://nces.ed.gov/programs/digest/d20/tables/dt20_318.20.asp

They promote their role as gateways to better jobs, inadvertently telling most school leavers they are second-class citizens. Bovens and Wille (2017) show how the 'new educational divide provides large advantages to the children of the professional class and makes it ever harder for working-class kids to work their way up', contributing to 'growing resentment toward universities and higher education among blue-collar workers'. This is reflected in support for anti-establishment nationalist movements, such as America First, Brexit and France's National Rally.

The journalists, lawyers and lobbyists who advocate for or against rules governing every area of life are mostly university educated. Again and again, research evidence on better, safer ways of doing things is resisted by university-educated professionals employed by industries that profit from the way things are. When researchers discovered the harms caused by pesticides, tobacco, fossil fuels, sugar and other substances, they campaigned to stop politicians from acting (Michaels, 2008; Oreskes and Conway, 2010). In *The Enablers*, Frank Vogel (2022), a former senior World Bank official, shows how professionals support kleptocrats and corruption. Chuck Collins (2021) gives an insider's account of how the 'wealth defence industry' manages 16 per cent of national wealth ($20 trillion) and minimises taxes for the richest 0.01 per cent of Americans. They exert undue influence on politics and universities through donations, lobbying and personal networks. Universities could earn trust by helping citizens to use knowledge and democratic politics to improve their lives and counterbalance the gross disparity of power that distorts democracy.

A major reason for teaching practical politics is that dissatisfaction with democracy is widespread (see Foa et al). The blunt reality is that it does not work for most people. Political incompetence causes immense suffering, cost lives and waste resources on a monumental scale (Tuchman, 1984; Crewe and King, 2013). Yet for all the blunders and injustices committed by liberal democracies, the independent rule of law and ability of citizens to challenge the powerful, elect lawmakers, hold rulers accountable, and change their government by peaceful means gives people more freedom to innovate, tackle collective problems and improve their lives.

Many young people want to use knowledge to make a difference. The World Economic Forum (WEF, 2017) *Global Shapers Annual Survey* of 18- to 35-year-olds across 186 countries identified climate change as their top global issue (49 per cent), followed by large-scale conflict (39 per cent) and inequality (30 per cent). Many jobs across disciplines require political skills and knowledge. Increasing political abilities could improve the quality of democratic governance and cut the cost of political incompetence, benefiting everyone. Universities that offer opportunities to learn how to address these issues will therefore attract students.

These reasons make a compelling case for universities to teach practical politics.

What is politics and what abilities do you need to do it?

Politics shapes almost every aspect of our lives, from personal relationships and work to global rules for trade, travel and warfare. American political scientist Harold Lasswell bluntly described politics as *Who Gets What, When, How* (1935). Bernard Crick called it 'the activity by which differing interests within a given unit of rule are conciliated' ([1962] 2000). Any organisation that decides who gets what is a 'unit of rule', from university departments to the United Nations. Most politics takes place within institutions, behind closed doors, between officials, and within parties rather than between parties. Citizens have little power under most systems, but in liberal democracies they elect representatives to direct civil servants, our permanent government, and hold the executive to account. Between elections, citizens can lobby and campaign for issues to be addressed. This takes skill and persistence. Even experienced politicians fail repeatedly, which is why everyone needs to learn how to do it better.

Political activity takes place at roughly four levels (Alexander, 2016, p 4):

1. *Governing*: the politics of running any organisation – charity, university, or state – and making things happen.
2. *Challenging*: the politics of influencing power holders, or trying to replace them, including opposition parties and pressure groups.
3. *Accepting* or supporting those in power or their challengers, as followers, employees or citizens.
4. *Submitting* to people in power by those who feel powerless.

Media coverage of politics is preoccupied with the first two levels, but most citizens experience politics at level four, submitting to decisions in which they have little say. People support a party, trade union, association, or campaign to gain more power in levels three or two, but most feel powerless and excluded from politics. Good political education can increase people's confidence and ability to take part and move up a level.

Core skills and knowledge for practical politics

Practical politics requires a different mindset from most academic study. To campaign successfully, you need to distil knowledge into a call for action and competency in seven areas:

1. Understand the issues, through the eyes of participants as well as observation and investigation.
2. Know your way round the power structures.

3. Understand systems that influence the power structures, including ideas, incentives, institutions, interest groups, finance, laws, networks, technologies, geography, demography and ecology.
4. Know why: clarity about your values and desired outcomes, as well as the values and motivation of others.
5. Political abilities to question, communicate, organise, lobby, persuade, negotiate, make decisions, build relationships, plan, analyse finances or data, and act effectively.
6. Storytelling and rhetoric to create and communicate narratives that build support and influence decision makers.
7. Character: be confident, resilient, trustworthy and persist despite setbacks.

Deep knowledge is invaluable, but without political ability it is useless. People can become successful politicians using shallow, partial, or false knowledge (that is, lies). Higher education should improve the quality and integrity of democracy by developing political skills with respect for evidence. The leadership of many countries is an indictment of the universities that educated them.

Universities as agencies for democracy

The rest of this chapter outlines models of provision to show how some universities help people learn how to right wrongs, protect nature, improve society, and strengthen democratic governance in humanity's great experiment to create a better world. The best provision enables people to:

- tackle issues in practice, not just in theory;
- deal with power, including how to get and use it effectively;
- influence decisions and make change stick.

Getting practical politics into the curriculum is a political task. The following sections identify eight levels at which to strengthen provision, with examples to show what is possible and where to find lessons and potential allies. They suggest a spiral of engagement, starting with initiatives any student or tutor can take, working outwards through pedagogical practices, course programmes, issue-based partnerships, brokerage models and university-wide models, to collaborative networks and the whole system.

Symbolic acts and social practices

The simplest and most powerful way to promote education for democratic politics is through small, repeated social practices that *increase people's sense of agency* as members of a democratic learning community. This starts with the image a university projects to attract learners and promote its role in society. How people join its community shows who is welcome, what is valued, expectations, norms and how to take part. The smallest acts convey compliance and conformity, or inspire people to think for themselves, question assumptions, seek reliable evidence, be open to challenge, curious about opposing views, and make a difference in the world. Symbolic actions, such as displaying flags, singing the national anthem, displaying statues, 'taking the knee' for Black Lives Matter, the #MeToo hashtag, or gay pride rainbow affirm or challenge beliefs, norms and values.

Set-piece events like a public lecture, inaugural speech, prize giving, graduation ceremony, commencement address and countless routines reinforce traditions or give new meaning and direction to an institution. Controversies over statues, free speech and identity are opportunities to review collective values and how they are communicated. Authoritarian regimes revel in awards, ceremonies, medals and parades because autocrats know the power of symbolic action. Challenging and changing symbolic practices are forms of political education that open doors to change.

Pedagogical practices, teachable moments and course enrichment

The next level is to develop political competence through *empowering pedagogical practices* in any subject. These include:

- encouraging students to share experiences, aspirations, thoughts and feelings about the subject, and connect on an authentic, human level;
- starting courses with questions and critical inquiry (what Paulo Freire called 'conscientisation') rather than authoritative answers from established authors, whether critics or exponents;
- electing class representatives and devils' advocates;
- using buzz groups, study buddies, huddles, affinity groups, peer coaching, mentoring and action learning sets to deepen understanding;
- exploring subjects in their social, political and historical context;
- showing respect for evidence, analysis, experience and arguments from different perspectives;
- inviting activists, elected representatives and practitioners to speak;
- basing assignments on real-life problems, projects or community service to learn how to apply knowledge;
- creating communities of practice beyond the university;
- twinning with learners in the local community or abroad;
- lecture and course programme;

- building systematic evaluation using Kirkpatrick's four levels evaluation model (Kirkpatrick and Kirkpatrick, [1993] 2006) or specialised methods (Tamkin et al, 2002; Torney-Purta et al, 2015) to estimate impact and improve provision.

These practices develop confidence, a sense of agency and the skills of inquiry, communication, leadership and teamwork, essential for effective citizenship.

Teachable moments are opportunities to learn practical politics in any context, often informal and unplanned. For example, whenever someone

- Asks a question or makes an open-ended comment about an issue, you can guide exploration of how to tackle it effectively.
- Says it is impossible to change something, they are powerless or afraid, you can find out why, explore what they want to change and the pathways to it.
- Notices a power dynamic or conflict, you can highlight different interests at play, possible scenarios, or routes to a resolution.

If people say something prejudiced or ignorant, encourage learning by asking questions:

- Do you really mean it (could you rephrase it)?
- What is your evidence, where is it from?
- Have you checked its reliability and looked at other sources?
- Have you considered ... (a counter example)?
- Put yourself in the opposite position.

Challenging ignorant, racist, or hateful views and behaviours is necessary for learning, but it is also important to respect the person, since blame, shame and censure are usually counterproductive. This differs from conventional political arguments, in which both sides entrench their views and learn little. Discussing differences in respectful ways can deepen understanding and uncover common ground but requires skill and experience.

Learning opportunities also arise from engagement with the many dimensions of oppression, such as class, gender, race and sexuality. These are contentious issues on many campuses, as well as established in courses and research on cultural studies, Marxism, sociology and what have been described as 'grievance studies' (Pluckrose et al, 2018; Pluckrose and Lindsay, 2020; Lagerspetz, 2021). Awareness of these issues can lead people to adopt a righteous orthodoxy that silences alternative views and insists on certain beliefs and behaviours. Challenging sexism, racism and exclusion has a vital role in transforming society, but academic preoccupation with oppression can be a symbolic substitute for action. Exploration of contrary views deepens understanding, so it is important to create safe spaces for serious disagreement over difficult issues. The following questions can help:

1. What are the benefits of your position on this issue for you?
2. How do you feel and react when you are told to think or behave in a certain way?
3. If you held (an opposing point of view) or did (objectionable action), what would change your mind or persuade you to behave differently?
4. Where in the world has this issue been addressed effectively and what can we learn from it? What evidence is there for actions or policies that make a difference in practice?

These issues are often intensely personal and difficult to deal with. They are attacked as 'woke', politically correct, or identity politics by people who feel threatened, or see electoral advantage in antagonising their proponents. Understanding action and reaction is a core political skill that can be explored through dialogue, roleplay and project work.

Course enrichment means exploring social purpose, values, interest groups, history, power relationships, funding and institutional dynamics within any subject area, as well as questions about 'decolonising the curriculum', gender biases and diverse perspectives (Page, 2017). It also means finding meaningful opportunities to develop experience through social engagement.

Course programmes

Most courses in advocacy, campaigning, practical politics and social change are outside academia, but provision is growing in response to demand. A good course is life-changing, but creating one requires ability to navigate academic labyrinths. There will always be questions whether universities can support action-oriented courses. Professor Alberto Alemanno's courses in lobbying for citizens at the business school HEC Paris now run through the non-profit The Good Lobby. His book, *Lobbying for Change: Find Your Voice to Create a Better Society* (2017), is an excellent guide for anyone who wants to run a campaign and has useful course material. When creating a new course programme, it is best to start with short courses like this, work with external partners, and join a community of practice to draw on experience, skills and support from outside the institution.

Types of courses can be loosely described in relation to the four levels of politics outlined above. Starting from the bottom up these are as follows.

Educational support for the least powerful

Creating courses to address issues facing the least powerful is difficult for institutions designed by and for the most privileged participants in education. Historically, most provision was developed outside higher education, such as the workers' education movement in Europe, citizenship schools to support civil rights in the US, and popular education in Latin America. The university settlement movement (Berry, 1986) and extramural education are part of a progressive tradition to develop education with the least fortunate in society. The closest equivalent today are courses in community organising, such as Citizens UK's Community Leadership Training for social justice, accredited by Newman University, Birmingham.

Civic education, community engagement and political literacy

The largest area of provision is generic civic education and support for people to develop confidence, skills and knowledge for civic life. Many dedicated educators have produced a wide range of resources. Rutgers University website Teaching Civic Engagement offers 'how to guides', with interactive platforms for educators preparing students to participate in democracy, with companion volumes from the American Political Science Association (McCartney et al, 2013; Matto et al, 2017; Matto et al, 2021). The Civic Engagement Research Group at the University of California, Riverside conducts research, develops resources and promotes equitable political participation. Educating for American Democracy is a collaboration among academics, historians, political scientists, educators and students to support civic learning.[3]

With these resources, universities have no excuse not to offer students and citizens courses in democratic citizenship.

Challenging: political skills, strategies and methods

Generic provision overlaps with courses that equip people to bring about social change. Scott Myers-Lipton, Professor of Sociology at San José State University, California, has taught students to take part in social justice campaigns since 2006. Lessons from this are in his books *CHANGE: A Student Guide to Social Action* (2017) and *A Guide to Teaching Social Action* (2021). His work informs the Social Action Course initiative, a community of practice network in over 65 US colleges. Similarly, experience from the Advocacy for Policy Change course at Brandeis University in 2009/10 is used by over 50 US higher education institutions through ENACT, the Educational Network for Active Civic Transformation. A few British universities now offer activists courses, such as the BA in Social Change at

---

[3] See Chapter 13 for more on Educating for American Democracy.

Essex, an MSC on Political Activism and Campaigning at Aberdeen, and Power, Participation and Social Change MA at Sussex.

Governing and civic roles

Courses such as Politics, Philosophy and Economics (PPE), Masters in Public Administration (MPA) and Government Studies were created for students from elite schools aiming for leadership roles in politics or the civil service, but many institutions now widen their catchment. For example, City University New York (CUNY) MPA has an explicit commitment to a 'social justice leadership practice that is values-driven and inclusive', guided by a commitment to undo systemic inequity, manage change in the public interest, collaborative problem-solving and support for grassroots movements.

Politics within a policy area

Courses on how to influence a specific policy area, such as health, international development and science, are also growing. Peace education and conflict resolution are well established, with over 60 courses worldwide. Environmental politics is another growth area, with programmes such as Leadership for Sustainability MA at Malmo, Sweden, Environmental Politics BA at Brighton, and Environmental Campaigns and Policymaking: Strategies and Tactics at Yale.

One day, most subjects will include modules on how to use knowledge as effective citizens and contribute better to our collective wellbeing.

Issue-based centres and partnerships

Many specialist centres bring academics and external experts together to provide expertise, research and support for citizens. However, thousands of academic centres publish research and policy analysis with little impact on outcomes. Engagement with citizens often amounts to public relations. The following seven questions can help identify whether a centre is primarily concerned with furthering academic careers or citizens' ability to resolve social problems:

1. *Accessibility*: Are they responsive to the public? Do they engage through events and outreach as well as social media?
2. *Inclusivity*: Do they work with the diversity of citizens affected by an issue?
3. *Solution-focus*: Do they focus on finding out what works and helping people bring about solutions, or are they more concerned with analysing problems and publishing papers?

4. *Persistence*: Do they work on problems until they are resolved? Many problems take decades to solve, so institutional memory and persistence matter.
5. *Capacity*: Do they work with other researchers, practitioners and citizens to achieve the scale necessary to solve problems?
6. *Reflexive*: Do they publish lessons from failures as well as successes? Do they welcome feedback?
7. *Impact*: Above all, are their outputs used by citizens to influence policy makers and make a difference?

Setting up and sustaining a citizen-facing centre takes skill and determination, due to institutional pressures to generate income, publish peer-reviewed papers and show short-term impact, so some become independent charities in order to thrive.

Effective issue-based partnerships focus on one or more of the following roles:

1. *Public information*, such as the Academic Freedom Monitoring Project, run by Scholars at Risk at New York University; the Costs of War Project at Brown University; or Participedia, a crowdsourcing platform for public participation and democratic innovations. Our World in Data is a project of the Global Change Data Lab, based in the UK, which publishes accessible information to make progress against the world's largest problems.
2. *Resource centres*, such as the Community Tool Box, run by the Center for Community Health and Development at the University of Kansas.
3. *Research, innovation, development and advocacy* (RIDA):
    - Stanford's Deliberative Democracy Lab has run more than 100 Citizens' Assemblies and Deliberative Polls across the world to resolve complex issues (Fishkin, 2018).
    - The Nobel Prize winning Abdul Latif Jameel Poverty Action Lab (J-PAL) at Massachusetts Institute of Technology (MIT) develops evidence-informed policy through an international network of professors.
    - Arizona State University's Global Institute of Sustainability and Innovation hub contributes to over 30 collaborative networks to bring about sustainability at scale by reaching millions of people.
4. *Pro-bono clinics* give students real-world experience by providing advice and support to the public under professional supervision, such as innocence projects, clinics in legal education or advice on campaigning, debt, environment, housing, planning, welfare and other problems. Few universities do this, but well-run pro-bono clinics deepen learning, provide direct benefits to citizens, and identify political issues arising from individual cases.

5. *Convening, hosting and facilitation* is when academics bring stakeholders together to act on an issue, neighbourhood, or city (Kuttner et al, 2019). For example, in 2021, five higher education institutions in Greater Manchester launched an agreement with the mayor to work on education, skills, jobs, growth, the digital economy, the cultural economy, net zero and inequalities. The Political Literacy Oversight Group supports the UK network of citizenship education providers and the All-Party Parliamentary Group on Political Literacy, while five universities sponsor the All-Party Parliamentary Climate Change Group.
6. *Policy development and advocacy* are undertaken by many of these centres.

University-based partnerships can help citizens and practitioners to make informed interventions in public life. Their impact is measured by outcomes rather than papers. Since many issues need large-scale engagement to tackle them effectively, centres need to work strategically with collaborative networks, described in below.

Brokerage models

Effective brokerage between citizens and higher education institutions can level the playing field with business or government agencies. Examples of different models include:

1. *Community partnerships*: At least 77 campuses across the US have civic engagement centres. In the UK, the University of Brighton's Community University Partnership Programme helps local community, voluntary, social enterprise and statutory organisations develop ideas into projects, offering start-up funding, student volunteers, access to knowledge and communities of practice, and support for evaluation. These partnerships enable academics, students and community partners to address local issues, and embed social engagement into teaching and research. Other brokerages include the University of East London's Civic Engagement and the University of Manchester's Public Engagement Programme. Although most involve little explicit political education, their tacit political skills are potential first steps.
2. *Issue or subject brokers*: For example, the Urban Institute in Washington, DC, which promotes the wellbeing of people and places across the US through research into social and economic issues, translating findings for diverse audiences, developing solutions to real-world problems, and sharing them in accessible ways with policy makers to improve decisions that affect people's lives.
3. *Dating agency model*: The Scottish Policy and Research Exchange (SPRE) is an independent broker between policy makers and academics, drawing

on a network of 27,000 academics. SPRE aims to work with early career scholars and increase the diversity of voices contributing evidence for policy. It also trains researchers on how to provide evidence to policy makers and offers a range of online resources.

Most universities facilitate relationships between academics and policy makers or the media at a senior level, rather than grassroots citizens, perpetuating social divisions. Connecting marginalised, excluded and low-income citizens with relevant researchers is more difficult but would strengthen their civic role and improve social outcomes.

University-wide models

Most universities are commercially oriented, market-driven institutions. They serve businesses, governments, professionals and academic communities rather than citizens or society at large. At best, they proclaim a public service mission, run token programmes in civic engagement, and enable a few disadvantaged students to escape from marginalised communities. Many do this well. MIT is one of the best. Its 'mind and hand' philosophy spurs real-world engagement to set up innovative businesses rather than strengthen democracy. Its many centres include the J-PAL, mentioned above. MIT's Climate Portal provides detailed knowledge about the science and policy options, but nothing about learning political skills to solve humanity's most critical issue. Like most universities, its excellent learning and research are more likely to perpetuate global inequalities through the corporate and political institutions that employ their graduates.

Liberal universities seriously underestimate the crisis of democracy, the risks of authoritarian rule and the dangers of systemic inequality. Despite extensive evidence and analysis of all these issues, few universities break the mould. The University of the Western Cape (UWC) is an exception – a 'system defying' or 'struggle university' under apartheid in South Africa, providing intellectual, moral and practical support for resistance following protests by students and the appointment of a coloured rector in 1975. UWC continues to 'seek racial and gender equality and contribute to helping the historically marginalised participate fully in the life of the nation' as part of its mission. It has a research unit (the African Centre for Citizenship and Democracy) dedicated to 'questions of governance and development from a citizen-centred viewpoint' and 'more inclusive, democratic policies'. This is the most developed example of the 'third mission' of most African universities (Walters and Openjuru, 2014).

Global inequality is greater than in apartheid South Africa because of structural inequality in global governance (Alexander, 1996). Africa has

17 per cent of the world's population, but just 3 per cent of global income, and few representatives in the upper echelons of world politics. Inequality within liberal democracies contributed to the rise of populist nationalists who challenge democratic norms (Norris and Inglehart, 2018; Levitsky and Ziblatt, 2019). In this context, we urgently need 'system defying' universities to increase citizens' ability to have an equal and effective voice in their neighbourhood, nation and global governance.

The Carnegie Foundation's Elective Classification in Community Engagement provides a detailed framework for US colleges and universities to assess themselves, but civic and political education are only a small part. Universities need to go beyond traditional community engagement by weaving knowledge in the service of democratic citizenship into their ethos, pedagogy, programmes and governance. This includes elevating political skills, service learning and 'Professors of Practice'. It also means changing incentives in academic careers (Jessani et al, 2020) and taking part in relevant networks.

Collaborative networks and professional associations

Collaborative networks enable people to build capacity across institutions and amplify their impact, such as:

- 'Good Lobby Profs' are European academics who provide pro-bono analysis, 'rapid response' opinions and support for citizens' lobbying to counter abuse of power and strengthen democracy.
- ENACT, Educational Network for Active Civic Transformation, at Brandeis University, runs non-partisan courses, workshops and mutual support for educators in more than 50 US higher education institutions to engage young people in civic activism for state-level legislative change.
- The Campus Compact, founded in the US in 1985, aims to promote public purposes of higher education and build democracy. It offers extensive online resources, practical initiatives, professional credentials for community engagement, support for civic action plans, and impact awards to recognize achievement. Its Research University Civic Engagement Network (TRUCEN) shares knowledge and an Engaged Scholarship Toolkit for public scholarship and community-based research.
- The Democracy Commitment (TDC) is a non-partisan network of 100 community colleges serving over 2.5 million students in 27 US states dedicated to making democratic skills available to students involved in local, state and national discourse and action. TDC also runs a civic network to expand capacity for civic learning and democratic engagement.
- The National Campaign for Political and Civic Engagement is a consortium of more than 35 colleges and universities, based at Harvard

University's Institute of Politics, to develop 'civic minded and politically engaged students'.
- The Talloires Network of Engaged Universities, based at Tufts University, is a growing global coalition of 426 university presidents, vice-chancellors and rectors across 85 countries that aims to strengthen the civic roles and social responsibilities of higher education and build a global movement of engaged universities.
- Global Public Policy Network is a partnership of seven prestigious universities in public policy. Its mission is 'to address the most pressing public policy challenges of the 21st century and, as a result, to have policy impact, to be influential in public policy education and training' (www.gppnetwork.org/about).

Some UK universities are creating collaborative networks for public engagement, such as:

- Founded in 2020, the Civic University Network (CUN) of about 130 British universities, based at Sheffield Hallam University, has a resources hub and Civic Impact Framework to map civic activities and co-create Civic University Agreements with local partners. Its case studies share lessons in citizens' participation, such as the 'Commission Model: Learning from the Poverty Truth Commissions' that bring people living in poverty together with local decision makers to explore poverty reduction.
- The UK's National Co-ordinating Centre for Public Engagement (NCCPE) was founded in 2008 to recognise, reward and build capacity for public engagement by publishing resources and evaluation reports and granting annual Engage Watermark awards to recognise strategic support for public engagement.
- The Universities Policy Engagement Network, UPEN, aims to increase the impact of research on policy, provide a contact point for policy makers, organise a collective response to requests for evidence, and share learning around knowledge exchange and policy impact between UK universities.

Collaborative networks and academic brokerage have a vital role in sharing lessons, providing mutual support, building capacity, and asserting a collective voice for civic engagement by universities. Although they tend to be underresourced and overstretched, they have the potential to influence the whole system.

System-wide models

Influencing national provision is the ultimate step to promote education for democracy. American universities have a stronger tradition than in Europe.

John Dewey's Laboratory School at the University of Chicago and his 1916 book *Democracy and Education* inspired generations of teachers. After the Second World War, President Truman's Commission on Higher Education for American Democracy (1948) created a network of community colleges to 'strengthen democracy at home and to improve our understanding of our friends and neighbors everywhere in the world'. American universities have invested in citizen engagement and education for democracy for decades. But this has not prevented social polarisation, the erosion of democratic norms, nor political stalemate over critical issues such as climate, healthcare, gun ownership, inequality and racism. Americans are the poorer for it. Their democracy has declined on several indexes, including the Economist Intelligence Unit's Democracy Index, from a 'full democracy' in 2006 to a 'flawed democracy' since 2020, compared with more modest declines across Western Europe.[4] National policies for higher education are largely determined by market forces and the funding priorities of the state and private donors, allowing democracy to decay.

Conclusion

Democratic politics are a public good, created through centuries of campaigning and protected by the rule of law. For all their flaws, liberal democracies increase freedom, respond better to citizens' demands, and can create more inclusive, innovative societies. In theory, they give people power to govern society as equals. In practice, powerful elites have learnt how to protect their interests and privileges, often at the expense of the majority. Universities have educated society's leaders, politicians and professionals for over a century. They share responsibility for the persistence of damaging political problems, accelerating existential threats, erosion of democratic norms, and rise of authoritarianism in Western societies. They could play a more robust role in equipping people to strengthen democracy. Governing in a complex, unequal and rapidly changing world requires considerable abilities, knowledge and political skill. This chapter summarises some of the ways universities are rising to the challenge. Universities can learn from and with existing models to develop a universal 'mission for democracy', alongside teaching and research, to make society work better for everyone.

References

Alemanno, A. (2017) *Lobbying for Change: Find Your Voice to Create a Better Society*, London: Icon Books.

---

[4] Economist Intelligence Unit, Democracy Index, 2020; Wikipedia: https://en.wikipedia.org/wiki/Democracy_Index

Alexander, T. (1996) *Unravelling Global Apartheid: An Overview of World Politics*, Oxford: Polity Press.

Alexander, T. (2016) *Practical Politics: Lessons in Power and Democracy*, London: UCL Institute of Education Press/Trentham Books.

Berry, M.E. (1986) *The Settlement Movement 1886–1986: One Hundred Years on Urban Frontiers*, Cleveland: United Neighborhood Centers of America.

Bostrom, N. (2014) *Superintelligence: Paths, Dangers, Strategies*, Oxford: Oxford University Press.

Bovens, M. and Wille, A. (2017) *Diploma Democracy: The Rise of Political Meritocracy*, Oxford: Oxford University Press.

Collins, C. (2021) *The Wealth Hoarders: How Billionaires Pay Millions to Hide Trillions*, Cambridge: Blackwell/Polity Press.

Crewe, I. and King, A. (2013) *The Blunders of Government*, London: Oneworld.

Crick, B. ([1962] 2000) *In Defence of Politics*, London: Continuum.

Dewey, J. (1916) *Democracy and Education: An Introduction to the Philosophy of Education*, London: Macmillan.

Economist Intelligence Unit (2020) *Democracy Index 2020: In Sickness and in Health*, London: EIU.

Fishkin, J. (2018) *Democracy When the People are Thinking: Revitalizing our Politics through Public Deliberation*, Oxford: Oxford University Press.

Foa, R.S., Klassen, A., Slade, M., Rand, A. and Collins, R. (2020) *The Global Satisfaction with Democracy Report 2020*, Cambridge: Centre for the Future of Democracy.

Jessani, N.S., Valmeekanathan, A., Babcock, C.M. and Ling, B. (2020) 'Academic incentives for enhancing faculty engagement with decision-makers: considerations and recommendations from one school of public health', *Humanities and Social Sciences Communications*, 7: 148: www.nature.com/articles/s41599-020-00629-1

Kirkpatrick, D.L. and Kirkpatrick, J.D. ([1993] 2006) *Evaluating Training Programs: The Four Levels*, 3rd edn, Oakland, CA: Berrett-Koehler Publishers.

Kuttner, P.J., Byrne, K., Schmit, K. and Munro, S. (2019) 'The art of convening: how community engagement professionals build place-based community–university partnerships for systemic change', *Journal of Higher Education Outreach and Engagement*, 23(1): 131–60.

Lagerspetz, M. (2021) '"The grievance studies affair" project: reconstructing and assessing the experimental design', *Science, Technology, & Human Values*, 46(2): 402–24.

Lasswell, H. (1935) *Who Gets What, When, How*, New York: Whittlesey House.

Levitsky, S. and Ziblatt, D. (2019) *How Democracies Die: What History Reveals About Our Future*, New York: Penguin Random House.

Matto, E.C., McCartney, A.R.M., Bennion, E.A. and Simpson, D. (eds) (2017) *Teaching Civic Engagement across the Disciplines*, Washington, DC: American Political Science Association.

Matto, E.C., McCartney, A.R.M., Bennion, E.A., Blair, A., Sun, T. and Whitehead, D.M. (eds) (2021) *Teaching Civic Engagement Globally,* Washington, DC: American Political Science Association.

McCartney, A.R.M., Bennion, E.A. and Simpson, D. (eds) (2013) *Teaching Civic Engagement: From Student to Active Citizen,* Washington, DC: American Political Science Association.

Michaels, D. (2008) *Doubt Is Their Product: How Industry's Assault on Science Threatens Your Health,* Oxford: Oxford University Press.

Myers-Lipton, S. (2017) *CHANGE!: A Student Guide to Social Action,* London: Routledge.

Myers-Lipton, S. (2021) *A Guide to Teaching Social Action,* London: Routledge.

Norris, P. and Inglehart, R. (2018) *Cultural Backlash: Trump, Brexit, and Authoritarian Populism,* Cambridge: Cambridge University Press.

Oreskes, N. and Conway, E.M. (2010) *Merchants of Doubt,* New York: Bloomsbury.

Page, S.E. (2017) *The Diversity Bonus: How Great Teams Pay Off in the Knowledge Economy,* Princeton, NJ: Princeton University Press.

Pluckrose, H. and Lindsay, J. (2020) *Cynical Theories: How Universities Made Everything About Race, Gender, and Identity – and Why This Harms Everybody,* Durham, NC: Pitchstone Publishing.

Pluckrose, H., Lindsay, J. and Boghossian, P. (2018) 'Academic grievance studies and the corruption of scholarship', *Areo,* 2 October.

Rees, M. (2003) *Our Final Hour,* New York: Basic Books.

Tamkin, P., Yarnall, J. and Kerrin, M. (2002) *Kirkpatrick and Beyond: A Review of Models of Training Evaluation,* IES Report 392, Brighton: Institute for Employment Studies.

Torney-Purta, J., Cabrera, J.C., Roohr, K.C., Liu, O.L. and Rios, J.A. (2015) 'Assessing civic competency and engagement in higher education: research background, frameworks, and directions for next-generation assessment', *ETS Research Report Series,* (2): 1–48.

Truman, H.S. (1947) Statement by the President Making Public a Report of the Commission on Higher Education, 15 December: www.presidency.ucsb.edu/documents/statement-the-president-making-public-report-the-commission-higher-education

Tuchman, B.W. (1984) *The March of Folly: From Troy to Vietnam,* New York: Knopf.

Vogel, F. (2022) *The Enablers: How the West Supports Kleptocrats and Corruption – Endangering Our Democracy,* Lanham, MA: Rowman & Littlefield.

Walters, S. and Openjuru, G. (2014) IV.2. University-Community Engagement in Africa, Report: *Higher Education in the World 2014,* 1 October http://hdl.handle.net/2099/15274

World Economic Forum (WEF) (2017) *Global Shapers Annual Survey 2017,* World Economic Forum Global Shapers Community.

PART III

How to make a lasting impact

10

The evidence on educational methods for political engagement

David Kerr and Bryony Hoskins

Introduction

Political engagement is central to the functioning of democratic society. An engaged citizenry is a sign of a healthy democracy. High levels of political and civic participation not only increase the chances of citizens' voices being heard on important issues but also confer legitimacy on elected officials and democratic institutions. However, in many countries, there has been a growing concern since the 1990s that increasing numbers of the public, particularly younger generations, are becoming disengaged from political and civic life.

This disengagement, or 'democratic deficit' as it is termed by political scientists, has brought an increased focus on the role of education in helping to reverse this trend by educating young people how to engage politically. It has led to countries strengthening the role of citizenship education in their school curricula over the past 20 years through teaching and learning approaches designed to help young people to develop the civic competences (knowledge, skills, values and dispositions) that encourage them to engage politically now and in the future.

In England, this concern saw the establishment of the Citizenship Advisory Group (CAG), chaired by Professor (Sir) Bernard Crick, in 1998, and the introduction of citizenship as a new statutory national curriculum subject for all 11- to 16-year-olds in 2002. In the CAG final report, known as the 'Crick Report', the Lord Chancellor was quoted from a speech he made earlier in the year: 'We should not, must not, *dare not*, be complacent about the health and future of British democracy. Unless we become a nation of engaged citizens, our democracy is not secure' (QCA, 1998, p 8). The Crick Report projected the benefits of effective citizenship education to be:

- For pupils – an entitlement in schools that will empower them to participate in society effectively as active, informed, critical and responsible citizens.

- For schools – a firm base to coordinate existing teaching and activities, to relate positively to the local community and to develop effective citizenship education in the curriculum for all pupils.
- For society – an active and politically-literate citizenry convinced that they can influence government and community affairs at all levels. (QCA, 1998, p 9)

The Citizenship Advisory Group was clear on how education would impact positively on levels of political engagement in society through young people getting their entitlement to citizenship education in schools.[1]

Given this context, this chapter explores the nature of the interrelationship between political engagement and educational approaches, particularly through citizenship education in schools. It draws on latest research evidence from a range of disciplines, including key findings from research on citizenship education, such as the National Foundation for Educational Research's (NFER, 2001–10) Citizenship Education Longitudinal Study (CELS) and the Institute of Economic Affairs' (IEA) International Civic and Citizenship Education Study (ICCS). There is a particular focus on the effect of social background on modes of political engagement, as that is highlighted in research analyses (Hoskins and Janmaat, 2019).

The chapter is structured around four key questions:

1. What is meant by political engagement? We start with establishing a clearer definition to enable the identification of the factors and contexts that impact on it, particularly social background and education.
2. What are the key principles of how young people learn to engage politically? We will look at the key principles of learning that influence political engagement and the contexts where it takes place, notably schools.
3. What methods of teaching and learning in school enhance young people's development of civic competences and their political engagement? We will identify what forms of learning in schools are particularly effective as well as which groups of young people they most benefit. Research has shown that not all social groups of young people are benefiting from these learning experiences in the UK and across Europe (Hoskins and Janmaat, 2019).
4. What are the implications for the future direction of citizenship education policy, practice and research in England? We conclude by exploring what the latest research evidence on educational methods for political engagement means for policy, practice and research in

---

[1] For more on the work of the Crick group, see Chapter 5 in this book.

citizenship education is important, because it is over 20 years since the Crick Report (QCA, 1998) and the introduction of citizenship into the school curriculum. Much has changed in that time in the nature and organisation of education, schools, approaches to citizenship education and the evidence base.

What is meant by political engagement?

To look at educational methods for political engagement and the processes of learning, it is first necessary to define the concept of 'political engagement'. There is considerable confusion around the term because scholars understand it in different ways. These differences mainly concern scope, with some using a definition that only comprises different forms of political participation (Macedo, 2005), while others entertain a much broader understanding including attitudes and dispositions, such as political interest, engaging in political discussions, keeping track of news, political efficacy and political trust (Norris, 2000; Solt, 2008).

The definition of political engagement we employ is developed from the current research base and is pragmatic. In line with Macedo (2005), we use political engagement in a narrow sense to refer only to adult political activities. We consciously exclude other elements, such as political efficacy and interest, from the definition as these are also often considered as predictors of participation (Blais, 2000). In addition, we see political activities at school as part of the learning component rather than the outcome of political activities.

The forms of political engagement we are interested in are voting, joining a political party, legal protest and illegal protest. Not only do these cover a range of political activities, but they also represent a good mix of conventional and alternative and accepted and controversial forms of engagement. Voting is an obvious choice. Although this conventional mode of participation is relatively unpopular among young people (Sloam, 2014), it is also the most common and widespread form of political activity among that age group (Keating and Janmaat, 2016). What makes this interesting is the social gap in participation, with the less well educated, as a rule, showing lower voting levels, and these inequalities widening over time (Sloam, 2013; Lawrence, 2015).

Similar to voting, party membership is often thought of as a conventional mode of engagement that has largely fallen out of favour among the electorate and particularly among the young (Inglehart and Welzel, 2005). Being the preserve of the highly engaged, it is a much rarer form of participation, but also one that is likely to be much more influential than voting.

The third form of participation we have an interest in is legal protest. It captures activities such as partaking in demonstrations, organising and signing petitions, boycotting products and wearing badges. This form is often labelled as 'alternative' and tends to be more popular among young people because of the more informal and egalitarian nature of these activities (Lichterman, 1996). These forms of collective action also allow for greater input from the participants, which may contribute to their sense of agency and efficacy. In the UK, social disparities in this form of participation are even starker than for voting. While UK graduates vote 1.1 times as much as the average citizen, they take part in demonstrations 2.6 times as much, suggesting that engaging in legal protest seems to be an elite affair (Sloam, 2014).

Illegal protest is the last form of participation in which we are interested. It includes partaking in a violent demonstration, blocking traffic and occupying public buildings. This form is controversial, as it involves civil disobedience and breaking the law. Consequently, the number of people engaging in this form of participation is very low. However, if some students or groups plan to engage in illegal activities to protest something they believe to be wrong and would like to see changed, such activities can be seen as a form of political engagement.

A conspicuous omission in the forms of political engagement we include is online participation. We have a pragmatic reason for this in that unfortunately the data sources investigating political engagement among young people are not currently available.

Educational approaches and political engagement

Before we move onto identify the key educational methods for enhancing young people's political engagement, it is important to acknowledge that there is considerable debate among researchers about the role of and relationship between social background and education in the learning of political engagement. There are broadly three competing theoretical viewpoints:

1. Those who argue that social class is the main factor influencing political engagement and that education merely proxies for social class (Persson, 2014; Lauglo, 2016).
2. Those who suggest that education exerts only an indirect effect on political engagement via educational qualifications that help people to acquire social positions in society and that, in turn, impact on their degree of political engagement (Nie et al, 1996; Campbell, 2006).
3. Those who argue that education does have a direct effect on political engagement, and via schools and teaching and learning approaches can be considered as one of the main drivers of political engagement (Niemi and Junn, 1998; Emler and Frazer, 1999).

It is useful to explore each of these viewpoints in turn because they help to situate the effect of both social background and education on political engagement and identify the key principles of how political engagement is learnt by young people through teaching and learning methods.

Recent research by political scientists and economists has claimed that educational attainment, years of education or expected education outcomes have no effect on levels of political engagement. The argument is that education is only an approximate measure that is capturing an individual's socioeconomic background. The behaviours and attitudes associated with particular class backgrounds are said to be developed through early socialisation experiences within the home and are then argued to influence certain choices in education and political engagement (Persson, 2014). Certainly, comparative data analysis from the ICCS study confirms that the effect of social background on various modes of political engagement is greater in England than in any other European country; this includes future voting intentions, legal protest and illegal protest, with young people from poorer backgrounds having lower engagement levels than their middle-class counterparts (Hoskins and Janmaat, 2019).

The suggestion from the no effect perspective is that national education systems are unable to mitigate or even intensify either the potential for educational success or the potential for political engagement, as both have been preprogramed by age five. However, we argue that considerable effort has gone into establishing the educational interventions that provide the opportunity to diminish socioeconomic inequalities in achievement and that the same possibilities exist regarding the learning of political engagement (Heckman and Masterov, 2007). We believe that education systems and the learning opportunities offered in schools can and do influence young people's chances of becoming politically engaged. This depends on the extent to which the learning as acquisition and learning as participation principles play their respective part in enabling young people to learn to engage politically in schools and through citizenship education.

Learning as acquisition

The basis for the key principle of *learning as acquisition* is that knowledge is a set of abstract objects that an individual can possess. Education is then understood as a system of codifying that knowledge. The codified system is the knowledge held within an education system through the curriculum, teachers and teaching materials.

The effect of an additional year of education is the additional acquisition of the necessary knowledge and skills to understand how to register and vote, follow politics and evaluate and assess campaigns and candidates, or, put another way, through every additional year of education, an individual gains the political knowledge and verbal cognitive proficiency to enable them to understand the world of politics better and to take more advantage of the opportunities it offers to defend one's interests (Nie et al, 1996).

There is a general assumption behind much of this literature that specific subjects, notably citizenship education, are more helpful in developing these skills than others as they directly aim at fostering political engagement. Citizenship education has been found to have a positive and significant effect on intentions to and actual levels of political engagement (Whiteley, 2014). One of the main strengths of the acquisition learning principle is that it can be used to define the knowledge, skills, values and dispositions for political engagement and establish levels of proficiency in these competences. These qualities are often referred to as *civic competences* (Hoskins et al, 2012; Council of Europe, 2018). The competences needed for civic engagement are relevant as a step in the learning process of becoming more politically engaged.

Learning as participation

An alternative approach to acquisition is the principle of *learning as participation* (Sfard, 1998). This principle typically understands learning as action and part of a joint social enterprise to build and transform communities (Lave, 1991; Wenger, 1998). The goal of learning is community building as opposed to the cognitive metaphor of individual enrichment, and instead of a student being a consumer of knowledge, they become an apprentice to the community they are joining.

The social processes of learning through open dialogue and practising political engagement have been widely cited as an effective way to learn the skills for political engagement (Hoskins et al, 2016; Keating and Janmaat, 2016; Knowles et al, 2018). Evidence using communities of practice and constructivist theories of learning suggests that young people learn to become politically engaged in real-world environments or contexts that reflect the real world (Biesta et al, 2009). For example, a quantitative study, using data from the IEA's Civic Education Study in five European countries (Hoskins et al, 2012), showed that knowledge and skills about democracy and participatory attitudes are learnt through the process of meaning making in discussions with parents and friends about politics, discussions inside the classroom (an open classroom climate) and social participation in school councils.

How the key principles of learning work in combination

It is important to recognise that these key principles of learning often work in combination in education and schools. The learning as acquisition principle positions the transmission of political knowledge from teachers to students as the first step in learning political engagement and then proposes that this enables young people to have a better understanding of politics and the ability to engage with it. Meanwhile, the learning as participation principle conceptualises political knowledge to be co-created through participatory learning processes, including discussions and debates within communities such as schools and families. It is this experience of participation and co-creation of meaning that develops young people's competences that lead to future engagement; for example, a political identity, political efficacy and a sense of belonging to a political community. We propose that these learning principles can be complementary in terms of understanding political learning and even a necessity within a citizenship education curriculum aimed at developing informed and politically engaged young people.

What methods of teaching and learning in school enhance civic competences and political engagement for young people?

The school can be understood as a participatory community for learning about living in a diverse society through living this experience in the school. It can also be seen as an environment for engaging in democratic practices, reflecting on these experiences and reflecting on experiences from outside school (Daniels, 2001). Using the learning acquisition principle, the school could then also have the responsibility to facilitate the process of learning political engagement for each young person and enhance the quality of their political engagement by providing each learner with the breadth of knowledge, skills, values and dispositions (civic competences) needed for effective and democratic political engagement. Educators can assess and evaluate the learning that is needed to enhance engagement and the quality of political engagement and can use subject lessons in citizenship education and learning processes within the school community to deliver the content and political learning.

Nevertheless, we also accept the reality that school communities are not always open and democratic environments. Often, young people are not treated by all teachers in a fair way, with differing expectations of students according to where they come from and the different social groups to which they belong (Reay, 2006). When young people do not feel able to engage openly in a classroom discussion or participate on an equal footing in a discussion or debate, the classroom becomes a restricted learning environment for this individual or social group (Fuller and Unwin, 2004). For a school to really be a democratic learning community, it will take time and effort to bring all voices into discussions and decision-making. Democracy has to be a priority in schools in order to devote sufficient time to the processes needed to learn and develop civic competences. In schools with regular high-stakes testing and where the priority is labour market preparation over preparation for living in a democracy, the possibilities for learning political engagement may be limited. This may well allow certain social groups (the more advantaged) to advance and socially reproduce political engagement, while other young people (the more disadvantaged) are left behind on the periphery of the community.

Indeed, comparative research using data from the ICCS study confirms that the impact of social background on learning opportunities for political engagement is greater in England than in any other European country (Hoskins and Janmaat, 2019). Those young people from lower social backgrounds have less access to civic participation activities and approaches in school compared to middle-class children. In England, the school environment thus enhances the already salient social gaps in access to learning between different groups of children. In fact, these social disparities widen more in England between the ages of 12 and 20 than in other European countries (Hoskins and Janmaat, 2019).

If we borrow from participatory theories of learning the understanding that the school is a community that young people join and participate in for the negotiation of meaning and norms of the community, then there are many methods in a school that can facilitate political learning and engagement.

An open classroom climate for discussion

The most frequently cited of these methods is an open classroom climate for discussion (Hahn, 1998; Torney-Purta, 2002; Quintelier and Hooghe, 2011). This refers to a situation where students feel free to ask questions, bring up issues for discussion, express their own opinions, feel able to make up their own minds, and perceive that teachers respect their opinion and present different sides to an argument. The characteristics of a classroom based on these principles clearly follow participatory approaches to learning, where learning happens through interaction, negotiation and joint enterprise. There is considerable research from citizenship education studies, such as ICCS and CELS, that has demonstrated that the open classroom method of learning is effective in enhancing the following: political engagement (Torney-Purta, 2002, Campbell, 2008; Keating and Janmaat, 2016; Knowles et al, 2018), positive attitudes towards political engagement (Geboers et al, 2013), critical thinking (Ten Dam and Volman, 2004), citizenship skills (Finkel and Ernst, 2005) and political knowledge (McDevitt and Kiousis, 2006).

Political activities in the school

The participatory processes of learning political engagement also happen when young people are offered the chance to practise political engagement and decision-making at school. These can be through activities such as class councils, school parliaments, clubs and societies and mock elections, and there is considerable evidence for their effectiveness (Hoskins et al, 2012; Keating and Janmaat, 2016). Youth participation activities are said to lead to the development of civic skills, such as deliberation, compromise, speaking in public, expressing an opinion, learning to work in groups, and assimilating other people's opinions (Quintelier, 2008). In addition, they are also argued to provide greater awareness of issues in their communities and build the efficacy needed to become involved in bringing change (McFarland and Thomas, 2006).

Citizenship education

Since most of the research evidence suggests that learning for political engagement takes place through participatory learning processes, it may be a surprise to identify the effect of having a specific subject and curriculum for political learning, as studying a subject could well be decontextualised (not situated) and limited in its interactivity. But as Haste (2010) notes, citizenship education can be understood in different ways according to the key principles of learning. First, using the learning as acquisition principle and the cognitive theories of learning, we can postulate that teaching political knowledge will lead to higher levels of political participation and reduce the cost/effort towards political engagement in the future. Second, organising political engagement activities in the class (simulation activities, mock elections and student-led debates), which are situated in relevant and current issues that affect young people's lives, allows students to actively construct their knowledge, skills, values and dispositions (civic competences) needed for future political engagement. The evidence weighs more heavily on the success of the participatory approaches to learning political engagement. Nevertheless, this does not imply that learning political knowledge is not important. It simply means that using a participatory approach to learning political knowledge is more likely to result in political action later on.

Research on citizenship education has identified both no effects and positive effects on political engagement, with different delivery methods likely to produce different effects. Experimental design research has shown that participatory learning inside citizenship education classes is effective. For example, the Student Voice programme in the US, which targeted disadvantaged urban schools, found that contextualising debates in local politics and using interactive methodologies were effective for enhancing political knowledge, political efficacy and political participation (Feldman et al, 2007). In Germany, research by Oberle and Leunig (2016), who also used an experimental design, found that using simulation games inside citizenship education classes were effective for teaching knowledge about the EU and increasing levels of trust, for more socioeconomically deprived groups.

In England, as already noted, citizenship has been a mandatory subject for 11- to 16-year-olds in the national curriculum since 2002. Schools are free to decide on the content, mode of delivery and volume of citizenship education. The CELS study highlighted how schools have used this freedom and flexibility to substantially vary their approach to citizenship education (Kerr et al, 2007). Some schools are offering it as a specific subject, some as a cross-curricular approach, others through a more participatory route by introducing citizenship activities into the whole school, and still others employ a combination of these approaches.

The CELS study underlined that how citizenship education is implemented in schools has consequences for its effectiveness. The study's final report concluded that there had been a marked and steady increase in young people's civic and political participation from 2001 to 2010, and there were indications that young people would continue to politically engage as adult citizens (Keating et al, 2010). It identified several factors that shape young people's citizenship learning outcomes including levels of 'received' citizenship education. It found that citizenship outcomes were strongest for those young people in schools where young people reported being taught citizenship at least once a week; the citizenship curriculum was planned, coordinated and taught by a trained citizenship teacher; and there was formal assessment of young people's learning outcomes in citizenship (Keating et al, 2010).

What are the implications for the future direction of citizenship education policy, practice and research?

Changed context in education, schools and citizenship education

This research evidence needs to be situated within the context of considerable changes in education policy and practice and in citizenship education since the introduction of citizenship into the curriculum in 2002, including:

- Greater diversity of schools with the growth of academies, multi-academy trusts and free schools that report directly to the government. They do not have to follow the national curriculum, meaning that many have removed citizenship education from their curriculum.
- Schools demarcated more along socioeconomic status lines, with middle-class parents taking advantage of school choice options for their children's schooling. This has led to increased social division between and within schools.
- Narrower curricula focus, increased academic setting and high-stakes testing, with schools concentrating on knowledge delivery, core subjects (maths, English and science), setting classes by academic ability, and preparation for the world of work and public exams (GCSE, A-levels). This has been at the expense of citizenship education as a curriculum subject.
- Increased scrutiny of schools and student outcomes in a centrally controlled accountability regime by the school inspectorate (Ofsted) and supported by the Secretary of State for Education. Citizenship education does not figure prominently in accountability measures and is not an Ofsted priority.

- Citizenship education practice in schools becoming more fragmented and uneven with great practice in some areas and no practice in others. This has been highlighted in reports by Ofsted (2010, 2013) and the House of Lords (2018, 2022).
- Greatly reduced citizenship education research base with no major addition since the CELS study in 2001 and England's participation in ICCS in 2009. England did not participate in the ICCS studies in 2016 and 2021, and there has been no follow up to CELS.

The cumulative effect of these changes continues to be considerable on citizenship education and educational methods for political engagement. It impacts on political engagement levels among young people, as well as the quantity, nature and quality of teaching and learning opportunities for political engagement in schools and classrooms and in citizenship education. It means that, overall, those young people from disadvantaged backgrounds have increasingly fewer opportunities for and access to political activities and an open classroom climate in school, while those more advantaged pupils tend to have more opportunities and access. In short, education and schools in England over the past 20 years appear to be facilitating the widening and reinforcement of social divisions in society rather than narrowing and compensating for them.[2]

Given the nature of this changed context, combined with the research evidence, what does this mean for the future direction of policy, practice and research in citizenship education? There is much that can be written but we will focus only on the main implications.

For policy makers

- Recognise the importance of democracy and place the need to prepare young people to politically engage as a central aim of the education system rather than focusing narrowly on preparation for employability.
- Promote inclusion, access and social justice as key principles that underpin how the education system operates at all levels, particularly in school choice, to help lessen current social divisions in education and schools.
- Ensure that all young people receive their statutory entitlement to citizenship education as enshrined with the introduction of citizenship as a compulsory subject in 2002.
- Make teaching and learning processes that help young people to engage politically compulsory in schools rather than optional. Provide more of

---

[2] See Chapter 2 for a detailed critique of this issue.

them, particularly in schools with a high concentration of young people from disadvantaged backgrounds.
- Ensure that Ofsted takes citizenship education and political engagement seriously and include them in accountability measures so that opportunities for and impacts on young people are closely monitored.
- Support efforts to strengthen the evidence base for citizenship education by commissioning and taking part in impact studies and evaluations at local, national and comparative levels.

For practice in schools/school leaders

- Pay more attention to the social background of young people and provide continuing professional development for teachers on its impacts on teaching and learning and political engagement opportunities in schools and classrooms.
- Make promoting democracy and the school as a participatory community a priority and foster a strong democratic school ethos that supports teaching and learning opportunities for political engagement for all young people.
- Promote citizenship education as a standalone curriculum subject with sufficient curriculum time, status and properly trained teachers to teach it.
- Ensure that there is no academic selection or grouping in citizenship education, so classes comprise a mixture of young people from social backgrounds.
- Provide more distinct opportunities for young people to gain political knowledge and organise activities, such as classroom discussion, school councils and mock elections, that allow young people to experience and practise democracy.

For practice in classrooms/teachers

- Understand the key principles of how young people learn to engage politically and construct regular teaching and learning opportunities that enhance young people's civic competences and intentions to politically engage.
- Be aware of the social background of young people in classes and the barriers that can prevent them from fully engaging in opportunities for political engagement in the school and classroom.
- Work to break down those barriers through creating classrooms based on an open classroom climate that encourages all young people to participate and learn equally.
- In political discussions, ensure that the voices of all young people are brought in and that they feel they are being treated fairly.

- Strive to ensure that all young people take up teaching and learning opportunities, particularly for participation, provided in the school and classroom, especially those from more disadvantaged backgrounds.

For research/researchers

- Recognise the considerable gaps that remain in our understanding of the nature of the links between education, citizenship education and political engagement among young people and work to fill in those gaps through more research studies.
- Focus explicitly and urgently on research that helps to explain the impact of young people's online political engagement and how that relates to more traditional forms of political engagement.
- Conduct more research studies on better understanding the effects of social background, particularly for young people, on modes of political engagement in schools.

Taken together, these implications call for a sizeable shift in the direction of travel of policy and practice in education and citizenship education in England to focus more centrally on democracy and participation. Such a focus is urgently needed to narrow the current large implementation gap between policy and practice in citizenship education in schools and enable young people from all social groups to learn how to politically engage and have their voices heard in schools and in society. It would also greatly increase the chances of fulfilling the ambition of the Crick Report that effective citizenship education practice in schools would help us to produce 'an active and politically-literate citizenry convinced that they can influence government and community affairs at all levels' (QCA, p 9). Given the current levels of political engagement of young people in England and the barriers that many have to overcome to learn how to participate in schools and classrooms, this is an ambition that is worth fighting for.

References

Biesta, G., Lawy, R. and Kelly, N. (2009) 'Understanding young people's citizenship learning in everyday life: the role of contexts, relationships and dispositions', *Education, Citizenship and Social Justice*, 4(1): 5–24.

Blais, A. (2000) *To Vote or Not To Vote: The Merits and Limits of Rational Choice Theory*, Pittsburgh, PA: University of Pittsburgh Press.

Campbell, D.E. (2006) 'What is education's impact on civic and social engagement?', in R. Desjardins and T. Schuller (eds) *Measuring the Effects of Education on Health and Civic/Social Engagement*, Paris: OECD/CERI, pp 25–126.

Campbell, D.E. (2008) 'Voice in the classroom: how an open classroom climate fosters political engagement among adolescents', *Political Behavior*, 30(4): 437–54.

Council of Europe (2018) *Reference Framework For Competences For Democratic Culture*, Strasbourg: Council of Europe.

Daniels, H. (2001) *Vygotsky and Pedagogy*. London: Routledge Falmer.

Emler, N. and Frazer, E. (1999) 'Politics: the education effect', *Oxford Review of Education*, 25: 271–92.

Feldman, L., Pasek, J., Romer, D. and Jamieson, K.H. (2007) 'Identifying best practices in civic education: lessons from the student voices program', *American Journal of Education*, 114(1): 75–100.

Finkel, S. and Ernst, H. (2005) 'Civic education in post-apartheid South Africa: alternative paths to the development of political knowledge and democratic values', *Political Psychology*, 26(3): 333–364.

Fuller, A. and Unwin, L. (2004) 'Expansive learning environments: integrating personal and organisational development', in H. Rainbird, A. Fuller and A. Munro (eds) *Workplace Learning in Context*, London: Routledge, pp 126–44.

Geboers, E., Geijsel, F., Admiraal, W. and ten Dam, G. (2013) 'Review of the effects of citizenship education', *Educational Research Review*, 9: 158–73.

Hahn, C. (1998) *Becoming Political: Comparative Perspectives on Citizenship Education*, Albany, NY: SUNY Press.

Haste, H. (2004) 'Constructing the citizen', *Political Psychology*, 25(3): 413–39.

Heckman, J.J. and Masterov, D.V. (2007) 'The productivity argument for investing in young children', *Applied Economic Perspectives and Policy*, 29(3): 446–93.

Hoskins, B. and Janmaat, J.G. (2018) *Education, Democracy and Inequalities: Political Engagement and Citizenship Education in Europe*, London: Palgrave.

Hoskins, B., Janmaat, J.G. and Villalba, E. (2012) 'Learning citizenship through social participation outside and inside school: an international, multilevel study of young people's learning of citizenship', *British Educational Research Journal*, 38(3): 419–46.

Hoskins, B., Janmaat, J.G., Han, C. and Muijs, D. (2016) 'Inequalities in the education system and the reproduction of socioeconomic disparities in voting in England, Denmark and Germany: the influence of country context, tracking and self-efficacy on voting intentions of students age 16–18', *Compare: A Journal of Comparative and International Education*, 46(1): 69–92.

House of Lords (2018) *The Ties That Bind: Citizenship and Civic Engagement in the 21st Century*, London: House of Lords.

House of Lords (2022) *The Ties That Bind: Citizenship and Civic Engagement in the 21st Century – Follow-up Report*, London: House of Lords.

Inglehart, R. and Welzel, C. (2005) *Modernization, Cultural Change, and Democracy: The Human Development Sequence*, Cambridge: Cambridge University Press.

Keating, A. and Janmaat, J.G. (2016) 'Education through citizenship at school: Do school activities have a lasting impact on youth political engagement?', *Parliamentary Affairs*, 69(2): 409–29.

Keating, A., Kerr, D., Benton, T., Mundy, E. and Lopes, J. (2010) *Citizenship Education in England 2001–2010: Young People's Practices and Prospects for the Future: The Eighth and Final Citizen Education Longitudinal Study (CELS)*, London: Department for Education.

Kerr, D., Lopes, J., Nelson, J., White, K., Cleaver, E. and Benton, T. (2007) *Vision Versus Pragmatism: Citizenship in the Secondary School Curriculum in England. Citizenship Education Longitudinal Study: Fifth Annual Report*, Slough: NFER.

Knowles, R.T., Torney-Purta, J. and Barber, C. (2018) 'Enhancing citizenship learning with international comparative research: analyses of IEA civic education datasets', *Citizenship Teaching & Learning*, 13(1): 7–30.

Lauglo, J. (2016) 'Does political socialization at home boost adolescents' expectation of higher education? An analysis of eighth-grade students in 35 countries', *Comparative Education Review*, 60(3): 429–56.

Lave, J. (1991) *Situating Learning in Communities of Practice*, Cambridge: Cambridge University Press.

Lawrence, M. (2015) *Political Inequality: Why British Democracy Must be Reformed and Revitalized*, London: IPPR.

Lichterman, P. (1996) *The Search for Political Community: American Activists Reinventing Commitment*, Cambridge: Cambridge University Press.

Macedo, S. (2005) *Democracy at Risk: How Political Choices Undermine Citizen Participation and What We Can Do About It*, Washington: Brookings Institution Press.

McDevitt, M. and Kiousis, S. (2006) 'Experiments in political socialization: kids voting USA as a model for civic education reform', Working Paper no. 49. CIRCLE, University of Maryland.

McFarland, D.A. and Thomas, R.J. (2006) 'Bowling young: how youth voluntary associations influence adult political participation', *American Sociological Review*, 71(3): 401–25.

NFER (2001–2010) *Citizenship Education Longitudinal Study*, Slough: National Foundation for Educational Research.

Nie, N., Junn, J. and Stehlik-Barry, K. (1996) *Education and Democratic Citizenship in America*, Chicago: Chicago University Press.

Niemi, R.G. and Junn, J. (1998) *Civic Education: What Makes Students Learn*, New Haven, CT: Yale University Press.

Norris, P. (2000) *A Virtuous Circle: Political Communications in Post-industrial Societies*, New York: Cambridge University Press.

Oberle, M. and Leunig, J. (2016) 'Simulation games on the European Union in civics: effects on secondary school pupils' political competence', *Citizenship, Social and Economics Education*, 15(3): 227–43.

Ofsted (2010) *Citizenship Established? Citizenship in Schools 2006/09*, London: Ofsted.

Ofsted (2013) *Citizenship Consolidated? A Survey of Citizenship in Schools*, London: Ofsted.

Persson, M. (2014) 'Testing the relationship between education and political participation using the 1970 British Cohort Study', *Political Behavior*, 36(4): 877–97.

QCA (1998) *Education for Citizenship and the Teaching of Democracy in Schools: Final Report of the Citizenship Advisory Group*, the Crick Report, London: QCA.

Quintelier, E. (2008) 'Who is politically active: the athlete, the scout member or the environmental activist? Young people, voluntary engagement and political participation', *Acta Sociologica*, 51(4): 355–370.

Quintelier, E. and Hooghe, M. (2011) 'The effect of compulsory voting on turnout stratification patterns: a cross-national analysis', *International Political Science Reviewer*, 32(4): 396–416.

Reay, D. (2006) 'The zombie stalking English schools: social class and educational inequality', *British Journal of Educational Studies*, 54(3): 288–307.

Sfard, A. (1998) 'On two metaphors for learning and the dangers of choosing just one', *Educational Researcher*, 27(2): 4–13.

Sloam, J. (2013) 'Voice and equality: young people's politics in the European Union', *West European Politics*, 36(4): 836–58.

Sloam, J. (2014) 'New voice, less equal: the civic and political engagement of young people in the United States and Europe', *Comparative Political Studies*, 47(5): 663–88.

Solt, F. (2008) 'Economic inequality and democratic political engagement', *American Journal of Political Science*, 52(1): 48–60.

Ten Dam, G. and Volman, M. (2004) 'Critical thinking as a citizenship competence: teaching strategies', *Learning and Instruction*, 14(4): 359–79.

Torney-Purta, J. (2002) 'The school's role in developing civic engagement: a study of adolescents in twenty-eight countries', *Applied Developmental Science*, 6(4): 203–12.

Wenger, E. (1998) *Communities of Practice: Learning, Meaning, and Identity*, Cambridge: Cambridge University Press.

Whiteley, P. (2014) 'Does citizenship education work? Evidence from a decade of citizenship education in secondary schools in England', *Parliamentary Affairs*, 67: 513–35.

11

Citizenship education: building for the future

Lee Jerome and Liz Moorse

Introduction

This chapter deals with many of the issues that are discussed in greater detail elsewhere in this book. It approaches them from the practical perspective of the Association for Citizenship Teaching (ACT)[1] in the UK, which is a membership organisation promoting high-quality citizenship education for all. As of 2022, citizenship had been a national curriculum subject in England for 20 years. This period generated a wealth of school-based experiments and saw the development of a cadre of experienced subject specialist teachers, which led to some principles that inform the work of ACT and underpin its planning for the future. Our starting point is that good citizenship teachers address the emotional dimension, the role of knowledge and rational argument, and the need for citizenship to be enacted. This approach continues to inform how teachers are responding to significant ongoing and emergent challenges. In considering five of these challenges, this chapter reflects on what the next 20 years might hold, and what citizenship in schools might look like in the near future.

The urgency of political literacy

Bernard Crick paved the way for citizenship education in England's national curriculum by calling for a programme of political literacy, by which he meant learning about the institutions, problems and practices of our democracy and how to make oneself effective as a citizen (Crick, 2000).[2] This task must be understood in the context of several profound challenges:

---

[1] More information about the Association for Citizenship Teaching can be found at: www.teachingcitizenship.org.uk

[2] See Chapters 5 and 10 in this book for more on Crick and the development of citizenship education in England.

1. We have to acknowledge the continuing decline in satisfaction with democracy among young people – partly because of the failure of democracy to prevent rising inequality, hardship and the associated frustrations of young people (Foa et al, 2020).
2. There is some evidence that this leads to greater support for 'outsider' candidates who promise to break the mould, potentially linked to the rise in populism (Sloam and Henn, 2018).[3]
3. Young people's political activity often happens in broad social movements or campaigns, which keeps political action alive, but potentially does little to refresh the institutional and party political infrastructure of democratic governance (Norris, 2004).[4]
4. The legacy of Brexit seems to be a more deeply divided and polarised political culture (Hobolt et al, 2020).
5. One result of that polarisation may well be an increased concern among rightwing parents that teachers cannot be trusted to teach politics impartially (Weinberg, 2021).
6. This leads to another challenge – the rise in government regulation of teachers' impartiality (DfE, 2022a), with the attendant concern that teaching about politics may be seen as a high-risk activity, with serious consequences if a school gets it wrong (see, for example, Ofsted, 2021).[5]

However, we do have some evidence that citizenship education can make a difference. The longitudinal research by Keating et al (2010) tracking the impact of citizenship education from 2001 to 2010 showed us that where students received 'a lot' of citizenship education, this improved their citizenship outcomes, including efficacy and intention to participate, over and above the impact of other background factors. A small extension of this work that followed students into young adulthood showed a lingering effect in boosting their actual levels of participation (Keating and Janmaat, 2016). Hoskins et al (2017) point out that children from lower socioeconomic backgrounds are less likely to experience the most impactful forms of citizenship education in school, such as open classroom discussion and participation, but their conclusion is that where schools do provide these opportunities as an entitlement for all students, citizenship education can help to close the civic gap. Weinberg (2021) has also demonstrated that more citizenship education, especially open classroom discussions of contemporary issues, can close the gap

---

[3] See Chapter 6 for a discussion of educational responses to different forms of populism.
[4] See Chapter 8 for the role of action learning in developing young people's political understanding and involvement.
[5] See Chapter 3 for a critical look at the issue of divisive concepts and political impartiality.

between socioeconomic groups in relation to intention to participate. Weinberg's research indicates that actually meeting politicians can be counterproductive for some students, but innovative programmes such as The Politics Project (2021) have demonstrated that when embedded in planned sequences of learning, such engagement can both increase the likelihood that students discuss politics at home and their belief that politicians care about what they think.

Case study 1 Power and community[6]

One school in West London has addressed these aspects of political literacy through the community organising approach, which combines learning about political institutions and processes with real problem-solving of significance to young people and their families. The teacher wanted to start small and then grow the work into a whole school approach that ensured that their students were empowered to lead the changes in the community that they wanted to see.

Students developed their understanding of the key community organising principles and how to apply these when undertaking action. The key community organising principles include:

- never do for others what they can do for themselves
- understand self-interest and what is in it for them
- build relationships.

The approach sits well with the objectives of citizenship education to 'develop active, informed and responsible citizens', build knowledge about 'the ways in which citizens work together to improve their communities', and to 'experience and evaluate different ways citizens can act together to solve problems and contribute positively to society' (DfE, 2013).

The students listened to those in the community using a range of strategies to 'listen with a purpose' and engaged with members of the school community (pupils, parents and staff) and those in the neighbourhood. Teachers worked with students to plan how to talk about the issues of concern and find issues that were 'winnable', so that students could experience some level of success. They worked on developing skills and knowledge about how to act, so that students developed the capacity to research, read, listen,

---

[6] The case studies in this chapter are adapted from articles, resources and presentations developed by teachers working with the Association for Citizenship Teaching. The references in each case lead to a fuller account of each project.

think critically, reason, negotiate and compromise. Students then worked in 'action teams' to create campaigns designed to address specific issues they had prioritised. Issues included building relationships with the school's neighbours to address local negativity about the school, local road safety, and improving student voice within the school community using a student council model.

Students became adept at relationship building and finding and using strategies to persuade local policy makers to take their ideas seriously and build empathy. They found creative ways to appeal to the emotions of those they met and talked to at the local council and developed campaigns that involved an element of surprise; for example, by attending local meetings and bringing cake for those who attended. Students had decided it would be harder for decision makers to say no when they brought homemade cake to a meeting and they spent time in advance to find out which flavour those attending the meeting preferred. They became known locally as 'Kidz with Cake!' but, more importantly, they got the right decision makers in the room and helped them make the right decisions.

Source: Doona, 2019

We need to redouble our efforts to raise students' critical understanding of the role of democratic politics in an age of rising scepticism. And we need to support teachers to manage this task while assiduously maintaining political impartiality. But impartiality does not mean neutrality and teachers need to be confident to explore democratic values and the various alternatives so students can think through what they gain, and potentially lose, because of the political system in which they live. Pagliarello et al's literature review (2021) suggests that citizenship education may promote political support for any party. While this supports the idea that it can be non-partisan, it also means that citizenship education does not operate in any simple way to defend democracy against populist parties trading in misinformation. The challenge for the next 20 years is to be more explicit about the value of democratic citizenship and to give more students the opportunities to routinely discuss political issues and to act politically. Teachers can be non-partisan but this should not undermine their commitment to facilitate students' own political development and democratic action.

Digital citizenship and media literacy

One aspect of this challenge that was barely mentioned at the beginning of our subject's arrival in the curriculum was digital media literacy. While our early curriculum included the study of the 'media and the internet in providing information and affecting opinion', Facebook wasn't launched until 2004 and the iPhone first appeared in 2007, so very few people had really begun to imagine how ubiquitous mobile technology and social media would become. Now, our familiarity with online information leads to overconfidence in assessing our capacity for criticality. Ofcom (2022) research indicates that around 70 per cent of adults and older adolescents are confident they can spot misinformation online, but only 22 per cent of adults and 11 per cent of adolescents are actually able to spot fake stories. This can be a matter of life and death when, as we saw during the COVID-19 pandemic, 40 per cent of information online comes from unreliable sources (Kivenen and Kivenen, 2020).

In looking ahead to the next 20 years, we can draw on the Council of Europe (2019) framework on *Digital Citizenship Education*; General Comment No. 25 from the UN Commission on the Rights of the Child (UN, 2021), outlining children's rights in the digital environment; and a growing body of work about education programmes that work. Anzalone (2020) describes a programme of news literacy that was developed in the US for undergraduates and has been taken to schools. After studying how the media works and the sources of mis/disinformation, students are empowered to engage even more with the news and to be more interested in politics. Similarly, Vogt (2020) describes how a programme developed for schools in Ukraine resulted in greater criticality towards news sources and an improved ability to distinguish between facts and opinions and to spot fake stories. In turn, this has inspired UK teachers to devise their own programme in schools.

Case study 2 Digital and media literacy through citizenship

Realising that the proliferation of misinformation and conspiracy theories was becoming a significant and harmful issue not just for their secondary students but for those in many schools across the country, two teachers from schools in the south of England worked together to develop a new approach for teaching digital and media literacy. Their model drew on the expertise of academics and journalists they engaged with during a teacher professional development visit to the US.

Starting with a lesson to introduce the media and its role and responsibilities in society, teaching begins by considering pupils' perceptions and behaviour using an analysis of their own consumption of information and media across different devices. Students are also encouraged to commit to a 24-hour media blackout to understand the way in which our lives are saturated by the media.

The teachers then designed their REVIEW model (Joy, 2020) to simplify the concepts and skills they wanted to teach. This includes the following elements to checking a media story:

- *Reputation*: Have you heard of the source? Have they been reliable before?
- *Evidence*: What facts are cited? Are there any holes?
- *Verify*: How does this source compare to others? Does everything match up?
- *Intent*: Why was the information/story published? Is it factual and impartial?
- *Emotions*: How do you feel about the story? Are you swayed by your feelings?
- *Weigh it up*: What do you now think about what you know? Does the information/story seem plausible?

Lessons develop knowledge and skills in relation to each part of the model; for example, lessons on 'information neighbourhoods' explore the key intent of the information/article to establish an understanding of and draw distinctions between misinformation, disinformation and malinformation. The teaching here draws on journalistic practices to test accountability, independence and whether information can be verified. Students sort and sift through a range of articles and social media posts to categorise the type of information, such as advertising, entertainment, propaganda, publicity, journalism or raw information, and to explore where information overlaps between categories.

Further lessons develop lateral reading techniques and evaluation of the accuracy of news reports and verification of information. For example, students are taught to compare a source with other sources, to establish what information is consistently reported and what is being embellished or missed, and then to verify by checking to see whether there is corroborating evidence and to establish whether the author is named and authoritative and cites sources for what is said.

We need to ensure that we equip young people with the skills to discern fact from opinion, and to distinguish between reliable and unreliable information, as the starting point for informed citizenship. But we also have to recognise that this is more than merely transferring legacy media skills to the online context. We need to address the knowledge dimension about how the internet works, who owns what and who profits from our involvement, the challenge of regulation, and the role of media in a democratic society (Moorse, 2022). We also need to tackle these issues in the light of children's rights, and learn how to balance our desire to protect children from online harms with the enjoyment to be derived from interaction and expression online. And teachers need to engage with the fact that the internet opens up new possibilities to develop identities as members of online communities, to build networks for action online, and to consider how citizens' roles are changing in an increasingly digital democracy. In maintaining our focus on political literacy, we also have to be alert to the temptations of 'clicktivism' (such as endless likes and reposts) and ensure that young citizens understand the difference between what one teacher memorably described as 'slacktivism' rather than 'activism' (Wright, 2011).

Equalities and social justice

It is almost a cliché to observe that young people are often motivated by a sense of fairness, but this commitment is undoubtedly linked to the popularity of issues-based campaigning politics we have already mentioned. In the UK, young people are at the forefront of the Black Lives Matter movement, School Strike for Climate and trans inclusion, but there is a backlash associated with the 'culture wars' attacking such positions as 'woke' and dangerously partisan (Leo, 2022). When citizenship education was introduced to the curriculum, there was a widespread consensus in government that institutional racism had to be tackled through the police, education system and other state institutions; indeed, citizenship education was seen as part of the response (Moorse, 2020). However, such explanations are now seen as more controversial by some (Commission on Race and Ethnic Disparities, 2021), meaning that teachers feel more susceptible to scrutiny and criticism. Similarly, while the Human Rights Act 1998 obliges schools to promote human rights and challenge discrimination and inequality, the topic of human rights has become more controversial as ministers are calling for substantial reforms, with a return to 'common sense' and 'typically British rights' (Ministry of Justice, 2021).

Once again, despite these challenges, there is some evidence about what works in this area. UNICEF UK has been promoting their Rights Respecting Schools Award programme for a number of years, with 5,000 schools (working with 1.6 million pupils) having signed up across the UK. As schools progress through the scheme, they build students' knowledge of rights, their sense of efficacy and their wellbeing (UNICEF UK, nd). This echoes earlier work in schools on the south coast of England where adopting a rights framework led to improved relationships, better attendance and happier staff (Covell and Howe, 2011). As with the work on political literacy, they also found that these effects could also counter some of the effects of social disadvantage, by promoting school engagement and building efficacy (Covell et al, 2011). Montague, who works with young human rights activists through Amnesty UK, has also documented how being a rights activist often leads to improvements in wellbeing, as young people are consolidated in their activist identity, reinforcing their efficacy, and strengthening their meaningful relationships with others (Montague and Eiroa-Orosa, 2017). Even without the experience of consistent external activism, the relationship between wellbeing and children's rights has been well documented (see, for example, Lloyd and Emerson, 2017). ACT's own work in promoting human rights defenders in schools documented a range of positive experiences, not least students' feeling of connectedness to a wider struggle for social justice (Jerome, 2017). Carlile's (2020) work also demonstrates how faith schools can use a human rights framework to promote LGBTQ inclusion in ways that build relationships with parents and local faith groups – particularly important when public demonstrations against schools have served as high-profile warnings to school leaders (Christian Institute, 2019).

Case study 3 Deliberating about equality

In England, schools are required to 'promote the fundamental British values' (FBVs), defined in statutory guidance as democracy, the rule of law, individual liberty and tolerance of religious beliefs. The Deliberative Classroom project, developed by ACT, aims to teach the FBVs as complex political concepts requiring discussion, evaluation and application in different contexts, as opposed to being values that can be simply promoted. It was designed to develop deeper political reasoning about toleration and religious freedom through deliberative discussion (ACT, n.d.).

In one Church of England school in the Midlands, the debate society agreed to participate in the project and a mixed age group of student volunteers joined a deliberative discussion on religious freedom in school. While the school had a Christian ethos, with religious assemblies and trips to the cathedral, a large minority of students were Muslim. The students discussed a motion about how their school should implement the principles of religious freedom and toleration in that context. These deliberative conversations demonstrated how issues of diversity and identity can be discussed in ways that are respectful, exploratory, responsive to others' ideas and experiences, and can lead to compromise about the best way forward.

One group of Muslim boys raised the following points:

Speaker 2: "I think people should get to wear what they want according to their religion."
Speaker 1: "To what extent though? You can't just come into school wearing a jilbab or something."
Speaker 2: "Well, obviously, it's a Christian school innit."
Speaker 1: "Yeah, you should abide by the rules that you chose."

Some of the non-Muslim students commented:

Speaker 2: "Personally, I think that if you are going to the cathedral, it doesn't matter whatever faith you are … you don't have to take part in the prayers or the hymns."

Speaker 4: "Yeah, it shouldn't be a sign of disrespect if they don't go up for a blessing or communion, if they just want to sit there they're not doing anything wrong. At least they've come."

This sentiment was echoed by a Muslim student who observed: "We sing but we don't actually mean any of it but, we're just singing to be respectful."

These pragmatic responses reflect Vertovec's (2007) account of how people manage the tensions that arise through diverse cultural, religious and ethical beliefs by establishing a 'veneer of civility' through everyday interactions. This does not necessarily reflect an act of self-denial or oppression; rather, as Gilroy (2004) describes it, it could be seen as an act of 'conviviality', where we move away from a reified sense of identity and embrace mechanisms for being different together.

Despite, or perhaps because of, the ongoing political debate about human rights standards and rights in school, citizenship teachers need to sustain their efforts to build this aspect of their work. Of all the elements of citizenship education, this one seems to speak most directly to the emotions of young people, as it engages with their concerns for fairness as a starting point for action (Engelmann and Tomasello, 2019). As research undertaken for the Equalities and Human Rights Commission concluded, such work involves explicit teaching about equality and human rights, opportunities for action, and a school culture in which students are treated equally and fairly (Culhane and McGeough, 2020). This means ensuring that citizenship education is seen as more than a few lessons in the timetable and a small element of the curriculum, but runs through the life of the school and guides schools' relationships with their communities. At the same time, we need to continue to develop our approach to deepening knowledge in this area, otherwise, as Parker (2018) has argued, we will fail to consolidate our curriculum position and build the knowledge base to move these debates on.

Extremism

A fourth challenge confronting teachers, which was barely even discussed when citizenship was being planned in the late 1990s, is how to position citizenship education in relation to efforts for countering violent extremism (CVE). While teachers saw the relevance of their subject for dealing with the aftermath of 9/11 and subsequent acts of terrorism, there has been a growing call for them to be more proactively involved in CVE through promoting democratic values as an antidote to extremism, countering extremist messages, and monitoring and reporting young people demonstrating signs of extremism. In the UK, this has led to the 'Prevent duty', which requires schools to report concerns about students to Channel panels, where cases are assessed with a view to offering individual interventions (Busher and Jerome, 2020). There are over 5,000 referrals each year and education currently accounts for more referrals than any other public service (including the police) and over half of all people referred are under the age of 20, with a quarter being younger than 16 years of age.

Against this backdrop, there has been a tendency to turn to a narrow safeguarding approach, where the political dimension is ignored, or to focus on promoting positive democratic values, where criticality is sidelined (Vincent, 2019). Dealt with as a depoliticised pastoral or whole school issue, it has been all too easy for Muslims and other minorities (both students and staff) to feel alienated by such policies, which is exacerbated by the proliferation of simplistic messages about Britishness and British values (Jerome et al, 2019). However, young people are clear that they value the opportunity to learn about terrorism and extremism in a broad political and comparative context. They report that they have no shortage of ways to hear about terrorist atrocities when they happen, but they need help to understand what it all means (Jerome and Elwick, 2019). There is a distinctive role for citizenship in the curriculum here, one which ACT has explored through its Building Resilience programme.

Case study 4 Citizenship in an age of extremism

As part of the Association for Citizenship Teaching's Building Resilience programme (ACT, 2022), a South London school wanted to create a sequence of lessons to help students think about politics in a world with extremism, radicalisation and acts of terror. Teachers were concerned about the myths and misinformation that young people encounter, and wanted to challenge the frequently expressed view that terrorism was a recent phenomenon that stemmed from religious beliefs, in particular Islam. The lessons were designed to:

- Define and understand the key terms 'extremism', 'radicalisation' and 'terrorism' and the different definitions that are used by government and in the media.
- Introduce students to case studies of groups that use extremist and terrorist actions to develop a concrete understanding of these abstract terms.
- Define and understand radicalisation, how people become radicalised and what can drive people towards extremist groups or behaviours. The teacher used a recent example of three young men who had been radicalised following their long-term experience of prejudice because of their religious beliefs.
- Consider whether terrorists are all the same, using critical questions to explore different notions of terrorism and groups who use terrorist methods. Two case studies of the

IRA (Irish Republican Army) and IS (Islamic State) were used to examine the different political and religious motivations and begin to consider what can be done to counter and prevent the harms caused by these groups.
• Examine whether a terrorist is always a terrorist, using a historical case study of the African National Congress in South Africa, to learn about apartheid and the anti-apartheid protest movement and discuss the labelling of terrorists and the notion of freedom fighters.

In the final lessons, students considered what government does to protect its citizens and the role of education in countering extremism and radicalisation. Students were asked to carefully examine the Prevent strategy and guidance to schools and develop their own critique with recommendations for improvements. The teacher used the actual policy document, with students gradually building their skills and confidence to interrogate and interpret a lengthy text. They examined the policy in pairs using a critical questioning template to help them structure their critical evaluation and identify the different types of interventions in the policy, assess the risks of doing nothing, and develop their own recommendations for where they felt the advice could be improved.

The students in this project helped us understand that citizenship education does not need to provide definitive explanations of why terrorism (or other forms of state-sponsored political violence) occurs, nor answers about what to do. But by developing a space for critical and informed investigation of both terrorism and counterterrorist measures, it can help young people build their own understanding of how to navigate citizenship in a world of terrorism and extremism. Citizenship education in the age of CVE has become more explicit about its contribution to safeguarding democracy and challenging the simplistic narratives that position certain groups (most notably Muslims) as outsiders or threats. These lessons demonstrate the importance of building knowledge and understanding about complex political phenomena, and not sweeping controversial issues under the carpet as an avoidance strategy.

Sustainable citizenship education

In the first version of the national curriculum, sustainability and Agenda 21 were explicitly referenced as core knowledge, but in the current version, written in 2014, these references have been removed. Belatedly, the Department for Education (DfE, 2022b) has issued *Sustainability and Climate Change: A Strategy for the Education and Children's Services System*, which suggests that schools have an important role to play – both in providing education for sustainable citizenship, and in managing the school estate in a sustainable way. As the Working Group III report of the Intergovernmental

Panel on Climate Change (IPCC, 2022) indicates, the next 20 years will be crucial for the future of life on the planet, and so citizenship education must play its part in equipping citizens with the capacity to act.

This means confronting some of the obstacles to effective education – not least the anxiety that many people feel about climate change, which can be an obstacle to internal efficacy (Trott, 2021). And second, we need to recognise that external efficacy can be undermined because some young people are deterred by high-profile disruptive activism, which can seem like it generates media coverage but achieves little change, and formal politics, which can feel like it is incapable of adopting solutions on the right scale (Dunlop et al, 2021).

Here, we are buoyed by the evidence from the field of environmental education that resonates with the approach taken by citizenship teachers. Monroe et al (2019) conducted a systematic review of the evidence and concluded that establishing a meaningful connection between learners and information about climate change was important, especially as a prelude to engaging in deliberative discussions and implementing school or community projects. In successful projects, children start to assuage their anxiety by finding positive action to undertake and through their collaborations with others feel a greater sense of hope that there are movements of like-minded people working for the future (Trott, 2021). Indeed, many young people engaging in environmental activism demonstrate a 'do it ourselves' attitude to politics, where they build their own global networks for direct action, bypassing traditional party political structures and nurturing efficacy and action (Pickard, 2022).

Case study 5 Sustainability in the citizenship classroom

A group of teachers devised a series of lessons around citizenship and sustainability, created for a joint conference organised by ACT and Parliament Education and Engagement team. The teachers recognised the importance of learning about the whole range of action available to citizens in relation to climate change and decided to focus more explicitly on how to engage with parliament, in addition to extra-parliamentary activism. These lessons engaged with a real-life parliamentary process around the Education (Environment and Sustainable Citizenship) Bill, a Private Members' Bill proposed by Lord Knight of Weymouth in the House of Lords.

The sequence of lessons included information on climate change and on the Bill, which called on the government to take sustainable citizenship education more seriously. Students learned about the draft Bill, the process of Private Members' Bills, and the role of education in climate change policy. Because the parliamentary process was ongoing, the students also had the opportunity to listen to parts of the debate, consider the variety of views being discussed, and follow up with parliamentarians who spoke to engage in the argument or express their support.

Through exploring the legislative framework, current proposed legislation and the detailed advocacy and debate undertaken by politicians, this project helped young people appreciate another way in which action for sustainable citizenship can be undertaken (Shortland, 2021).

If humanity has any hope of turning around the impending climate catastrophe, it is highly likely we will need to tackle it through as many approaches as possible. Young people (along with everyone else) will have to consider the implications for how they consume, what jobs they seek, how they travel, how they live, and how they behave as citizens. To some extent, they will need to learn that citizens need to 'do it ourselves', but they also need to think beyond individual responsible actions to find methods to influence and hold to account those with power to change political and economic systems through national government and international processes. Building the sense of efficacy to promote action (and reduce anxiety) is one necessary step. Building the political literacy to determine where to focus one's efforts is as important. And facilitating opportunities to get involved in some meaningful activity may well be the most important contribution that citizenship teachers play in securing our future.

Conclusion

The citizenship education community in England, and more broadly across the UK, has embraced the challenge of introducing a new subject into the curriculum, creating a professional identity, a rich set of practices, and a strong body of evidence over 20 years. As new challenges arise, so citizenship teachers have to rearticulate their subject, and develop their practices to stay relevant and engage with real-world issues. In this chapter, we have sketched out five priorities that will shape our practices for the next 20 years, and indicated how we can build on established foundations.

In looking ahead, we are clear that sustaining and improving our democracy requires citizens who believe that a democratic life is better than the alternatives, and who are willing to invest time and effort to strengthen it and defend it from threats. In part, this is instrumental – democracies need to deliver better results for citizens and they need to rise to the challenges we have outlined in this chapter. But democracy itself can enhances citizens' wellbeing, or flourishing – through their freedom of expression, through free association with kindred spirits, through a sense of belonging and purpose, and through the optimism that drives democratic renewal. These benefits contribute to what we think of as a sense of 'democratic wellbeing'. While schools are far from perfect institutions, for many young people they offer a relatively stable, consistently caring and nurturing environment where equality and inclusion are consciously promoted, and where good social relations are fostered. In that context, we aim to make a contribution to the wellbeing of our democracy and to nurture the democratic wellbeing of our young people.

References

ACT (Association for Citizenship Teaching) (n.d.) The Deliberative Classroom: www.teachingcitizenship.org.uk/resource/the-deliberative-classroom-project/

ACT (2022) Building Resilience: www.teachingcitizenship.org.uk/act-building-resilience-project

Anzalone, J. (2020) 'Citizenship and news literacy', *Teaching Citizenship*, 51: 20–3.

Busher, J. and Jerome, L. (eds) (2020) *The Prevent Duty in Education: Impact, Enactment and Implications*, Cham: Palgrave Macmillan.

Carlile, A. (2020) 'Teacher experiences of LGBTQ-inclusive education in primary schools serving faith communities in England, UK', *Pedagogy, Culture & Society*, 28(4): 625–44.

Christian Institute (2019) 'More parents rail against LGBT issues being taught in primary schools', 20 March: www.christian.org.uk/news/more-parents-rail-against-lgbt-issues-being-taught-in-primary-schools/

Commission on Race and Ethnic Disparities (CRED) (2021) *The Report of the Commission on Race and Ethnic Disparities*, London: Her Majesty's Government.

Council of Europe (2019) *Digital Citizenship Education*: www.coe.int/en/web/digital-citizenship-education/home

Covell, K. and Howe, B. (2011) *Rights, Respect and Responsibility in Hampshire County: RRR and Resilience Report*, Sydney, Nova Scotia: Cape Breton University, Children's Rights Centre.

Covell, K., Howe, B. and Polegato, J.L. (2011) 'Children's human rights education as a counter to social disadvantage: a case study from England', *Educational Research*, 53(2): 193–206.

Crick, B. (2000) *Essays on Citizenship*, London: Continuum.

Culhane, L. and McGeough, E. (2020) *Respect, Equality, Participation: Exploring Human Rights Education in Great Britain*, London: Equality and Human Rights Commission.

Department for Education (DfE) (2013) *National Curriculum in England: Citizenship Programmes of Study*. London: Department for Education.

DfE (2014) *Promoting Fundamental British Values Through SMSC*. London: Department for Education.

DfE (2022a) *Guidance: Political Impartiality in Schools*, London: Department for Education.

DfE (2022b) *Sustainability and Climate Change: A Strategy for the Education and Children's Services System*, London: Department for Education.

Doona, N. (2019) 'Community organising: student led approaches to making change in their community', *Teaching Citizenship*, 49: 20–3.

Dunlop, L., Atkinson, L., McKeown, D. and Turkenburg-van Diepen, M. (2021) 'Youth representations of environmental protest', *British Educational Research Journal*, 47(6): 1540–59.

Engelmann, J. and Tomasello, M. (2019) 'Children's sense of fairness as equal respect', *Trends in Cognitive Sciences*, 23(6): 454–63.

Foa, R.S., Klassen, A., Wenger, D., Rand, A. and Slade, M. (2020) *Youth and Satisfaction with Democracy: Reversing the Democratic Disconnect?*, Cambridge: Centre for the Future of Democracy.

Gilroy, P. (2004) *After Empire: Melancholia or Convivial Culture?*, Abingdon: Routledge.

Holbolt, S., Leepetr, T. and Tilley, J. (2020) 'Divided by the vote: affective polarization in the wake of the Brexit referendum', *British Journal of Political Science*, 51(4): 1476–93.

Hoskins, B., Janmaat, J.G. and Melis, G. (2017) 'Tackling inequalities in political socialisation: a systematic analysis of access to and mitigation effects of learning citizenship at school', *Social Science Research*, 68: 88–101.

IPCC (Intergovernmental Panel on Climate Change) (2022) *Climate Change 2022: Mitigation of Climate Change*: www.ipcc.ch/report/ar6/wg3/

Jerome, L. (2017) *Speak Truth to Power: Evaluation Report of a Pilot Project in Ten Schools in England of Resources from the Robert F. Kennedy Centre for Justice and Human Rights*, London: Association for Citizenship Teaching.

Jerome, L. and Elwick, A. (2019) 'Identifying an educational response to the prevent policy: student perspectives on learning about terrorism, extremism and radicalisation', *British Journal of Educational Studies*, 67(1): 97–114.

Jerome, L., Elwick, A. and Kazim, R. (2019) 'The impact of the prevent duty on schools: a review of the evidence', *British Educational Research Journal*, 45(4): 821–37.

Joy, B. (2020) 'Media literacy: theory to practice', *Teaching Citizenship*, 51: 43–47.

Keating, A. and Janmaat, J.G. (2016) 'Education through citizenship at school: Do school activities have a lasting impact on youth political engagement?', *Parliamentary Affairs*, 69(2): 409–29.

Keating, A., Kerr, D., Benton, T., Mundy, E. and Lopes, J. (2010) *Citizenship Education in England 2001–2010: Young People's Practices and Prospects for the Future*, Research Report DFE-RR059, London: Department for Education.

Kivenen, E. and Kivenen, K. (2020) 'How to protect ourselves from the infodemic?, *Teaching Citizenship*, 51: 31–32.

Leo, B. (2022) 'Brainwashed: woke council "indoctrinating" schoolkids by teaching them they're not "racially innocent"', *The Sun*, 30 January.

Lloyd, K. and Emerson, L. (2017) '(Re)examining the relationship between children's subjective wellbeing and their perceptions of participation rights', *Child Indicators Research*, 10(3): 591–608.

Ministry of Justice (2021) 'Plan to reform Human Rights Act', press release, 14 December: www.gov.uk/government/news/plan-to-reform-human-rights-act

Monroe, M., Plate, R., Oxarart, A., Bowers, A. and Chaves, W. (2019) 'Identifying climate change education strategies: a systematic review of the research', *Environmental Education Research*, 25(6): 791–812.

Montague, A. and Eiroa-Orosa, F. (2017) 'In it together: exploring how belonging to a youth activist group enhances well-being', *Journal of Community Psychology*, 46(1): 23–43.

Moorse, L. (2020) 'Citizenship education in England: policy and curriculum', in A. Peterson, G. Stahl and H. Soong (eds) *The Palgrave Handbook of Citizenship Education*, Cham: Palgrave Macmillan, pp 375–402.

Moorse, L. (2022) 'Teaching media literacy through citizenship: an urgent priority for schools', *School Librarian*, 70(1).

Norris, P. (2004) 'Young people and political activism', paper delivered at the conference, Civic Engagement in the 21st Century, University of Southern California, 1–2 October.

Ofcom (2022) 'The genuine article? One in three internet users fail to question misinformation', 29 March: www.ofcom.org.uk/news-centre/2022/one-in-three-internet-users-fail-to-question-misinformation

Ofsted (2021) *Inspection of the American School in London*, London: Ofsted.

Pagliarello, M., Aniol, M., Sanjuro Hanck, L. and Zonta, T. (2021) 'Populism, democracy and the role of civic education: bridging the gap between academia and policy practice', 89 Initiative: http://89initiative.com/

Parker, W. (2018) 'Human rights education's curriculum problem', *Human Rights Education Review*, 1(1): 5–24.

Pickard, S. (2022) 'Young environmental activists and do-it-ourselves (DIO) politics: collective engagement, generational agency, efficacy, belonging and hope', *Journal of Youth Studies*, 25(6): 730–50.

Politics Project (2021) *Digital Surgeries Wales: Impact Report 2020–21*: www.thepoliticsproject.org.uk

Shortland, S. (2021) 'Sustainability in the citizenship classroom', *Teaching Citizenship*, 54: 45–50.

Sloam, J. and Henn, M. (2018) *Youthquake 2017: The Rise of Young Cosmopolitans in Britain*, Cham: Palgrave.

Trott, C. (2021) 'Climate change education for transformation: exploring the affective and attitudinal dimensions of children's learning', *Environmental Education Research*, 28(7): 1023–42.

UN (2021) *General Comment No. 25 (2021) on Children's Rights in Relation to the Digital Environment*, New York: UN Committee on the Rights of the Child.

UNICEF UK (nd) *Rights Respecting Schools Award Impact: The Evidence*: www.unicef.org.uk/rights-respecting-schools/the-rrsa/impact-of-rrsa/

Vertovec, S. (2007) *New Complexities of Cohesion in Britain: Super-Diversity, Transnationalism and Civil-Integration*, report to the Commission on Integration and Cohesion, Wetherby: Department for Communities and Local Government.

Vincent, C. (2019) *Tea and the Queen: Fundamental British Values, Schools and Citizenship*, Bristol: Policy Press.

Vogt, K. (2020) 'Learn to discern: integrating critical information engagement skills into the curriculum', *Teaching Citizenship*, 51: 24–5.

Weinberg, J. (2021) *The Missing Link: An Updated Evaluation of the Provision, Practice and Politics of Democratic Education in English Secondary Schools*, London: Shout Out UK.

Wright, J. (2011) 'Slacktivism or activism?', *Teaching Citizenship*, 31: 18–21.

12

Reversing democratic decline through political education

Murray Print

Democracy is in decline in established democracies, and more so in the newer democracies of the past half-century, but that decline can be reversed through political education. If democracy is to survive in a viable form, this decline must be reversed. The decline is addressed elsewhere, although Freedom House (2021) captures the essence of the problem. The focus here is on the role schools can play in a reversal process, with particular emphasis on the school curriculum in its multiple forms. Political education as a school subject is rare, but civics education (US), citizenship education (England) or even civics and citizenship education (Australia) are more common vehicles for learning about and practising democracy in schools and, as such, act as a proxy for more explicit political education. However, in recent years, these subjects have been under direct threat in schools and through system curricula controlled by state curriculum bodies.

The role of the school in creating and sustaining democratic citizens has been well accepted by democratic governments for over a century. Dewey's ([1916] 1997) work early last century epitomised this connection between schools and learning democracy. Indeed, as democracy is not a natural human condition, and unlikely to be nurtured in home and family environments, it needs to be encouraged and practised in the security of school environments and through the school curriculum. This chapter considers what can be done to address this disastrous, potentially existential political situation of democratic decline. It will use a model of political and civic learning (Print, 2009a, 2012) and survey the latest relevant research. It will draw out the lessons from the research into approaches that can help counter democratic decline, such as:

- formal school curriculum as developed by an expert, non-partisan group;
- informal school curriculum;
- situated learning – incorporating formal, informal and extracurricular elements.

Threats to democracy

The threats to democracy in modern society are now well documented, although they appear somewhat disguised to large sections of the general population as there seems to be a lack of widespread concern over the current situation. The problem, typified by the publication *Democracy under Siege* (Freedom House, 2021), has been compounded by:

- Increasing disparity and inequality in Western democracies over the past three decades, stimulated by the neoliberal ideology of conservative governments.
- The rise of social media as an information source for young people excessively affected by 'celebrities' and influencers, with a concomitant decline in the use of traditional media as information sources by the young.
- The rise of fake news and malicious misreporting by biased media, especially social media, with the intention of persuading young people.
- Decline in trust of politics, political parties and politicians writ large.
- Apparent disdain for political education in schools by conservative governments. The deliberate decline of citizenship education in the English curriculum since 2010 and the 2014 Australian curriculum review, which were deliberately political in nature and had the effect of reducing the opportunity of students to learn about the political system (ACARA, 2014). In Australia, this was reinforced by the 2020–21 ACARA review of the Australian curriculum, which further eroded possible political education and reinforced the decline of political education in schools on the grounds of streamlining the 'overcrowded' school curriculum (ACARA, 2020/21).

Numerous sources have analysed these threats in detail, including *Challenges to Democracy: Ideas, Involvement and Institutions* (Dowding et al, 2001). This edited work identified three key areas of challenge – equality and satisfaction of people, changing patterns of political involvement (mostly decline), and changing state and political institutions. More recently, challenges have come from the rise of the internet and social media as vehicles for information (or misinformation) dissemination, globalisation, the impact of fake news and conspiracy theories, and the relentless persistence of corruption that has further eroded trust in government, politics and politicians.

Special mention needs to be made of the impact of the COVID-19 pandemic, which exacerbated democratic backsliding in most regions of the world. The Economist Intelligence Unit's Democracy Index recorded its lowest measure since the organisation began tracking the quality of governance in the world in 2006 (*The Economist*, 2022). Similarly, Freedom House (2021) reported that its global index of civil liberties and political rights had declined for the 15th consecutive year. More than fifty countries, representing 38 per cent of the world's population, now live in autocracies, representing the highest share since 2006.

A further impact of the COVID-19 pandemic, identified by the International Institute for Democracy and Electoral Assistance (International IDEA), was that almost 80 of the roughly 210 countries and territories scheduled to hold elections between February 2020 and July 2021 postponed them due to health reasons (International IDEA, 2022). Holding elections to determine a government is a central feature of democracies, and the curtailment of any election should raise concerns.

The case of Australia is a good example of the threats to an established democracy, ones that are often difficult to detect. It has long been argued that democracies rely for their continuance on an informed, engaged polity (Civics Expert Group, 1994; QCA, 1998; Print, 2007a). This need for informed, engaged citizens identifies future generations as an important source for democratic stability. In turn, this requires an understanding of the political education received by students in schools. In Australia's federation, responsibility for schools is constitutionally vested with the states – a situation common with other federations such as Germany, the US and Canada. However, unlike most federations, Australia has a means of obtaining systematic student performance data at a national level. The National Assessment Program has existed for more than two decades through sample assessment tests and later with a census test in literacy and numeracy called NAPLAN (National Assessment Program Literacy and Numeracy). The National Assessment Program – Civics and Citizenship (NAPCC) was initiated after a government report (Print and Hughes, 2001) and commenced three-yearly sample tests of Australian Year 6 and 10 students in 2004.

The latest NAPCC report has revealed an ongoing problem with Australian students learning political (non-partisan) education at school. At a national level, only 38 per cent of Year 10 students (about 15 years old) achieved at or above a proficiency standard labelled 'challenging but reasonable' for such students (ACARA, 2020). Yet within two or three years, these same students will be required by law to compulsorily vote in a federal (national) or state-level election, and most likely a local-level election as well.

Why are the NAPCC results so poor in a country with a well-established compulsory voting requirement of citizens? When we use the concept 'opportunity to learn', we can investigate the school curriculum to identify what and how students can learn through political education in whatever form it may take – civics education, civics and citizenship education, citizenship education, society and culture, studies of society, possibly history and so on. In the case of learning political education through the school curriculum, young Australians simply don't have the opportunity to learn about democracy and politics in schools (Print, 2007b, 2009b; Saha and Print, 2010). A detailed case study of primary schools in New South Wales (Neoh, 2019) found that it was difficult for students to learn about civics and government as teachers tended to not deliver it as part of the formal curriculum. Instead, when any form of civics and citizenship education was available, it was 'disguised' as something else (Australia Day, Remembrance Day) other than explicitly political education.

We can verify this through curriculum analysis and the data from the NAPCC assessments. Similar to the US NAEP (National Assessment of Educational Progress), the NAPCC identifies student knowledge and attitudes and we find that, in general, students know and understand little about politics, political processes and elections. This is an ongoing pattern that the NAPCC data have demonstrated since 2004 (Reichert and Print, 2017, 2019).

A key response to the decline in Britain was the Crick Report (QCA, 1998), following an earlier Australian report *Whereas the People: Civics and Citizenship Education* (Civics Expert Group, 1994), which made a strong and detailed case for the inclusion of citizenship education as a compulsory school subject. The Crick Report was initiated by a Labour government in Britain in response to the growing evidence of decline in civic engagement, as was the earlier decline in Australia. This trend in declining civic engagement has been explained by a number of different factors, including declining community cohesion and solidarity, a growing mistrust of government and politicians, a detachment of ordinary people, particularly youth, from politics in general, and a decline in the key political organisations of civil society such as political parties. Where voting is optional, unlike Australia, the decline was most evident in electoral participation (Whiteley, 2014). As Whiteley (2014, p 514) noted, from 84 per cent voting in the 1950 general election, participation had fallen to 59 per cent in 2001 and most of the decline was in the youngest cohort of voters.

In Australia, one of the very few countries with compulsory voting, sanctions for not voting and large numbers of people from quasi- and non-democratic backgrounds, learning democracy through a form of school-based political education should be compulsory. Furthermore, Australian governments appear to be aware of the need to educate young people about democracy. Every national declaration of education since 1988 has acknowledged that schools should educate 'active and informed citizens'. The clearest statement came from the 2008 Melbourne Declaration: 'Australian governments commit to working in collaboration with all school sectors to support all young Australians to become … active and informed citizens' (MCEETYA, 2008, p 8). Yet research shows that young Australians know little about Australian democracy (Print, 2007b, 2009b; Saha and Print, 2010; Reichert and Print, 2017, 2019; ACARA, 2020).

Addressing democratic decline through political education

Despite this concerning situation, there is some evidence that democratic decline can be addressed through forms of political education in schools. Two qualifications should be borne in mind. First, direct teaching of political education is rarely found in schools. There is a real and distinct fear among some educators, politicians and parents that explicit political education as such would probably brainwash or bias young people according to the teacher's views. Consequently, political education, which may be found within subjects designated in the school curriculum such as civics, citizenship, history, social studies and so on, should be restricted or/and controlled in their content. Second, evidence-based approaches to learning about democracy are problematic due to their dearth. There are simply very few studies that exhibit rigorous empirical evidence to identify a causal relationship between learning political education/civic and citizenship education and young people's political behaviour.[1] Experimental or randomised controlled trials (RCTs) are rare in political education research within schools. There are some studies of civic education programmes external to the normal school curriculum that have some experimental design qualities, such as Project Citizen by the Center for Civic Education in Calabasas, US. However, this example, and others, are optional, voluntary and invariably not integrated officially into the formal school curriculum.

Nevertheless, there are some positive findings from the political education research that can help to address democratic decline. Learning democracy can be achieved in multifarious ways but the most informed, non-partisan and engaging way for the population in general, and young people in particular, is through our schools and the school curriculum. This seems so obvious, so logical and yet, apparently, is so difficult. If democracy is not a natural human behaviour and it requires learning, then it seems obvious that it should be taught in schools. In *Democracy and Education* ([1916] 1997), John Dewey argued that the purpose of schools was to prepare democratic citizens, for if democracy was to work, it required informed, knowledgeable and wise citizens and, therefore, education had a moral purpose. He believed that democracy was not just a political system but an ethical ideal, indeed a way of life, with active informed participation by citizens. Dewey's arguments have been, in large measure, widely accepted by democracies worldwide in the 20th and 21st century.

Can political education, in whatever form, address democratic decline? We argue that there are three approaches to improving the effect of political education in school contexts:

---

[1] However, see Chapter 10 in this book.

- formal school curriculum developed by an expert, non-partisan group
- informal school curriculum
- situated learning – incorporating formal and informal curriculum elements.

To make sense of these approaches, there is a model available that links political and civic learning to subsequent political and civic behaviours (Print, 2009c, 2012). In other words, what kind of democratic citizen could be expected through school experience? The model identifies a set of school factors that significantly impact on a student's political and civic learning. These school factors can be divided into the formal curriculum and the informal curriculum, where the former consists of planned school subjects with their knowledge, skills and values, and the latter (planned learning activities that are not subjects) consists of instrumental elements, such as student councils, student elections, student assemblies and student newspapers, and expressive elements, such as clubs, sports, bands and social activities, which have varying effects on student political and civic learning (Print, 2012, pp 116–21).

Formal school curriculum

The Australian curriculum, adopted by all Australian educational jurisdictions, offers multiple opportunities to learn political education in different forms. The most logical is known as Australian Curriculum: Civics and Citizenship, located within the formal Australian curriculum across Years 3–10, which addresses three key themes that support learning about democracy and elements of political education:

- democracy and government;
- law and citizens;
- citizenship, diversity and identity.

When these curricula themes are applied through the formal curriculum, they offer students the opportunity to learn about and practise Australian democracy in school contexts and so contribute to resisting the democratic decline. What does the research say of the contributions of such formal school curriculum programmes to building democracy and reversing democratic decline?

The seminal study in the US on civic education effectiveness was published more than two decades ago. Dick Niemi and June Junn argued in their classic book *Civic Education* (1998) that it makes a difference for young people to learn civic knowledge and democratic understandings. Niemi and Junn found that the study of civic education in schools was linked positively with voting, political engagement as well as volunteering and joining civic associations, which are also measures of positive social capital (Print and Coleman, 2003). These conclusions were drawn from systematic analysis of National Assessment of Educational Progress (NAEP) test data from students in grades 4, 8 and 12. The strength of this study was the use of rigorous NAEP test data as compared with many studies that employ attitudinal data through surveys.

Similarly, political scientists Neundorf and colleagues (2016) argued that civic education is considered an important influence on political interest and orientations of young people, as schools, especially in the US, are expected to play a crucial role in creating and maintaining civic equality. They analysed data from the Belgian Political Panel Study (2006–11) and the US Youth–Parent Socialization Panel Study (1965–97), both of which contain information on the political attitudes and behaviours of adolescents and young adults, those of their parents, and the educational curriculum of the young respondents. Their findings reveal that civics education makes a difference to learners generally and, more specifically, civics education in schools compensates for inequalities in family socialisation with respect to political engagement. This conclusion holds for two very different countries (the US and Belgium), at very different points in time (the 1960s and the 2000s), and for a varying length of observation (youth to old age). Panel studies have greater rigour than cross-sectional studies, typically surveys, but they are not experimental and their findings are not causal.

Meanwhile, Whitely (2014) found positive effects of political education in England, where citizenship education was introduced as a statutory subject in the English school curriculum in 2001. After the Crick Report (1998), citizenship education subjects were developed in England for primary and secondary schools. After the 2010 general election, the Conservative–Liberal Democrat coalition government launched a review of the national curriculum, including the citizenship subject, which, it was feared, would be removed. Although citizenship was retained as a statutory subject, there were changes in focus and scope . Overall, Whitely (2014) concluded that citizenship education had a positive impact on three key components of civic engagement, namely efficacy, political participation and political knowledge and as such would serve to promote democratic participation among young people. Thus, through citizenship education, English students received a form of political education, albeit indirectly, that would serve them later to hopefully reverse democratic decline.

Berson et al (2014), noting a decline in democratic participation by American youth, claim that youth civic engagement is recognised as an essential component necessary for the preservation of democracy. However, the authors noted that persistently inadequate levels of youth civic participation were widespread in the US. In evaluating a civic education programme, they found an increase in students registered to vote and students' intent to register to vote after civic education was included in the school curriculum. This type of finding is quite common in these types of studies, namely that when exposed to a form of political education, students subsequently are more likely to register to vote and be involved in other forms of political participation.

Similarly, Galston's influential review of civic education (2007) identified a plethora of problems in American democracy that were reflected in declining levels of political participation. He also argued that political knowledge could be taught and that school-based civic education does make a significant difference in developing civic knowledge, skills and attitudes and, as such, could address democratic decline. Galston (2007, p 639) further argued that recent findings suggested 'formal, classroom-based civic education provides an effective means of teaching civic knowledge. Contrary to a longstanding scholarly consensus concerning the dim prospects for civic education, the recent wave of research furnishes a basis for hope and a guide for action.'

In their comprehensive and sophisticated meta-analysis of the effects of citizenship education, Geboers et al. (2013) reported on the differential effects of four different types of citizenship education. They distinguished between 'curriculum in school', that is, classroom activities that form part of the formal curriculum, 'curriculum out of school', such as organised government visits, the 'pedagogical climate', and 'extracurricular activities', such as voluntary service activities, school clubs and sports teams. They found that among 13- to 16-year-old adolescents, curriculum in school and extracurricular activities were most likely to facilitate democratic activities. 'Citizenship education that includes classroom activities carried out as part of a formal educational method or program such as civics instruction can also promote the development of citizenship' (Geboers et al, p 170).

Most of these studies are based on major surveys or national assessments with statistical analysis identifying significant differences that can be attributed to the impact of civics/citizenship education. However, a clear lack of RCTs or experimental designs exists, which are required in order to have confidence in identifying important causal relationships. Nevertheless, there are clear links between having the opportunity to learn about political education in some forms and young people's level of political knowledge and engagement.

More recently, Fitzgerald et al (2021) undertook a systematic review of the past decade of civic education research in the US. They found that political education, although taught in American schools through civic education, was in need of revitalisation, given the increasing polarisation of youth and American society in general. They argued that research showed the need for 'reconfiguring civic education to address inequitable civic learning opportunities and celebrate diverse civic strengths; the second illuminates the increasing need for civic education amid heightened intolerance and exclusion' (Fitzgerald et al, 2021, p 235).

In sum, the evidence for the beneficial effects of students participating in classes learning political education through civic education, citizenship education or civics and citizenship education is persuasive. Students acquire more political knowledge, more engaged political attitudes and are more likely to actively participate in political activities from voting to running for office. Major studies such as NAEP, NAPCC and ICCS (International Civic and Citizenship Education Study) have found similar results (Schulz, et al, 2010).

Although using path analysis of longitudinal data from the Citizenship Education Longitudinal Study (CELS), Avril Keating and colleagues (2016) found that school-based political activities can indeed have a positive and independent effect on electoral and expressive political engagement among young people in England, it was nonetheless found that, following a CELS cohort, students were more likely to have positive attitudes and intentions towards civic and political participation if they reported receiving high levels of citizenship education.

The study overlapped with the possible effects of citizenship education after it had become a compulsory subject in English schools. These effects were apparent even after the participants had left school and had become young adults, and above and beyond the effects of prior dispositions or other known predictors (such as socioeconomic status) that were included in the models as controls. The CELS was a significant study of citizenship education in England that ran from 2001 to 2010, occurring at the same time as citizenship education was initiated as a compulsory subject in the school curriculum (Keating et al, 2016).

The informal curriculum

The informal curriculum includes potentially important political education learning opportunities, particularly through instrumental activities, such as student councils, student elections, student newspapers and school assemblies (Print, 2009c, 2012; McFarland and Starmanns, 2009). These are planned learning activities for students that are not school subjects, and are therefore excluded from the formal curriculum, but offer experience in learning about and participating in political activities and democratic processes. Consequently, they should enhance democratic resilience among young people through the very experience of political education in practice. So what works in the informal school curriculum to promote learning about democracy?

In a study for the Australian Electoral Commission, researchers found that the role of the student council was an important potential source of political education through practical participation (Saha and

Print, 2010). The researchers found that how the school administration provided realistic opportunities for student governance was a key factor in determining how meaningfully students engaged with the student councils and student elections to those councils. Indeed, the researchers go so far as to claim that:

> We have provided evidence to support the notion that school elections may be the 'cradle' of democracy, since it is here that students experience a fundamental democratic practice. We have demonstrated empirically that students who do vote or run for office, are also more prone to feel prepared to vote as adults, to actually intend to vote, to know more about politics, and to have already experienced some form of political activism, such as attending rallies or letter writing. (Saha and Print, 2010, p 31)

This form of political education is widespread within educational jurisdictions and, if taken seriously in schools, clearly has potential significance for reversing the decline in democracy.

Similarly, in their study of US high school student councils, McFarland and Starmanns (2009) found the effects of those councils positive, although highly variable, in terms of political education. A key variable was the type of school, where certain schools (mostly private schools) offered students greater opportunities to participate realistically in student governance.

In their analysis of the effects of civic learning in school, Reichert and Print (2018) found that at the student level, civics learning through the formal curriculum, participation in student governance activities and in the community are the most significant predictors of intended future participation. However, some effects are conditional on whether more conventional or issue-related civic participation is the focus of active citizenship. Galston's (2007) review of civic knowledge, civic education and civic engagement found that participation in student organisations (including student councils) promoted a sense of civic efficacy and, combined with increased political knowledge, represented support for his claim that these would contribute to support democratic practice.

In summary, research shows that student participation in the informal curriculum is clearly related to engaging young people in positively relating to democracy and encouraging later political and civic life (Galston, 2007; McFarland and Starmanns, 2009; Saha and Print, 2010; Reichert and Print, 2018). Hart et al (2007) found that participation in the informal curriculum, as well as community service, was associated with higher rates of volunteering and voting in presidential elections in early adulthood. There is indeed a substantial literature on the effects of service learning, the combination of learning objectives with community service, although little in relationship directly to political education, with most relating to forms of civic engagement of the more social form (Hart et al, 2007).

Classroom climate

The evidence for creating a positive, open classroom climate that encourages respectful discussion is powerful, given the multitude of studies claiming that it positively facilitates student understanding and attitudes towards political knowledge and attitudes leading to enhanced political engagement. For example, David Campbell (2008) analysed data from CIVED,[2] a major study of civic education conducted in 1999, and found that an open classroom climate had a positive impact on adolescents' civic knowledge and appreciation of political conflict, even when controlling for numerous individual, classroom, school and district characteristics. Furthermore, an open classroom environment fostered young people's intention to be an informed voter when they reached voting age.

Similarly, Campbell found that while past research has shown that taking civics courses correlates with greater civic knowledge (Niemi and Junn, 1998), his analysis of the CIVED data indicated that it was more the nature of political discussion within the classroom, not simply the frequency of formal political education, for example through social studies instruction, which had the greater effect. Campbell (2008, p 450) noted that: 'A classroom environment which fosters a free, open, and respectful exchange of ideas is positively related to young people's level of knowledge about democratic processes.'

In their review of the effects of citizenship education, Dutch researchers Geboers and colleagues (2013) found those types of citizenship education that enhance the pedagogical climate and include dialogue and discussion in the classroom were able to promote the development of citizenship, political understanding and 'acting democratically (political)' (Geboers et al, p 163) among secondary school students.

Furthermore, Galston's review of the CIVED data (the IEA Civic Education Study, a comprehensive study of 90,000 14-year-olds in 28 countries and 50,000 17- to 19-year-old students in 16 countries throughout 1999 and 2000) found that school-based civic education does make a significant difference in developing civic knowledge, skills, and attitudes and that 'a classroom climate that encourages respectful discussions of civic and political issues fosters both civic knowledge and engagement' (2007, p 639). Overall, then, the research findings for schools and teachers offering

---

[2] Civic Education Study, carried out by IEA (International Association for the Evaluation of Educational Achievement).

a positive, open classroom climate that encourages respectful discussion is powerful in enhancing political knowledge, skills and engagement in their democracy. As such, this finding reinforces the value of conducting political education in schools through the various options in the formal curriculum, such as civics education, citizenship education, social studies, civics and citizenship education and so on.

Situated learning

An additional method can be considered as a way to address the democratic decline being experienced in modern democracies, although the research evidence is not yet conclusive. Situated learning, or what Mulder (2021) calls 'on-site citizenship education', refers to learning about democracy through participating in experiences in government institutions. For Mulder, on-site citizenship education consists of compulsory activities that usually take place outside the classroom context, such as a visit to a government institution (such as the House of Representatives, court, prison, police station), interaction with government officials (MPs, city councillors, judges, police officers), or the re-enactment of government institutions (simulated debating and voting on a law, re-enacting a lawsuit). It may also cover visiting a (interactive) democracy museum, or participating in informative quizzes and games about democracy and politics. Australia has excellent examples of these institutions in Canberra, such as the Parliamentary Education Office in the Australian Parliament, the Museum of Australian Democracy, the Constitutional Education Centre at the High Court, and the electoral education programme at the Australian Electoral Commission. However, rigorous research on the impact of these examples of situated learning on students does not exist.

Similarly, Mulder (2021) found the results rather problematic, namely the main Dutch on-site citizenship education programme has had, at best, limited impact on the political attitudes and behaviours of youngsters. The on-site citizenship programme does, however, have a robust, lasting effect on political knowledge. Also, on-site citizenship education generally does not have a differential effect on advantaged and disadvantaged adolescents (Mulder, 2021).

Conclusion

Democracy in the world today is indeed in peril. The evidence for a democratic decline, among both newer and established democracies, is overwhelming. This chapter has only addressed this phenomenon briefly, as it was intended to act as an entrée into possible ways for addressing this decline through political education.

What works is clear within certain methodological limitations. The formal curriculum reveals through well-established evidence that a form of political education (civics or citizenship education) will make a positive difference to student political knowledge and behaviour. That is, of course, if students are exposed to such a learning opportunity. For example, the Australian Curriculum: Civics and Citizenship, by addressing three key themes – democracy and government; law and citizens; and citizenship, diversity and identity – provides extensive opportunities for learning about democracy, although, in some Australian states, it is difficult to locate in the applied school curriculum.

The informal curriculum has the potential to positively engage students and increase political knowledge, although there is need for more experimental/RCT studies to determine the nature of those benefits. Similarly, a positive classroom climate appears to have positive effects on students, although these effects would not be limited to forms of political education. Where they are applied, however, the effect on student knowledge and engagement is positive. Service learning is an interesting possibility but given that most of what is included in this extracurricular area is tangentially related to political education, again more research is required. Finally, there are national assessments, such as the NAEP and NAPCC, which may have stimulatory effects on student political education as well as international assessments, such as the International Civic and Citizenship Education Study.

References

ACARA (2014) *Review of the Australian Curriculum*, Sydney: ACARA: https://docs.acara.edu.au/resources/STATEMENT_Review_of_the_Australian_Curriculum_20140324.pdf

ACARA (2020/21) *Review of the Australian Curriculum*, Sydney: ACARA: https://acara.edu.au/curriculum/curriculum-review

ACARA (2020) *NAP Civics and Citizenship 2019: National Report*, Sydney: ACARA.

Berson, M., Rodriguez-Campos, L., Walker-Egea, C., Owens, C. and Bellara, A. (2014) 'Youth engagement in electoral activities: a collaborative evaluation of a civic education project', *Journal of Education and Training Studies*, 2(1): 81–7.

Campbell, D. (2008) 'Voice in the classroom: how an open classroom climate fosters political engagement among adolescents', *Political Behavior*, 30: 437–54.

Civics Expert Group (1994) *Whereas the People: Civics and Citizenship Education*, Canberra: Commonwealth of Australia.

Dewey, J. ([1916] 1997) *Democracy and Education: An Introduction to the Philosophy of Education*, ebook edn: www.gutenberg.org/ebooks/852

Dowding, K., Hughes, J. and Margetts, H. (2001) *Challenges to Democracy: Ideas, Involvement and Institutions*, London: Palgrave Macmillan.

The Economist (2022) 'A new low for global democracy', 9 February: www.economist.com/graphic-detail/2022/02/09/a-new-low-for-global-democracy

Fitzgerald, J., Cohen, A., Maker Castro, E. and Pope, A. (2021) 'A systematic review of the last decade of civic education research in the United States', *Peabody Journal of Education*, 96(3): 235–46.

Freedom House (2021) *Freedom in the World 2021: Democracy under Siege*, Washington DC: Freedom House.

Galston, W. (2007) 'Civic knowledge, civic education and civic engagement: a summary of recent research', *International Journal of Public Administration*, 30(6–7): 623–42.

Geboers, E., Geijsel, F., Admiraal, W. and ten Dam, G. (2013) 'Review of the effects of citizenship education', *Educational Research Review*, 9: 158–73.

Hart, D., Donnelly, T., Youniss, J. and Atkins, R. (2007) 'High school community service as a predictor of adult voting and volunteering', *American Educational Research Journal*, 44(1): 197–219.

International IDEA (2022) 'Global overview of COVID-19: impact on elections': www.idea.int/news-media/multimedia-reports/global-overview-covid-19-impact-elections

Keating, A., Kerr, D., Benton, T., Mundy, E. and Lopes, J. (2016) *Citizenship Education in England 2001–2010: Young People's Practices and Prospects for the Future: The Eighth and Final Report from the Citizenship Education Longitudinal Study (CELS)*, Research Report DFE-RR059, London: Department for Education.

MCEETYA (Ministerial Council on Education, Employment, Training and Youth Affairs) (2008) *Melbourne Declaration on Educational Goals for Young Australians*, Melbourne: MCEETYA.

McFarland, D. and Starmanns, C. (2009) 'Inside student government: the variable quality of high school student councils', *Teachers College Record*, 111(1): 27–54.

Mulder, L. (2021) 'On-site citizenship education: An effective way of boosting democratic engagement and reducing inequalities among young people?', *Political Behavior*: https://doi.org/10.1007/s11109-021-09710-0

Neoh, Y. (2019) 'The practice of civics and citizenship education in New South Wales primary schools', PhD thesis, University of Sydney, Australia.

Neundorf, A., Niemi, R.G. and Smets, K. (2016) 'The compensation effect of civic education on political engagement: how civics classes make up for missing parental socialization', *Political Behavior*, 38(4): 921–49.

Niemi, R. and Junn, J. (1998) *Civic Education*, New Haven, CT: Yale University Press.

Print, M. (2007a) 'Citizenship education and youth participation in democracy', *British Journal of Educational Studies*, 55(3): 325–45.

Print, M. (2007b) 'Learning political engagement in schools', in M. Print, L. Saha and K. Edwards (eds) *Youth Participation in Democracy*, Rotterdam: Sense Publishers, pp 95–112.

Print, M. (2009a) 'Connecting youth political participation and civic education in school', in M. Print and H. Milner (eds) *Civic Education and Youth Political Participation*, Rotterdam: Sense Publishers, pp 123–42.

Print, M. (2009b) 'Teaching political and social values', in L. Saha and G. Dworkin (eds) *International Handbook of Research on Teachers and Teaching*, New York: Springer, pp 1001–14.

Print, M. (2009c) 'Civic engagement and political education of young people', *Minority Studies*, 1: 63–83.

Print, M. (2012) 'Teacher pedagogy and achieving citizenship competences in schools', in M. Print and D. Lange (eds) *Schools, Curriculum and Civic Education or Building Democratic Citizens*, Rotterdam: Sense Publishers, pp 113–28.

Print, M. and Coleman, D. (2003) 'Towards understanding social capital and citizenship education', *Cambridge Journal of Education*, 33(1): 123–49.

Print, M. and Hughes, J. (2001) *National Key Performance Measures in Civics and Citizenship Education*, report to the National Key Performance Measures Taskforce, Ministerial Council for Education, Training and Youth Affairs (MCETYA), Canberra.

QCA (1998) *Education for Citizenship and the Teaching of Democracy in Schools. Final Report of the Advisory Group on Citizenship*, the Crick Report, London: Qualifications and Curriculum Authority.

Reichert, F. and Print, M. (2017) 'Mediated and moderated effects of political communication on civic participation', *Information, Communication & Society*, 20(8): 1162–84.

Reichert, F. and Print, M. (2018) 'Civic participation of high school students: The effect of civic learning in school', *Educational Review*, 70(3): 318–41.

Reichert, F. and Print, M. (2019) 'Participatory practices and political knowledge: how motivational inequality moderates the effects of formal participation on knowledge', *Social Psychology of Education*, 22(5): 1085–108.

Saha, L. and Print, M. (2010) 'Student school elections and political engagement: A cradle of democracy?', *International Journal of Educational Research*, 49(1): 22–32.

Schulz, W., Ainley, J., Fraillon, J., Kerr, D. and Losito, B. (2010) *ICCS 2009 International Report: Civic Knowledge, Attitudes, and Engagement Among Lower-Secondary School Students in 38 Countries*, Amsterdam: IEA.

Whiteley, P. (2014) 'Does citizenship education work? Evidence from a decade of citizenship education in secondary schools in England', *Parliamentary Affairs*, 67(3): 513–35.

13

Towards civic learning for all

Kei Kawashima-Ginsberg

Inequality in wealth, income, educational attainment and access to many essentials such as proper healthcare and basic safety is well documented in numerous studies. Access inequity in high-quality civic preparation is one such condition that arguably contributes to many of these outcomes through a domino effect.[1] Young people who receive high-quality civic learning experience are *democratic actors*, capable of evaluating available information to formulate a plan for addressing public problems and execute the plan well while working with other stakeholders with varying interests. If a given neighbourhood or community is filled with these democratic actors, then that community should be able to fare better in challenging times and address numerous challenges that arise. In fact, previous studies have found that, on various outcomes, communities with strong civic engagement and social cohesion fare better than those that are not (Knight Foundation, 2010;[2] Kawashima-Ginsberg et al, 2012; Sampson, 2013). Furthermore, individuals who are civically involved show better health and economic outcomes, even after controlling for various socioeconomic factors (Kim, Kim and You, 2015). It follows, then, that a society full of these thriving civic communities would, in turn, have more representative government representatives who make decisions that elevate all of its members. This rationale is why the first public school systems in the US prioritised civic education as its central mission (Mann, 1849).[3]

---

[1] I define high-quality civic preparation as one in which a young person, through a web of institutional and/or relational networks, is exposed to diverse and meaningful opportunities for democratic practice and forms a strong working knowledge of the ways in which civic and political institutions function and can, therefore, leverage these systems for public good.

[2] https://knightfoundation.org/sotc/

[3] In his report to the Massachusetts Board of Education, where he proposed the concept of common schools, Mann (1849, pp 78–9) noted: 'It may be an easy thing to make a Republic but it is very laborious thing to make Republicans; and woe to the republic that rests upon no better foundations than ignorance, selfishness, and passion ... but if such as Republic be devoid of intelligence, it will only the more closely resemble an obscene giant who has waxed strong in his youth, and grown wanton in his strength; whose brain

What is the problem?

In recent decades, civic education has not only been inadequate but also severely inequitable, causing many Americans to be unprepared and distrustful of constitutional democracy itself. Among many causes of political polarisation and institutional and intergroup distrust in the US is likely a lack of civic preparation and civic practice among Americans (Pew Research Center, 2019, 2021). On the one hand, there are some indications that basic civic knowledge (being able to name three branches of the US government and say what their basic rights are) is held by a higher proportion of Americans than several years ago (Annenberg Public Policy Center, 2021). On the other, only 59 per cent recall taking a civics course in high school (Annenberg Public Policy Center, 2021). A survey of a nationally representative sample of young adults indicates that well less than half of young American adults report ever having worked on a community issue with others or been part of a deliberation about spending public funding.[4] As of 2021, 52 per cent of young Americans described American democracy as 'in trouble' or 'failed', while 34 per cent described it as 'somewhat functioning' or 'healthy' (Harvard Institute of Politics, 2021).

Why is this happening?

Over the past few decades, the public infrastructure to prepare youth for civic life in the US crumbled slowly but surely, with the No Child Left Behind policy shaping how time is allocated to maths and English language arts (Winthrop, 2020) and first-year college students increasingly viewing obtaining a well-paid job as their main concern.[5] Insufficient commitment to equitable civic learning has only helped the expanding disparities in voice and influence of American people, divided by class, race, gender, religion, educational attainment, geography and other factors.

---

has been developed only in the region of the appetites and passions and not in the organs of reason and conscience, and who, therefore, is boastful of his bulk alone and glories in the weight of his heel and in the destruction of is arm ... and all good men of after-times would fain to weep over its downfall, did not their scorn and contempt at its folly and its wickedness, repress all sorrow for its fate.'

[4] Carried out by the Center for Information and Research on Civic Learning and Engagement (CIRCLE).

[5] Author's analysis of the time-series data of the CIRP Freshman Survey by the Higher Education Research Institute at UCLA. Data retrieved from: https://heri.ucla.edu/heri-data-archive/

What is the solution? Five pathways for civic education to thrive and expand

In short, we as a society have to be much more serious about providing all students with the quality and quantity of learning and practice that prepare them fully for civic life. I have long maintained that

> civic education of American children and youth has always been essential, but the value of deeper civic education cannot be overemphasized in the current political climate. Strong civic education develops young people's capacity to grapple with contentious, possibly divisive, issues such as immigration reform and gun regulations in an informed, rigorous, yet civil manner. (Kawashima-Ginsberg, 2016, p 19)

Since 2019, I have been working on the collaborative project, Educating for American Democracy (EAD), with colleagues from Harvard, Arizona State University, Arizona State Department of Education and iCivics, a non-profit education organisation. We have discussed how to bring about the kind of civic education that prepares students for a life as democratic citizens, which added richness and nuance to the core idea through EAD. Importantly, we worked together through, and because of, our disagreements. The resulting report and companion guides and teaching resources represent one of the most promising solutions to our ailing democracy.

> Our large network of participants—including teachers, scholars, students, and leaders from private and public sectors—was professionally, demographically, and ideologically diverse. We charged ourselves with grappling with, rather than avoiding, the complexities of the important subjects under our care. Where we could, we found compromises; where arguments ran deep, we presented the principled tensions explicitly so that educators and students can join the conversation, and can experiment with ways of resolving the competing priorities and goals that characterize history education and civic learning. With compromise where possible and honesty about the hardest challenges, we reached consensus on a substantial educational vision. (Educating for American Democracy, 2021a, p 8)

EAD is powerful because this large network of stakeholders engaged constructively with disagreements and produced a powerful inquiry-learning framework that can be used by educators from kindergarten (in the US, around age 5) through to 12th grade (age 17 and 18) classrooms, and has already inspired a large number of informal education sites (museums, libraries and historical sites) to shape their visitors' learning experiences. The EAD initiative is an ambitious endeavour with a goal of preparing 60 million students, 1 million teachers and 100,000 schools over the next decade. It is clear that multifaceted and cross-ideological collaboration is needed to achieve such reach. In the following sections, we will explore five promising pathways in which theories and research in the EAD reports *Educating for American Democracy* (2021a), *Pedagogy Companion to the Roadmap to Educating for American Democracy* (2021b) and *Roadmap to Educating for American Democracy* (2021c) can be put into practice to advance this movement to fundamentally shift civic preparation of American students.

Before going into specific milieus in which the EAD ideas can come alive, let us look at a few major shifts that EAD attempts to make that are most relevant for the purpose of this chapter.

First, the scale of EAD targeted impact compels us to think differently about whom we serve through this initiative. At this scale (60 million), we must abandon the idea that motivated or high achievement students are the ones who should receive the best civic education, and instead commit to serving all students, irrespective of their racial/ethnic background, any disability and learning differences, or where they live. Second, the scope and rigour of the EAD Roadmap means that students need to begin their civic preparation in earnest much earlier than they typically do today (which is in junior-high or middle-school grades, ages 12–15 or so) and using every opportunity, including those that exist outside social studies time. Third, the EAD framework explicitly compels educators and students to explore and grapple with contentious issues and tensions in American history and contemporary society, all while our society continues to polarise. This means that we need to ask educators to shift how they teach and interact with students on a daily basis without alienating some students or further fuelling tensions. These shifts are important distinguishing features of the EAD initiative that can drive our shared goal and hope for a more perfect union. The pathways described below will help advance these shifts.

Pathway 1: Expand the meaning of 'civic learning' first by using a classroom as a mini polity

American adults often have a narrow definition of civic education, thinking of one class called 'civics' or 'American government' offered in high school social studies, where the teachers 'delivered' content to them. We have no reason to limit ourselves to such a small window of opportunities, when in fact a classroom can be seen as a microcosm of our society on the first day of preschool.

Despite common misconceptions, research finds that youngsters are engaging in meaningful civic life even in the preschool playground (Payne et al, 2020). Payne observed how young children were engaged in early forms of self-governance. In one case study, she noted that children observed one another carefully as they faced a possible conflict, intervene when there is injustice and negotiate a best solution. In this particular case, children were catching bugs on the playground and one of them felt he didn't get a fair share. Just when the conflict heats up, a child in the group goes to get another bug and hands it to him. There is no adult present at any point. The children detected a grievance emerging in their 'community', assessed a problem and found a solution, so that they can keep on playing.[6]

Educators play an essential role in helping young students gain an awareness of self as citizens in more ways than 'being a good person' when they design a classroom as a mini polity (Mindes, 2015). In these teachers' classrooms, students develop knowledge about how they and their fellow classmates manage their 'community', in which they learn, work, eat and play together. From an early age, children can learn to use tools to make decisions in inclusive and fair ways and begin to form a foundational understanding of how citizens share resources, handle different priorities and wants in their community, and ask themselves the two key questions of civic life: 'How should we live (learn) together?' 'What should we do?' (Levine, 2013, 2022).

Educators may need to adopt a different approach to their students, from that of a 'sole leader' to that of a 'wise facilitator' who will not offer a solution to every little problem students have, but help them build skills and commitment to do so by normalising the idea that students share ownership of their learning space, and that they contribute to their collective thriving by learning to work and make important decisions with other students.

For example, I learned from Dr Sylvia Rousseau[7] who, as a high school principal, not only told her students and staff that they co-owned their space but made it a felt experience through the school embodying student ownership and stewardship. In her school, students fully operated a supply store in the school, from conducting marketing research to managing inventory and running the store itself. Students were not only learning important life and career skills, but also feeling that their school leaders trusted young people's capacity to provide services to the school that students needed and made decisions on their own.

---

[6] This information was provided by Katherina Payne in a presentation she gave at CIRCLE (Center for Information and Research on Civic Learning and Engagement).

[7] Dr Rousseau is someone whom I consider as my mentor.

Pathway 2: Civic education as content, pedagogy and applied practice

What can a group of students, who have been socialised to think of themselves as democratic citizens and stewards of their own school and then community, do? A whole lot, it turns out. Once we start to expand the vision of what 'civic learning' is, educators often find that the content and practice of civic life are intrinsically linked. Students must have a working knowledge of how our institutions and policies are used to sustain a healthy community, know how to discern relevant and accurate information to inform their opinions and decisions, and then they are able to drive that knowledge home when they have a chance to apply knowledge to practice. The EAD Roadmap comes with a pedagogy companion (Educating for American Democracy, 2021b), which contains six principles of teaching the Roadmap (Figure 13.1). Principles 1 and 2 relate to the need for a paradigm shift in whom we as educators are accountable for, while Principle 3 underscores the need to establish an optimal and inclusive civic learning environment by building relationships and trust within classrooms and with the larger community. Principles 4 and 5 refer to instructional strategy that combine rigorous content learning through deep inquiries and application of the core knowledge to solve real-world problems, and using knowledge of democratic processes to make collective decisions or engage in productive discourse about real-world issues. Finally, Principle 6 helps students and educators assess and reflect on their learning experiences and outcomes to improve their learning experience for the future, reaffirming the first principle, Excellence for All, by this commitment for continuous improvement.

This idea has been around at least since Dewey ([1899] 2017) argued that students learned best when they had a chance to apply the abstract concepts they had learned directly to solve real-world problems. Civic learning is an ideal vehicle to facilitate students' learning in the community through real-world problem-solving. This type of pedagogy is already used in several civic education curricula, although names differ (informed action through service learning, action civics, some forms of expeditionary learning). They share features such as student-led decision-making and problem-solving in a local context. Typically, students decide on a focus issue/challenge, conduct research about the issue and develop plans for solving that problem. Programmes like Public Achievement (PA) have not only scaled up within the US but several large universities in Japan uses PA-style curriculum as a requirement (Horimoto and Ninomiya-Lim, 2020). This process often requires students to engage multiple community stakeholders and school or municipal administrators. Through this type of opportunity, students learn, through experience, what it is like to take care of one's community using civic and political processes. Importantly, students should reflect on

Figure 13.1: Six Pedagogy Principles for the EAD Roadmap

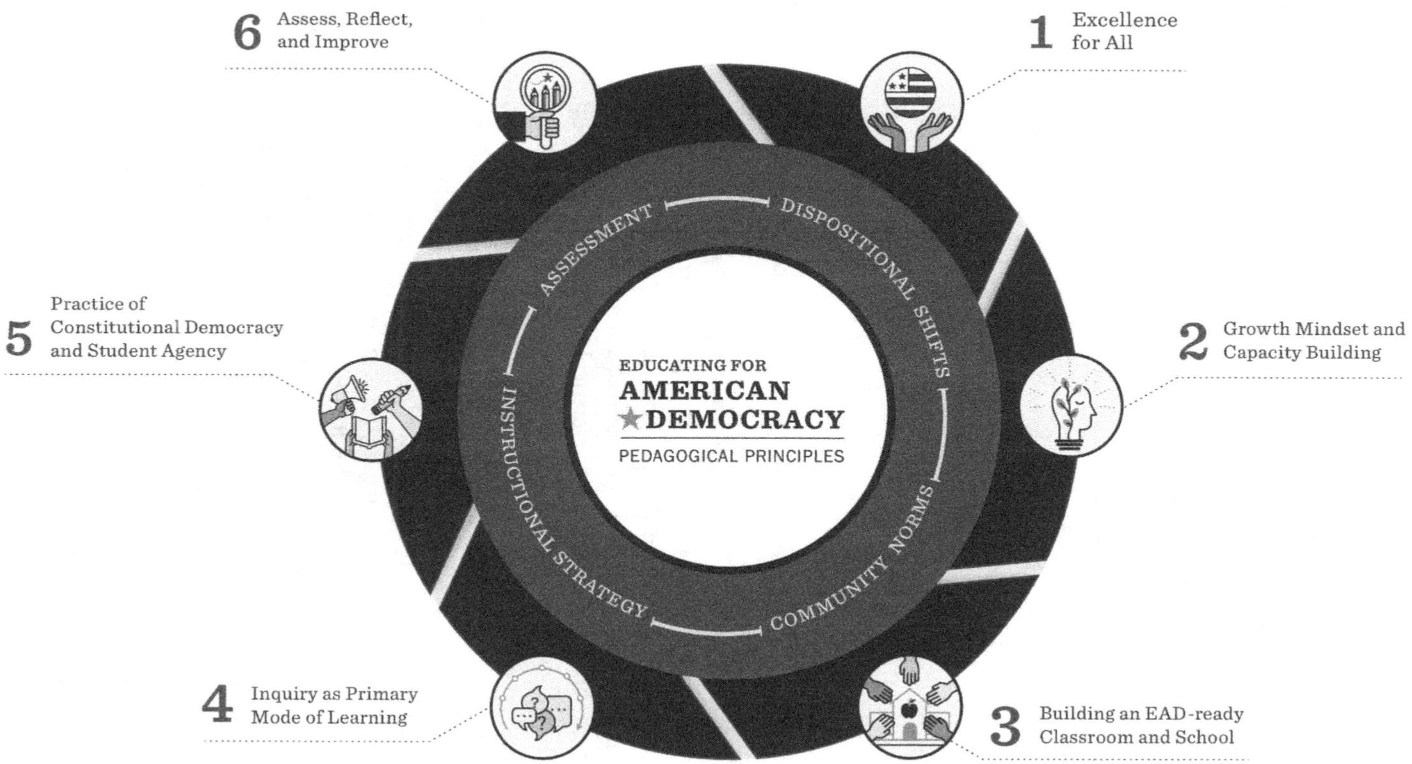

1. Excellence for All
2. Growth Mindset and Capacity Building
3. Building an EAD-ready Classroom and School
4. Inquiry as Primary Mode of Learning
5. Practice of Constitutional Democracy and Student Agency
6. Assess, Reflect, and Improve

EDUCATING FOR AMERICAN DEMOCRACY — PEDAGOGICAL PRINCIPLES

DISPOSITIONAL SHIFTS • COMMUNITY NORMS • INSTRUCTIONAL STRATEGY • ASSESSMENT

Source: Educating for American Democracy, 2021b. Reproduced with the permission of Educating for American Democracy

the project they just worked on and connect their particular local issue with more abstract civic concepts that tie back to a larger inquiry about how people and institutions in a constitutional democracy operate and develop their sense of identity related to civic life.

Not surprisingly, student-led civics pedagogy engages students well. They find it exciting to work directly on a challenge they see every day. There are some pitfalls that educators must avoid. First, 'working on an issue' means conducting thorough research about the issue from multiple perspectives and carefully developing plans that utilise the full range of civic tools that people have available. While student enthusiasm is an important part of learning, educators need to incorporate inquiry, which offers opportunities to teach numerous relevant skills, such as primary source analysis, media literacy, perspective-taking, and knowledge about the various mechanisms citizens use to effect change in their communities. Second, educators often say that it is difficult to save time for reflecting on the lessons learned in doing the project, and tying back to the abstract concepts/content that project tapped into. Strong curriculum guides would provide space for these reflections.[8]

Pathway 3: Thinking developmentally about civic readiness

It is not uncommon for educators and experts to hold the view that 'lower-elementary grade educators do not explore societal issues with students because they are not ready for such topics' (Scott et al, 2020). However, research and veteran teachers disagree, as children, even in preschool, have demonstrated their capacity for critical thinking, analysis of an issue and collaborative problem-solving (Hall and Rudkin, 2011; Krechevsky et al., 2015; Payne et al, 2020). The National Council of Social Studies has issued multiple position statements that emphasise the need for social studies education to start in the early grades. Elementary social studies experts agree that societal issue discussion and inquiry in kindergarten will likely look quite different from those that are happening in a high school US government course. For instance, young children may generate a question in the context of play or a stroll around the school yard with their friend. Educators can leverage these natural wonderings and students' curiosity about certain topics as an entryway into deep inquiry and content learning. Experts further recommend that the civic learning be relevant and meaningful to students of diverse backgrounds, so that their civic learning is founded on a positive affirmation of who they are and where their ancestors come from. For

---

[8] Illinois Civics Hub, for instance, offers a Service Learning Toolkit, which emphasises analysis and exploration of the topic from multiple perspective and presents numerous examples across disciplines: www.illinoiscivics.org/curriculum-toolkit/service-learning/

instance, Rodriguez and Swalwell (2021) take many common examples of early elementary social studies activities (holidays such as Thanksgiving and Christmas, and children's books that often attribute major social movements to one individual/hero) and show how these examples can be more inclusive and holistic.

The EAD Roadmap provides inquiry examples that touch on a number of key topics with increasing depth and complexity over time, so that students, as they progress from elementary grade level, will have numerous opportunities to revisit questions that are core to their civic knowledge and identity development. For instance, the EAD Roadmap's first theme, 'civic participation', touches on the basic question of citizenship: 'How can I help?' Students explore this question from multiple angles, sometimes through historical examples and at other times in real-life civic life, in an increasingly complex context. K–2 (kindergarten, children aged 5 in the US) students will explore their basic sense of identity and attachment to communities, and how they have helped people and communities closest to them. By 3–5th grades (around age 8–10), they deal with how people might see injustice in the decisions made for a community and learn about ways in which they can work with others to help make positive changes. By high school, students explore what civil society is and how people's civic actions interact with institutions and laws. Finally, they come back again to the idea of 'how can I help?' by reflecting on the opportunities and responsibilities of citizens in 21st-century society. Students must also have opportunities to make sense of what is happening around them, both in their classrooms and the world around them. Case examples, such as the 'Places to Play in Providence (Rhode Island)' project, demonstrate their capability. In this project, children, upon receiving a request for ideas from their mayor, go on to produce a complex park design and rules for park use by conducting research, interviewing stakeholders and then making a 3-D model of their park to showcase at the city hall (Mardell and Carpenter, 2012).

Pathway 4: Community schools and place-based collaborations

In the US, community schools share a philosophy of education, and commit to meeting students' needs holistically. For example, the inner-city community school my three school-aged children attend provides free lunch to all students, dentists come to provide preventive care each year and it offers affordable afterschool care.[9] They have a longer school day than

---

[9] Community schools often offer services provided by community organisations, such as dental check-ups, food pantry and social service agencies. Some community schools are also charter schools (as is the one my children go to) but not all charter schools subscribe to the community school philosophy.

surrounding schools and the school academically outperforms other schools in the city, although the school has just as many, if not more, students who are English learners and/or come from low-income families and over 90 per cent of the students are students of colour. These characteristics, as well as strong academic performance, are consistent with the findings from mounting research showing that community schools are effective at reducing persistent racial inequality in outcomes such as students' disciplinary action and school engagement (Moore et al, 2018; Johnston et al, 2020). Although it has been around since the early 20th century, the community school has evolved with the leadership of pioneers like Jane Addams, John Dewey and Dorothy Cotton (Benson et al, 2009). The modern iteration of community schools is one that is built on the evidence about how students from diverse backgrounds learn – and emphasises culturally relevant instruction and offers a variety of services that are traditionally offered in the community (and through private care), such as preventive medical and dental care and food pantries (Benson et al, 2017; Quinn and Blank, 2020).

There are emerging opportunities with community schools. Several communities of practice, organised by different names used for versions of community schools ('community-in-schools', 'alliance for community schools' and so on), have developed a consensus-based framework for effective community schools, while attempting to expand access to community schools from just 8,000 schools to 100,000 (Harper et al, 2020). The expansion of access to community schools could help more students feel safe and valued for what they bring to the classroom, while having more direct opportunities to interact with and learn from local communities.

If community schools of the next few decades are able to integrate community connection with community-based learning and problem-solving, they will contribute significantly to civic preparation of our students, especially those who are farthest from opportunities (inner-city schools, schools in rural communities). One of the greatest assets of the community school movement is its application of findings from rigorous and multidisciplinary studies of teaching and learning to the design of the framework and instructional guidance. Community schools' commitment to evidence-based practice is helpful, because community schools often serve marginalised communities that tend to be outperformed by their more privileged peers. Community schools work to bring all students to excellence by providing resources and materials and medical care and employing the best, evidence-based pedagogical approach to be responsive to students' lived experience, including trauma and cultural wealth and experience. This approach to instruction is referred to as 'trauma-responsive' and 'culturally responsive' teaching in the literature (Hammond, 2015; Urban Education Institute, 2017). These approaches are not only evidence based, but also necessary in the context of civic learning that will touch on contentious issues and ask students and educators to grapple with the complexities of American society, past and present, which will often involve historical and current events that have been, and still are, a source of trauma for various groups in the US. The coalition-building and evidence-based approach to building consensus (with community inputs) to scale up community schools holds promise, especially if the development of civic readiness, particularly through community-based problem-solving and collaboration, can become a major pillar of its renewed vision.

Pathway 5: Educational policies and role of parents and carers

Since I wrote about the legislative mandates for civic education in the states of Florida and Illinois (Kawashima-Ginsberg, 2016), my colleagues and I have been involved in three more local district or state-wide networks working to incorporate a new mandate into instruction as their evaluation partner. We learned numerous lessons along the way. There is no doubt that state laws to advance civic learning can be a powerful lever to ensure that educators across diverse types of communities come to achieve a shared set of goals, knowledge and motivation. Consequently, students gain foundational civic knowledge and positive attitudes towards civic engagement (Hayat and Kawashima-Ginsberg 2020). And we are starting to understand the essential elements of educator capacity-building that make teachers resilient against the COVID-19 pandemic, and even ideological and culture war (Kawashima-Ginsberg et al, 2022).

We are also learning about what can get in the way of educators shifting practices and the kind of support they most need (Daneels et al, 2019; Kawashima-Ginsberg et al, 2022). Synthesising all those lessons, we find that successful policy implementation design requires partnering with educators. This means that the policy designers take educator inputs and when the time comes to implement the new mandates, educators should be trusted but also supported with content – and technical resources *and* social and moral support.

A need to walk with educators and providing what they need when they need it has become increasingly important, especially as other kinds of law, so-called 'CRT Ban'[10] laws have begun to appear since the summer of 2021. According to Chalkbeat, an education news outlet, these critical race theory bans are efforts to restrict 'education on racism, bias, the contributions of specific racial or ethnic groups to US history, or related topics', and they are in place or in progress in 36 states, while 17 have ongoing efforts to expand coverage of the same topic.[11]

---

[10] 'CRT' refers to 'critical race theory'.
[11] For detailed information about each state, see: www.chalkbeat.org/22525983/map-critical-race-theory-legislation-teaching-racism

Recently, parents have organised to have their voices heard in education policy making. The most parent-organised groups featured in the media have spoken against these topics being covered in public schools.[12] Meanwhile, surveys of parents at large show two clear findings: a vast majority of parents, regardless of race, want to make sure students learn about American slavery in school, but they are, at the same time, against critical race theory.[13] Many experts would argue that good, in-depth teaching about slavery would inevitably touch on the idea of racism and its impact on American society. It is clear that parents have become more familiar than ever with what their children are learning at school after being thrown into a home teacher role during the COVID-19 pandemic, and it is understandable that they want to have a voice over what and how children learn at school.

We must find a way to proactively inform and seek inputs from parents and carers about the civics curriculum because they are essential to ensuring that civic learning at school is reflected and solidified at home. One thing I hope parents will remember is that students are the top priority of our education agenda, and students are not to be pulled into and out of a specific content or curriculum simply as a display of a political tug of war. Our students deserve clear messages about what it is they are learning and, even more, deserve to understand, through diverse views and narratives, what happened in American history, that the very essence of US constitutional democracy is forging a political people out of a diversity of types.

Final words: young people's desire to steward our planet and bring justice is a hope for the future

At the end of the day, education is an investment in the future. Individuals who obtain more educational credentials and skills enjoy more economic success in life (Torpey, 2021). Civic education is not only an investment in personal future but an investment in the sustainability of the republic, because without educated and engaged citizens who can work with all levels of government to perform its functions, and who possess general civility and the capacity to work with others on public problems, the American constitutional democracy would collapse. Several reputable columnists and scholars argue that it is already on the brink of collapse, likening it to other national regimes that collapsed shortly after displaying traits they

---

[12] See an example in Loudoun County, Virginia: www.loudountimes.com/news/teacher-accuses-parent-group-of-racism-after-group-criticizes-lcps-equity-efforts/article_69469b9a-9d49-11eb-b2c1-bff954bdd342.html

[13] www.usatoday.com/story/news/education/2021/09/10/crt-schools-education-racism-slavery-poll/5772418001/

observe in the US today (see, for example, Homer-Dixon, 2022; Stroop, 2022; and those citing Levitsky and Ziblatt, 2018), or at least is backsliding (International IDEA, 2022).

Young people have been at the forefront of the countermovement to the threats to American democracy, by marching, occupying and voting. The number of young people who say they have attended marches and demonstrations increased fivefold between 2016 and 2020, from 5 per cent to 27 per cent nationally, and now 60 per cent of young adults say that they associate themselves with one or more social movements (CIRCLE, 2020a). Involvement in a movement is associated with a higher likelihood of voting (CIRCLE, 2020a). As a youth cohort, the Gen Z voters (those who are born in 1995 and later) have shown much stronger voter turnout than any of the previous generations (CIRCLE, 2021a). Young adults we have surveyed in the past few years have named climate change, affordability of healthcare and racism as top issues, although issue priorities do vary by race and ethnicity. In spite of their doubts about the authenticity of American democracy, the COVID-19 pandemic, economic hardship and mental health challenges, young Americans are poised to remain civically engaged (CIRCLE, 2020b, 2021b).

Although evidence suggests that less time has been spent on social studies at elementary and secondary levels, and social studies time is spent on more rote and repetitious tasks (McMurrer, 2007; Vogler and Virtue, 2007; Winstead, 2011; CCSSO, 2018), demanding rigorous and relevant civic education has not been a major advocacy priority among young people, but I wish it were, because it needs to be championed by all stakeholders, including young people themselves, if it is to make a significant and scalable shift. Listening to educators through my work in civic education research and evaluation often reminds me that it takes a lot of training, skills and confidence to provide students with the kind of relevant and rigorous civic education that my colleagues and I hoped for all students when we developed the Educating for American Democracy roadmap and pedagogy companion. My friends in civic education often lament the fact that most everyday Americans, young and old, like and accept having civics in schools but do not actively advocate for it. But if demands are not coming from young people or families, it will not be lifted up as a key priority of the American education system.

I imagine this scarcity of 'civics champions' is in part caused by the fact that not enough students and their families have the opportunity to understand what they deserve to experience through civic learning during their school years. It is possible that the systemic erosion of civic education has been so severe that too few understand what it means to be fully civic life ready, and what schools can and should offer to achieve this goal. We have to start building a deep bench of students who, alongside older people, know what it means to be fully prepared for civic life and will advocate accordingly so that more students have access to this opportunity. Although I am hopeful that Educating for American Democracy, with championing teachers and organisations, has begun to do this, we have much to do in developing informed policy, teacher capacity and student voice at scale, so that an emerging movement led by a coalition of civic and social studies education organisations can become a societal demand to prepare all students for productive, active and lifelong participation in civic life.

References

Annenberg Public Policy Center (2021) *America's Civics Knowledge Increases During a Stress-Filled Year*: www.annenbergpublicpolicycenter.org/2021-annenberg-constitution-day-civics-survey/

Benson, L., Harkavy, I., Johanek, M.C. and Puckett, J. (2009) 'The enduring appeal of community schools', *American Educator*, 33(2): 22–47.

Benson, L, Harkavy, I., Puckett J. et al. (2013) *Knowledge for Social Change*, Philadelphia, PA: Temple University Press.

CIRCLE (Center for Information and Research on Civic Learning and Engagement) (2020a) *Poll: Young People Believe They Can Lead Change in Unprecedented Election Cycle*, 30 June: https://circle.tufts.edu/latest-research/poll-young-people-believe-they-can-lead-change-unprecedented-election-cycle

CIRCLE (2020b) *Young People Turn to Online Political Engagement During COVID-19*, 20 October: https://circle.tufts.edu/latest-research/young-people-turn-online-political-engagement-during-covid-19

CIRCLE (2021a) *2020 Election Center*: https://circle.tufts.edu/2020-election-center

CIRCLE (2021b) *Despite Pandemic, Civically Engaged Youth Report Higher Well-Being*, 7 July: https://circle.tufts.edu/latest-research/despite-pandemic-civically-engaged-youth-report-higher-well-being

CCSSO (Council of Chief State School Officers) (2018) *The Marginalization of Social Studies*: https://ccsso.org/resource-library/marginalization-social-studies

Daneels, M.E., Kawashima-Ginsberg, K. and Healy, S. (2019) 'From paper to practice: lessons from the #CivicsIsBack campaign', *Success in High-Need Schools Journal*, 15(1): 58–69.

Dewey, J. ([1899] 2017) *The School and Society: Being Three Lectures*, ebook edn: www.gutenberg.org/ebooks/53910

Educating for American Democracy (EAD) (2021a) *Educating for American Democracy: Excellence in History and Civics for All Learners*: www.educatingforamericandemocracy.org

EAD (2021b) *Pedagogy Companion to the Roadmap to Educating for American Democracy*: www.educatingforamericandemocracy.org

EAD (2021c) *Roadmap to Educating for American Democracy*: https://www.educatingforamericandemocracy.org/wp-content/uploads/2021/02/Roadmap-to-Educating-for-American-Democracy.pdf

Hall, E.L. and Rudkin, J.K. (2011) *Seen & Heard: Children's Rights in Early Childhood Education*, New York: Teachers College Press.

Hammond, Z. (2015) *Culturally Responsive Teaching and the Brain: Promoting Authentic Engagement and Rigor Among Culturally and Linguistically Diverse Students*, Thousand Oaks, CA: Corwin.

Harper, K., Jonas, S. and Winthrop, R. (2020) *Education Inequality, Community Schools, and System Transformation: Launching the Task Force on Next Generation Community Schools*: www.brookings.edu/blog/education-plus-development/2020/11/10/education-inequality-community-schools-and-system-transformation-launching-the-task-force-on-next-generation-community-schools/

Hayat, N. and Kawashima-Ginsberg, K. (2020) 'Building for better democracy together: final report on the Illinois #CivicsIsBack civic education initiative', unpublished technical research report, Medford, MA: CIRCLE.

Homer-Dixon, T. (2022) 'The American polity is cracked and might collapse. Canada must prepare', *The Globe and Mail*, 2 January: www.theglobeandmail.com/opinion/article-the-american-polity-is-cracked-and-might-collapse-canada-must-prepare/

Horimoto, M. and Ninomiya-Lim, S. (2020) 'Nurturing citizenship in higher education: public achievement-style education at Tokai University', *Educational Studies in Japan: International Yearbook*, 14: 29–38.

International IDEA (2022) *The Global State of Democracy 2021: Building Resilience in a Pandemic Era*: www.idea.int/gsod/sites/default/files/2021-11/the-global-state-of-democracy-2021_1.pdf

Johnston, W.R., Engberg, J., Opper, I.M. et al. (2020) *Illustrating the Promise of Community Schools: An Assessment of the Impact of the New York City Community Schools Initiative*, Santa Monica, CA: RAND Corporation.

Kawashima-Ginsberg, K. (2016) *The Future of Civic Education*, Washington, DC: National Association of State Boards of Education: https://nasbe.nyc3.digitaloceanspaces.com/2016/09/Future-of-Civic-Education_September-2016-Standard.pdf.

Kawashima-Ginsberg, K., Daneels, M. and Hayat, N. (2022) 'Preparing teachers for current and controversial issue discussion', in J. Lo (ed) *Making Discussions Work: Methods for Quality Dialogue in the Social Studies*, New York: Columbia University Press.

Kawashima-Ginsberg, K., Lim, C. and Levine, P.L. (2012) *Civic Engagement and Unemployment II: The Case Builds*. Washington, DC: National Conference on Citizenship.

Kim, S., Kim, C.Y. and You, M.S. (2015) 'Civic participation and self-rated health: a cross-national multi-level analysis using the world value survey', *Journal of Preventive Medicine and Public Health*, January, 48(1): 18–27.

Krechevsky, M., Mardell, B. and Reese, J. (2015) *Children are Citizens*, Cambridge, MA: Harvard University Graduate School of Education.

Levine, P. (2013) *We Are The Ones We Have Been Waiting For*, Oxford: Oxford University Press.

Levine, P. (2022) *What Should We Do?: A Theory of Civic Life*, Oxford: Oxford University Press.

Levitsky, S. and Ziblatt, D. (2018) *How Democracies Die: What History Reveals about our Future*, New York: Crown Publishing.

Mann, H. (1849) *Twelfth Annual Report to the Secretary of the Massachusetts State Board of Education (1848)*, Boston, MA: Dutton and Wentworth, State Printers.

Mardell, B. and Carpenter, B. (2012) 'Places to play in Providence: valuing preschool children as citizens', *Young Children*, 67(5): 76–78.

McMurrer, J. (2007) *Choices, Changes, and Challenges: Curriculum and Instruction in the NCLB Era*, Washington, DC: Center on Education Policy.

Mindes, G. (2015) 'Preschool through grade 3: pushing up the social studies from early childhood education to the world', *Young Children*, 70(3): 10–15.

Moore, K.A., Lantos, H., Jones, R. et al. (2018) *Making the Grade: A Progress Report and Next Steps for Integrated Student Supports*, Child Trends Report: www.childtrends.org/wp-content/uploads/2017/12/ISS_Child Trends_February2018.pdf

Payne, K.A., Adair, J.K., Colegrove, K. et al. (2020) 'Reconceptualizing civic education for young children: recognizing embodied civic action', *Education Citizenship and Social Justice*, 15(1): 35–46.

Pew Research Center (2019) *Trust and Distrust in America*: www.pewresearch.org/politics/2019/07/22/trust-and-distrust-in-america/

Pew Research Center (2021) *Public Trust in Government: 1958–2021*: www.pewresearch.org/politics/2021/05/17/public-trust-in-government-1958-2021/

Quinn, J. and Blank, M.J. (2020) 'Twenty years, ten lessons: community schools as an equitable school improvement strategy', *VUE*, 49(2): 44–53.

Rodríguez, N.N. and Swalwell, K. (2021) *Social Studies for a Better World: An Anti-Oppressive Approach for Elementary Educators*, New York: WW Norton.

Sampson, R. J. (2013) *Great American City: Chicago and the Enduring Neighborhood Effect*. Chicago: University of Chicago Press.

Scott, N., Foley, A. and Kawashima-Ginsberg, K. (2020) Educator Listening Tour Report for Educating for American Democracy Project, unpublished report.

Stroop, S. (2022) 'Is American democracy on the brink of collapse?', *Open Democracy*, 28 January: www.opendemocracy.net/en/5050/is-american-democracy-on-the-brink-of-collapse/

Torpey, E. (2021) 'Education pays, 2020', *Career Outlook*, US Bureau of Labor Statistics: www.bls.gov/careeroutlook/2021/data-on-display/education-pays.htm

Urban Education Institute (2017) *Practicing Trauma-Responsive Teaching*, Chicago: University of Chicago: https://uei.uchicago.edu/sites/default/files/documents/UEI%202017%20New%20Knowledge%20-%20Practicing%20Trauma-Responsive%20Teaching.pdf

Vogler, K. and Virtue, D. (2007) '"Just the facts, ma'am": teaching social studies in the era of standards and high-stakes testing', *The Social Studies*, 98: 54–58.

Winstead, L. (2011) 'The impact of NCLB and accountability on social studies: teacher experiences and perceptions about teaching social studies', *The Social Studies*, 102(5): 221–7.

Winthrop, R. (2020) *The Need for Civic Education in 21st-Century Schools*, Big Ideas: www.brookings.edu/policy2020/bigideas/the-need-for-civic-education-in-21st-century-schools/

14

Conclusion

Lessons for democratic health

Henry Tam

Political education: challenges and opportunities

We have seen how democratic self-governance can be seriously undermined by the lack of civic competence in shaping public policies or electing representatives. The problem has been exacerbated by politicians who seek to reduce even further the influence of citizens who are economically disadvantaged, socially marginalised and/or discriminated against by prevailing institutional attitudes and practices. Through gerrymandering, facilitating donations from the wealthy elite, manipulation of conventional and social media, imposition of restrictions to deter poor voters,[1] and subversion of oversight institutions,[2] they erode democracy to ease their path to power. They are able to do this because too many people possess neither the skills nor the understanding to see through such manoeuvres, let alone oppose them.

Recent decades have shown that democracy cannot be sustained by the vote alone.[3] When there are so many ways to mislead people about what options are on offer, or nudge them towards giving up on engaging with politics altogether, it is hollow to insist that all is still well just because everyone has a vote. If citizens are truly to shape their own governance, they must learn about the issues that matter, what to make of rival claims, and how to establish and pursue their common objectives. To achieve that, political education is indispensable.

---

[1] For example, the introduction of photo ID for elections when it is known that identity fraud at the electoral booth is not a problem in reality, while the requirement for a photo ID would prevent many people (from poorer background with neither a driving licence nor a passport) from voting.

[2] Such as the Electoral Commission and other bodies tasked with ensuring the fairness of elections.

[3] For an overview of the challenges facing democracy, see Tam (2018a).

However, those who fear that political education could shine a light on their anti-democratic ploys have come up with a number of countermeasures to hamper its development. First, there is the cynical invocation of freedom to justify the teaching and promotion of false, misleading and vicious claims. On the surface, the argument rests on the premise that there should be no limit on what can be taught and discussed in a free society, especially when it takes place in an academic institution.[4] But, on reflection, it is clear that the freedom to communicate does not extend to the putting forward of malicious slanders, discredited dangerous claims, confidential information, statements to incite violence and others that are ruled out in every free society. Proponents of 'no limit' on what can be said in educational institutions would not hesitate to back the banning of attempts to teach the necessity of overthrowing the government in the name of communism or Islamic fundamentalism. Yet they seem to want to give a free pass to the promotion of the prejudices and oppressive attitudes (racism, sexism and homophobia) that their political supporters are in tune with.

Second, the need to cultivate a shared identity and culture is used to justify the teaching of certain favoured interpretations of history, values and beliefs.[5] But while a sense of shared identity and culture is important for the development of civic solidarity and the pursuit of common purpose, it does not follow that it is embodied in a monolithic conception defined by some outmoded 19th-century, colonial, alpha male worldview. For example, it is hardly plausible to suggest that the teaching of bygone military triumphs is essential but learning the lessons from past atrocities and exploitation is superfluous.

Third, the notion of 'impartiality' is brought in to exclude targeted ideas. Any exposition or criticism that challenges prevailing dogmas is deemed to be 'contested' and teachers should not be allowed to incorporate any of it in their lessons unless they want to be castigated as 'biased'. But the veneer of neutrality barely stands up to inspection. Politicians who are so keen to exclude critiques of racist culture, or arguments for the drastic reduction of reliance on fossil fuel – on the grounds that they are contested by others – are equally ready to defend the teaching of evangelical views, or the presentation of their favoured historical figures as flawless – when these

---

[4] The Republican governor of Florida, Ron DeSantis, signed into law a requirement on colleges and universities, in the name of 'intellectual diversity', to ensure that conservative ideas and claims, regardless of their credibility, are taught to counterbalance teachings not favoured by conservatives (Henderson, 2021a).

[5] For example, in the US, the Republican governor of Texas (Greg Abbot) signed into law a project that promotes 'patriotic education' as defined by Republicans, and another law that bans any teaching relating to a project that aims at raising awareness of slavery and racism in American history (Henderson, 2021b).

are also contested by others. Impartiality is achieved neither by stepping back from everything that is contested (there would be very little left to teach otherwise), nor by leaving one sect of partisan politicians to decide what is 'incontrovertible' or not.

Finally, political education can be derailed by anti-liberal propagandists who regard the mission of their culture war as putting an end to what they disparagingly dismiss as 'politically correct' or 'woke'. Any discussion that strikes them as oversensitive to 'innocuous' banter or the misrepresentation of vulnerable people is deemed an unacceptable intrusion into the education of young minds. Dropping any pretence to 'freedom for all views' or 'impartiality', this approach unabashedly stigmatises ideas, not on any societal grounds, but on the anti-liberal agenda adopted by those politicians who seek to weaken democracy through diluting its core ingredients such as equal respect and mutual concern.

To have the political education required for good democratic health, we must not shy away from articulating and defending the lessons we have learnt from history on what it takes for people to share power and responsibility in their own governance. 'Freedom' cannot be treated as a blanket licence for every form of behaviour – in academic institutions or anywhere else. Within democratically coherent boundaries, where preventable harm and irresponsible misinformation can be objectively assessed and held in check, there should be a general presumption in favour of the open and reasoned exploration of diverse claims to seek agreed answers where possible, or deepen understanding of irreconcilable differences otherwise. The shared identity and culture we need is that of democratic citizenship, which connects us through engagement as equals and communication via civil discourse. The research, investigative and judicial institutions underpinned by this culture enable us – not to abstain from passing any judgement on contested claims – but to make judgement impartially so as to support or reject the dissemination of different claims accordingly. Culture warriors' assault on liberal ideas would then be seen as no more legitimate than the anti-liberal attacks launched by authoritarian extremists or fundamentalist fanatics.

Learning to be democratic citizens

Looking at the variety of ideas and practices considered in the foregoing chapters, we can in summary set out broadly three areas that an effective form of political education should address: civic togetherness, civic objectivity and civic efficacy.[6]

---

[6] More details on political literacy and the importance of developing empathic thoughtfulness, cognitive thoughtfulness and volitional thoughtfulness can be found in Tam (2016).

Civic togetherness

For democracy to function, people need to be able to engage in shared missions for their common wellbeing. This requires a genuine appreciation of the value of taking each other's concerns and perspectives on board, and is why interdependence is an asset. It cannot be taken for granted that people will collaborate well without learning to interact with others cooperatively, especially when self-centred individualism has encroached on much of contemporary culture and the ethos of many schools, where attaining higher test scores than others is the prime measure of a student's quality. With lingering prejudices and new divisive manoeuvres in society, mutual respect needs to be taught, not as an abstract notion, but as an everyday form of relationship that is sustained by attitudes, rules and enforcement that are visible in promoting reciprocity and tackling discrimination.[7] An understanding of the rights and responsibilities of group membership should be progressively developed from what one can expect in being a member of a teacher's class, their school, through being a part of one's neighbourhood to being a citizen of one's country and a member of the global community. This would ensure that the obligations individuals and the group have to each other are properly recognised rather than (in most cases, groundlessly) assumed.

The cultivation of civic togetherness involves the acquisition of a shared identity that underpins the 'we' in how we govern ourselves democratically. This civic identity goes beyond the diverse personal identity markers associated with culture, gender, belief, religion, economic status, ethnicity, language, place of birth, locality, family, work and so on. It means that for all our individual differences, our readiness as fellow citizens to stand by others as we expect them to stand by us is not to be pushed aside through the invocation of any other affiliation or 'higher' value.

Learning to develop empathic thoughtfulness and recognise our mutual responsibility is indispensable to the formation of democratic relationships. Our actions can impact on each other, and just as we would not want others to behave thoughtlessly with no regard for the consequences on us, we should be mindful of how our attitudes and actions may affect others. Through group projects, action learning, community outreach and perspective-sharing exercises, those involved may come to see that there are many issues that can only be effectively dealt with when people take each other's ideas and concerns into consideration and work together on finding a satisfactory way forward.

---

[7] For example, mere words in a school's mission statement about mutual respect have little value if they are not backed by practical initiatives and arrangements that can effectively deal with offensive and discriminatory behaviour.

Civic objectivity

Democracy can only operate when deliberations, decision-making and dispute resolution are anchored by objectivity that is made possible through cooperative enquiry. Attempts to sow confusion over what should be allowed in the name of freedom, or what must not be permitted for the sake of impartiality, should be tackled with reference to the objective systems of evaluation that are already relied on in our everyday life. Systems such as scientific research, scholarly analysis, forensic investigation, judicial assessment and public service reporting exemplify how the acceptability of claims in different fields can be objectively and reliably determined. People need to learn how to draw information from cooperative enquiry systems and apply the approach of evidence sharing and cross-checking to their discussion with others about the merits of contrasting claims. They should understand that the reliability of these systems has nothing to do with infallibility (which no system possesses), but is derived from the extent to which they are open to external scrutiny, thorough reviews in the light of new findings or interpretations, and the possibility of revision if warranted. This reliability is what enables society to differentiate responsible communication from lies, fallacies and prejudicial claims. It can accordingly guide us on what should or should not be shared widely in learning institutions.

Citizens need to be trained from an early age so that they can differentiate reliable assertions from deceitful or fallacious claims.[8] It is also important to be able to recognise when a belief or decision should be revised in the light of new findings, especially through critical exploration with others. This goes beyond basic reasoning skills, and covers competences for dealing with rhetorical misdirection, seeing through deceptive propaganda and biased reporting, as well as seeking out dependable sources of information, assessing evidence and the veracity of testimony, and weighing up rival interpretations.

Cognitive thoughtfulness needs to be developed for citizens to engage in cooperative enquiry to solve the problems they face. This requires a learning culture that facilitates hypotheses-making, careful observations, experimentation and informed revisions, without repression or groundless dismissal, so that we can reach a reasoned consensus on what warrants our acceptance.[9] It also needs to be backed by institutional arrangements that

---

[8] For example, we would not want anyone to believe that drinking bleach is a cure for coronavirus infection, or that global warming is a hoax concocted by unscrupulous people – two widely reported falsehoods promoted by Donald Trump when he was president of the US.

[9] Or, where agreement on the details cannot be reached, at least a shared understanding of how we can live with our conflicting views.

provide for transparent processes of collaborative exchange, structured adjudication with built-in capacity for re-examination, and protection from manipulative distortion.

Civic efficacy

Democracy relies on those under its jurisdiction exercising meaningful influence over its workings. If citizen participation is to be more than an aspiration, people need the skills and opportunities to work with others to formulate and pursue their objectives. A crucial yet often overlooked factor is the role of power relations. A school that routinely ignores the concerns of its teachers and pupils cannot convincingly promote student input in shaping its activities and policies. The same applies to any public body at the local or national level. It is essential for participatory arrangements – from deliberative exercises to the election of representatives – to be underpinned by a commitment to take on board the considered views of the participants. Such arrangements need to be transparent and accessible so that people can be confident in taking part in them with the knowledge that it is possible to make a difference to the outcome. This, in turn, requires parity of influence in that no individual or group can take undue advantage over others by using their wealth, status or capacity for intimidation. People should learn how power inequalities in institutions and society more widely need to be curtailed, and why those entrusted with power to serve the public must be subject to effective accountability mechanisms.

Accountability is a vital and complex issue that is seldom explained to those who are integral to its effectiveness. On a wide range of matters, we have to hand power to others to make decisions on our behalf or execute our collective decisions. To ensure that power is exercised responsibly, there has to be a good understanding of what procedural and institutional arrangements are needed to hold those in positions of power to account, the extent to which those arrangements are in place, and how to make use of them. Ignorance in this area could fuel misguided demands for unfettered political leadership (John, 2019).

Education should foster volitional thoughtfulness that steers us, when making decisions that affect others, to seek the views and concerns of others rather than acting unilaterally. The disposition to treat others as one would have them treat one is critical for democratic collaboration. This needs to be developed along with a sophisticated grasp of how to engage with others expressing divergent views, manage the emotional dimensions of verbal exchange, and explore common ground when total agreement cannot be reached. Feedback on participatory exercises – on what worked well or did not, and their actual impact – is a key learning tool that should be consistently built into them.

The role of political leadership

Many politicians who value democracy as a principle nonetheless overlook its parlous state in practice. They point to the urgency of needing to deal with other problems such as climate change, poverty, the energy crisis, economic instability, threats to our health, risks to national security and so on. However, in order to tackle these challenges effectively, the necessary policies are only ever likely to gain sufficient public backing if there is much wider informed engagement by citizens. So long as large numbers of people remain detached from politics or misled as to what and how problems are to be solved, the critical issues we face will continue to be inadequately addressed. It is because we need urgent solutions that politicians who care about securing democratic support to advance the common good should make it their priority to support the development of political education. This would involve using their power and influence to strengthen the conditions for improving citizens' understanding of democracy in the following areas:

- educational practices;
- electoral arrangements;
- engagement processes;
- epistemic institutions.

Educational practices

The civic role of schools should be highlighted. Instead of pressing educators to focus narrowly on individual competitiveness in terms of performance in examinations, there should be a policy shift towards collaborative groupwork, where students learn to deal with problems in diverse team settings, and evaluate possible solutions through mutual checks and exchange. This applies to all subjects to broaden understanding of how to determine what is correct, and work through competing answers to arrive at reasoned agreement.

Schools need to be directed at social goals rather than private interests. There should be tighter restrictions over the setting up of schools by private groups, which, in the absence of any democratic accountability, can neglect the needs of disadvantaged children, discard citizenship teaching in favour of their chosen ideology, or look primarily to their own pecuniary interests – paying associates and relatives any salary they wish regardless of their actual contribution. All schools should be required to be inclusive in their intake[10] and supportive in seeking and responding constructively to the views expressed by students following informed discussions.

---

[10] For example, selection on the basis of religion would not be accepted.

Practical skills for political engagement should be inculcated in schools and beyond. Universities, as we have seen, can do a lot more on campus and with communities to enhance citizens' competence in considering public issues, reflecting on diverse comments, and working with others to identify and pursue actions that can make a positive difference. This should be carried out with partners such as voluntary groups and local authorities in action learning programmes for all ages.

Clear guidance and quality training for teachers and school leaders should be mandated, so that the effective approaches for providing political education,[11] which have been well documented, can be systematically disseminated and applied in all learning institutions. This must be backed by a general inspection regime that requires such application to be demonstrated in those institutions' annual performance. In recent decades, the neoliberal emphasis has been to reduce education to little more than a means to get a job, when, in truth, without a good political education, each new generation will end up too often with governments that leave many of them poor and marginalised, with little hope of ever getting a decent job or a home of their own.

Electoral arrangements

What is taught about democratic values must be aligned with safeguards that will uphold such values. Accordingly, electoral arrangements for public office at all levels should be reviewed and reformed to ensure that they connect authentically with ideas disseminated about democracy in schools. In the UK and the US, there is no shortage of politicians who want pupils to be familiarised with their country's commitment to democracy, but have no hesitation in using their legislative power to weaken democracy by placing a variety of barriers before targeted groups to hinder them from influencing electoral outcomes. The disjunction between verbal commendation of democracy in the classroom and its dysfunctional manifestation in practice inevitably breeds disillusionment.[12]

Politicians should ensure that weaknesses in the system for democratic accountability are made clear, along with explanations of how they can be rectified. For example, changes to electoral registration arrangements, which have led to a major decline in the number of people registered to vote, should be remedied (James, 2016). Better methods should be considered with, for example, a system directly linked to the requirement for compulsory education for all children. As they go through their stages of education, pupils

---

[11] Or by other names such as 'citizenship education' or 'civics'.

[12] Lack of political efficacy fuels disillusionment. See, for example, Helm (2022).

will learn about their right to vote and how they can activate that right when they become eligible to vote. Any checks for identification when voting can be based on the security verification built into the registration system, eliminating any spurious requirement such as photo ID. This would facilitate access to voting by postal and electronic means, and counter attempts to put certain people off voting.

The rules for elections should be taught to everyone, and any anomaly should be highlighted as priorities for reforms rather than glossed over in schools. Students should learn about what a fair and inclusive system of representation would involve, and what political leaders are doing to attain it. Issues to consider will include: voting constituencies or districts ought to be comparable in influence as reflected in their size, population and number of representatives; gerrymandering practices that have led to some parties requiring far more votes to win a seat should be stopped after it has been explained how substantial disadvantages would have been brought in by manipulative boundary drawing; and how some methods of voting can lead to voter preferences being given as close as possible to equal influence on the outcome,[13] while others would allow the preferences of a minority to trump those of everyone else in 'safe seats'.

Finally, in addition to the efficacy of one's vote, interest and confidence in engaging in political activities are also affected by the scope of what can be done before and after elections. There should be political assurance to young people that their vote really matters – backed by statutorily guaranteed independent bodies to scrutinise and adjudicate on electoral legitimacy and terms of office (including the recall of politicians who have breached public trust). Without such independence, the broad exposition of democracy by educators would be undercut by partisan manipulation that uses the cloak of electoral mechanisms to hide anti-democratic subversions.[14] This calls for urgent reforms to ensure that public bodies and officials with oversight responsibility for electoral matters can act diligently without undue interference from unscrupulous demagogues.

---

[13] As made possible under different types of proportional representation.

[14] For example, the UK Conservative government's move to usurp the independence of the Electoral Commission and exert control over what one political party would deem to be acceptable or unacceptable political campaigns poses a serious threat to what citizens can do in organising themselves to promote political goals (Renwick, 2021). In the US, Trump's pressing of Republican state officials to help him overturn the results of the 2020 presidential election highlights the danger of allowing people who hold their position on a partisan platform to have the power to determine if electoral outcomes should be endorsed or rejected (Gellman, 2021).

Engagement processes

Participation in engagement processes carried out by authorised decision-makers, as we have seen, can be highly effective in raising confidence in and understanding of such processes. There is considerable scope to provide more opportunities for engagement with public policy, but those involved must be supported by clear guidance, quality control, systematic provision of training in the required skills, and help with best practice adoption. Otherwise, an engagement event could just come across as a token exercise that, disappointingly, makes little difference.

Public bodies should be tasked with collaborating with schools, colleges and community groups to seek the views of the public. They need to make sure that the engagement processes they set up focus on matters that are specific enough for a meaningful discussion to take place (for example, broad surveys asking how people may want to rank, say, the environment, crime, housing, transport, in order of importance are vacuous); are genuinely open to alternative options (as opposed to where a public body is already bound by an existing piece of legislation or externally set budget that it cannot opt for a different course the public may demand); and can be decided by those who take responsibility for the engagement exercise (so that what is put forward by those engaged would not simply be filed away with no actual decision-maker responding to it).

In addition to spelling out the parameters at the outset, there should be mandated guidance and training to ensure that engagement practices are deliberative and inclusive, so that participants will learn through them how they can examine public policy options, formulate an informed preference and put it forward for consideration. This means that the practices will have to be supported by a skilled facilitator; rules for honest and civil exchange can be enforced; adequate time is allowed for questioning and deliberation; encouragement is given to the respectful sharing of ideas and experiences; and an explanation given on how the exercise will be concluded – by a majority vote, a priority list, an overall consensus, or key agreement and disagreement noted – and responded to by the public body in question.

Whether the issues discussed concern the policies of an external public body, or are matters for a school to decide, those who organise the engagement should pay attention to the selection of participants – how to get a good cross-section of people in a group that is neither too large nor too small to deliberate together – and the giving of feedback afterwards – people need to know what happens as a result of their participation, and whether or not there will be further opportunities to discuss the matter if their views were rejected. The feedback should be given not just to the participants, but to all those who may be affected by the decisions taken, so that the role of deliberative engagement is more widely recognised.[15]

Epistemic institutions

Education in general, and political education in particular, has to be anchored by the work of epistemic institutions, such as independent research organisations, peer-endorsed scholars, professionally recognised experts, judicial bodies, and investigators and reporters with proven credentials. The information they provide underpins claims made in medicine, engineering, criminal trials and so on. When claims are thus supported, they cannot be invalidated by people who contest them without sound argument or relevant evidence. It is vital that the role of epistemic institutions is properly protected in law and widely explained in schools, colleges and universities.[16]

The democratic legitimacy of a government is intertwined with the robustness and objectivity of the epistemic institutions in existence. The nature of critical enquiry and how it connects to reliable findings should be taught in schools, so that instead of blind faith in every pronouncement by some self-styled expert or groundless scepticism towards any statement one feels like dismissing, what people learn to believe in is related to the open searching, sustained scrutiny, safeguards from bribes and intimidation, and readiness to revise, in the light of relevant findings, the processes that generate belief assessments.

Members of all educational bodies should be given training in how to check claims against recognised epistemic sources, and protected from accusations of bias or indoctrination when their work is backed by established epistemic consensus. Society cannot function if, for example, no vaccine against a dangerous virus can be rolled out just because some people contest it without sound reasons; or no warning can be given about the activities of an extremist group because someone rejects it, irrespective of the evidence. Teachers should not be left in a position where they are deterred from explaining anything as a result of some individual or group dismissing what they say without any objectively good grounds.[17]

---

[15] For more details on effective engagement with citizens, see Tam (2019).

[16] For more on the issues relating to assessing the reliability of beliefs in society, see Tam (2018b).

[17] The UK government, for example, issued guidance in 2022 suggesting that the teaching of policy ideas for tackling climate change would not be advisable because these might be contested – regardless of the soundness of these ideas or on what basis they might be contested (Adams, 2022).

Political leadership is needed to ensure that, through a combination of peer scrutiny, statutorily guaranteed independence and external review and recognition, epistemic institutions can collectively provide the intellectual checks and balance to shield educators from lies, distortion and misinformation. This is particularly important to develop in view of two notable trends. One is the tendency to invoke 'faith' or some unquestionable custom to justify objections to certain matters being taught, despite the lack of good reasons to reject the teaching in question.[18] The other is the tactic of funding people to write false or highly misleading reports – based on manipulated data or views given by those paid to express support – to dispute findings that are inconvenient for certain corporations.[19] Individual teachers may not easily stand up to these assaults on learning, but they can with the structured support of epistemic institutions.

The future of democracy

The UK and the US, once at the forefront of promoting the culture of democracy after the Second World War, have, in recent decades, become highly vulnerable to anti-democratic manoeuvres that pave the way for corrupt and authoritarian practices. Unscrupulous politicians, counting on most people not recognising the threat they pose, have been using their legislative and executive powers to place more barriers to disrupt the democratic participation of citizens who might otherwise vote for their rivals (Yang, 2022).

Political understanding is needed more than ever to see why and how we should engage in shaping public decisions, and what obstacles are being devised to disrupt our engagement. Civic-minded educators and policy makers must recognise the strength and urgency of the case for enhancing the provision of political education, draw on innovative ideas and proven practices to help demonstrate the impact it can make to democratic engagement, and build alliances with other civil society groups and campaign organisations to press for the necessary changes.

The inculcation of civic competence is a necessary condition for citizens to assess political options and consider how to influence the selection of those options by legitimate means. Of course, education cannot by itself halt

---

[18] This has happened often; for example, with objections raised to the teaching of evolution, despite it currently being the most critically developed account of how different forms of life emerge and change.

[19] From challenging the health risks of smoking to the planetary dangers of carbon emission, the world has witnessed the emergence of a whole industry of corporate-funded think tanks to serve particular business interests.

the different moves designed to weaken democratic arrangements, spread misinformation and widen power inequalities. But it is more likely that such moves would face stronger opposition with a citizenry equipped with the skills to scrutinise and respond accordingly to them.

When we hear the mantra, 'keep politics out of education', we should remember that it makes sense if it is applied to keeping partisan edicts and autocratic interference out of schools and other learning institutions. When it is a matter of improving awareness of why politics affects us and how to engage with it as members of a democratic society, the priority is to keep educating citizens about politics.

References

Adams, R. (2022) 'Guidance on political impartiality in English classrooms "confusing" say teachers' unions', *The Guardian*, 17 February: www.theguardian.com/education/2022/feb/17/guidance-on-political-impartiality-in-english-classrooms-confusing-say-teachers-unions

Gellman, B. (2021) 'Trump's next coup has already begun', *The Atlantic*, 6 December: www.theatlantic.com/magazine/archive/2022/01/january-6-insurrection-trump-coup-2024-election/620843/

Helm, T. (2022) 'Young adults have dramatic loss of faith in UK democracy, survey reveals', *The Guardian*, 10 April: www.theguardian.com/politics/2022/apr/10/young-adults-loss-of-faith-in-uk-democracy-survey

Henderson, A. (2021a) 'GOP "indoctrination" law aimed at Florida colleges is a "disgraceful" attack on free speech: First Amendment experts', AlterNet, 27 June: www.alternet.org/2021/06/free-speech/

Henderson, A. (2021b) 'Historians slam Texas governor for "patriotic education" law that promotes propaganda over facts', AlterNet, 27 June: www.alternet.org/2021/06/greg-abbott-2653567926/

James, T. (2016) 'Millions are missing from the UK's electoral registers', Open Democracy, 12 February: www.opendemocracy.net/en/opendemocracyuk/millions-are-missing-from-uk-s-electoral-registers/

John, T. (2019) 'More than half of UK voters want "strong, rule-breaking" leader, says survey', CNN, 8 April: https://edition.cnn.com/2019/04/08/uk/hansard-strong-leader-brexit-poll-gbr-intl/index.html

Renwick, A. (2021) 'The Elections Bill's proposals on Electoral Commission governance: risks to electoral integrity and devolution', the Constitution Unit, 30 September: https://constitution-unit.com/2021/09/30/the-elections-bills-proposals-on-electoral-commission-governance-risks-to-electoral-integrity-and-devolution/

Tam, H. (2016) *Political Literacy and Civic Thoughtfulness*, Sheffield: Centre for Welfare Reform, free download available: https://citizen-network.org/uploads/attachment/525/political-literacy-and-civic-thoughtfulness.pdf

Tam, H. (2018a) *Time to Save Democracy: How to Govern Ourselves in the Age of Anti-Politics*, Bristol: Policy Press.
Tam, H. (2018b) *What Should Citizens Believe: Exploring the Issues of Truth, Reason & Society*, Sheffield: Citizen Network.
Tam, H. (ed) (2019) *Whose Government Is It? The Renewal of State-Citizen Cooperation*, Bristol: Bristol University Press.
Yang, M. (2022) 'Report raises alarm on "insidious" effort to undermine US democracy', *The Guardian*, 13 April: www.theguardian.com/us-news/2022/apr/13/insidious-effort-to-undermin

Index

1619 Project 37, 39

A

Abdul Latif Jameel Poverty Action Lab (Massachusetts Institute of Technology) 136
academic freedom 6, 50–61, 136
academies (England) 20, 21, 22, 25, 156
active learning/action learning 8, 112–13, 131, 215, 219
Addams, Jane 204
Advocacy for Policy Change (Brandeis University) 134
African Centre for Citizenship and Democracy (University of the Western Cape) 138
agonistic approaches 8, 97, 103–7
Albermarle Report (England & Wales) 116
Alemanno, Alberto 133
Alexander, Titus 9
Alinsky, Saul 44, 45
All About Arsenic project (US) 91
Allen, Danielle 41, 42
Alternative vote system *see* proportional representation
Anzalone, J. 167
Arthur, J. 100
Association for Citizenship Teaching (ACT) 67, 163, 170, 172, 174
Australia 11, 180, 181–83, 185, 192
Australian Curriculum: Civics and Citizenship 185, 192

B

Backer, D.I. 103, 104
banking (mode of) education 7, 82, 85–87, 93
Begum, Halima 60
Belgian Political Panel Study 186
Ben-Porah, S. 54, 59
Bergamini, Matteo 112
Berson, M. 186
Black Lives Matter (BLM) 28, 57, 71, 113, 114, 116, 122, 131
Blunkett, David (Lord) 64
Bovens, M. 128
Brazil 21, 50
Breslin, Tony 6–7
Brexit 2, 70, 96, 128, 164
Brighouse, Tim 17
Britain *see* UK
British values (teaching of) 7, 56, 65, 98, 99, 100, 170, 172

C

Caballero Dávila, L. F. 104
Callan, E. 54, 59
Campbell, David 87, 150, 154, 190
'cancelling' people (culture of) 35
Cantle, Ted 70
Carlile, A. 170
Catalonia 96, 99
Center for Information and Research on Civic Learning and Engagement (CIRCLE) (US) 196, 199, 207
Cento Bull, Anna 104
charter schools (US) 20, 21, 203
Citizenship Advisory Group (England) 147–48
Citizenship Education Longitudinal Study (CELS) 148, 154, 155–56, 157, 188
Citizenship for 16–19 Year Olds in Education And Training report (England) 64
Civic Education Study (CIVED) 152, 190
civic efficacy 217
Civic Engagement Research Group (University of California) 134
civic objectivity 216–17
civic togetherness 215
Civic University Network (UK) 140
civility 36, 40–41, 44–47, 171, 206
Claes, E. 27, 28
classroom climate 10, 11, 152, 154, 157–58, 190–92
collaboration (in learning) 12, 22, 25, 44, 90–91, 174, 203, 205
collaborative networks 139–140
Collins, Chuck 128
Colombia 99, 104–5
communitarian 70, 101
community cohesion/social cohesion 5, 7, 64, 65, 67, 71, 97–100, 103–6, 117, 183, 195
Community Leadership Training (Citizens UK) 134
community organising 134, 165
community partnerships (with universities) 137
community schools (US) 203–5
Community University Partnership Programme (University of Brighton): 137
contentious issues (including divisive concepts) 5, 28, 35–47, 51, 91–2, 102, 105, 131, 204–5, 214
Corbyn, Jeremy 70, 114
Cotton, Dorothy 204

course enrichment 133
Crick, Bernard 6–7, 64, 65, 67–70, 73, 75, 129, 147, 163
Crick report 64, 147, 149, 159, 183, 186
'Critical Race Theory' (CRT) 37, 38, 205
critical thinking 5, 21, 22, 23, 24, 26, 27, 56, 57, 61, 154
culture war 4, 169, 205, 214
curriculum 11, 12, 17, 22, 26, 27, 37, 38, 46, 55, 61, 65–8, 70–5, 86, 87, 91–3, 99–102, 122, 130, 133, 147–58, 163, 166, 169–75, 180–92, 200, 202, 206

D

Dansich, R. 36, 40, 41, 43
Declaration of Principles on Academic Freedom and Academic Tenure (US) 52
deliberative (approaches/practices) 8, 44, 97, 100, 102–6, 117, 124, 136, 170–1, 174, 217, 221, 222
Deliberative Democracy Lab (Stanford University) 136
The Democracy Commitment (TDC) (US) 139
Denmark 23
Dewey, John 5, 27–8, 46, 54, 58, 141, 180, 184, 200, 204
Digital Citizenship Education (Council of Europe) 167
divisive concepts *see* contentious issues
divisive legislation 36, 38–40, 42, 46, 213
Dorling, Danny 29
Dufour, Barry 68
Dutch 190, 191

E

Educating for American Democracy (EAD) 11, 134, 197, 198, 200, 201, 207, 208
Educating for Civic Reasoning & Discourse report (US) 82
Education for Citizenship and the Teaching of Democracy in Schools report (England) *see* Crick report
Education Network for Active Civic Transformation (ENACT) (US) 134, 139
equality *see* inequality
Elective Classification in Community Engagement (Carnegie Foundation) 139
electoral arrangements 219–20
Electoral Commission (Australia) 188, 191
Electoral Commission (UK) 2, 212, 220
Emler, N. 150
engagement processes 221–22
England 5, 6, 17–18, 20–8, 54–61, 64–75, 98, 159, 175, 180, 181, 188; *see also* UK

epistemic institutions 222–23
Estonia 5, 25, 26
Extremism 7, 10, 171–73, 214

F

Farrell, Anna 90–91
Finland 5, 23, 25, 26
Fitzgerald, J. 187–188
Foa, R.S. 128, 164
Follett, Mary Parker 7–8, 82, 85–7, 88, 90, 93
Frazer, E. 150
Freire, Paulo 5, 7, 23, 24, 82, 84, 86, 87, 88–89, 131

G

Galston, William 187, 189, 190
Geboers, E. 154, 187, 190
Germany 155, 182
Gilroy, P. 171
Global Institute of Sustainability and Innovation hub (Arizona State University) 136
Good Lobby Profs 139
Guidance: Political Impartiality in Schools report (England) 51, 54–7

H

Habermas, J. 102
Hahn, C. 154
Haste, H. 155
Hess, Diana 39, 42, 91–92
Higher Education: Free Speech and Academic Freedom report (England) 51, 54, 57–9
Hodgson, Robin (Lord) 72–3
Hong Kong 98–99, 100, 102
Hooghe, M. 27, 28, 154
hooks, bell 24, 104
Hoskins, Bryony 9, 18, 21, 148, 149, 152, 164
House of Lords Select Committee on Citizenship and Civic Engagement 22

I

identity (civic/national) 8, 97–107, 213, 215
Illinois Civics Hub 202
impartiality 3, 51, 55–60, 164, 166, 168, 213, 214, 216
inequality 8, 10, 18, 19, 24, 69, 96, 113, 128, 138, 139, 149, 151, 169–71, 181, 186, 195, 204, 217, 224
Inglehart, R. 139, 149
International Civic and Citizenship Education Study (ICCS) 148, 151, 154, 157, 188, 192

J

Janmaat, J.G. 18, 19, 21, 148, 149, 152, 154, 164
Jerome, Lee 10
Junn, June 150, 185, 190

K

Kahne, J. 23
Kawashima-Ginsberg, Kei 11
Keating, A. 19, 149, 152, 154, 156, 164, 188
Keith, W.M. 36, 40, 41, 43
Kerr, David 9, 67, 156
King Jr, Martin Luther 45, 114
Kiwan, Dina 6
Knight Abowitz, Kathleen 7, 104, 105
Knowles, R. T. 152, 154

L

learning as acquisition 151–52, 153, 155
learning as participation 152, 154, 155
Lee, C.D. 82, 84
Leunig, J. 155
LGBT/LGBTQ+ 117, 121, 170
Lo, M. 89–90, 104, 105
local authorities (local government) 8, 9, 17, 25, 74, 113, 115–18, 120, 122, 124, 219
local government *see* local authorities

M

Macedo, S. 149
Making Sense of Citizenship (manual) 67
Mann, H. 195
Mansson, N. 21, 28
Mamlok, D. 104, 105
Mårdh, A. 104–5, 106
Martinez, Raoul 22
McFarland, D. 188–89
media literacy 166–69
Melbourne Declaration (2008) 183
misinformation 10, 166, 167–68, 172, 181, 214
Monbiot, George 19
Monroe, M. 174
Moorse, Liz 10, 55
Mouffe, C. 81, 96, 97, 98, 103
Mulder, L. 191
Myers-Lipton, Scott 134

N

National Assessment of Educational Progress (NAEP) (US) 183, 186, 188, 192
National Assessment Program: Civics and Citizenship (NAPCC) (Australia) 182–83, 188
National Campaign for Political and Civic Engagement (US) 139
National Co-ordinating Centre for Public Engagement (NCCPE) (UK) 140
neoliberal 4, 5, 12, 17, 20, 23, 59, 181, 219
Neundorf, A. 186
The New and the Old report (England) 64
Niemi, Dick 150, 185, 190
Norris, Pippa 139, 149, 164

O

Oberle, M. 155
Ofsted (the Office for Standards in Education, Children's Services and Skills) (England) 74, 75, 156–58, 164
Operation Black Vote 116

P

Pagliarello, M. 166
parents/parental 5, 12, 17, 25, 37, 55, 68, 99, 152, 156, 164, 165, 170, 184, 186, 205, 206
Parker, L. 87
Parker, W. 171
participation 7, 9, 10–12, 17, 18, 20–22, 24, 26, 40, 44, 68, 74, 91, 103, 112–14, 117, 118, 123–24, 134–36, 140, 147, 149–59, 164, 183, 184, 186–89, 203, 217, 221, 223
Payne, K.A. 199, 202
pedagogy 5, 12, 24, 56, 60, 68, 82, 84, 85, 89, 90–93, 100, 103–5, 106, 131–33, 187, 190, 198, 200, 202, 202, 204, 207
Personal, Social and Health Education *see* PSHE
Phipps, A. 59
photo ID (for voting) 1, 212, 220
political communities 97–98
political engagement 9, 13, 17–19, 28, 98, 106, 113, 142–59, 185, 186, 188, 190, 219
political literacy 6, 7, 10, 18, 26, 64–75, 104, 121–24, 134, 137, 163, 165, 168, 169, 175, 214
Political Literacy Oversight Group (UK) 137
populist/populism 7, 81–82, 83, 88, 164
power relations/structure 43, 86, 87, 129–30, 133, 217
Prevent (strategy, UK) 65, 99, 172, 173
Print, Murray 11, 182, 183, 186, 189
Programme for International Student Assessment (PISA) 26
Project Citizen (the Center for Civic Education, Calabasas, US) 184
proportional representation 2
protest(s) 1, 9, 70, 114, 122, 138, 149–51, 173
PSHE (Personal, Social and Health Education) 65, 66, 68, 71, 72, 73
public sensemaking 89–90

Q

Quintelier, E. 154, 155

R

race issues 18, 35, 37, 43, 60, 112–24, 132, 141, 205
Reay, Diane 5, 153
Reichert, F. 23, 183, 189
The Research University Civic Engagement Network (TRUCEN) (US) 139
Rodriguez, N.N. 203
Rousseau, Sylvia 199
Ruef, J. 89–90
Runnymede Trust 60, 116

S

Safstrom, C. 21, 28
Sahlberg, Pasi 25
Sant, Edda 8, 81–82, 83, 84–85
school council(s)/student council(s) 11, 68, 69, 73, 81, 121, 152, 158, 166, 185, 188, 189
Scotland 17, 106
Sellers, Kathleen 7
sexism 37, 39, 40, 59, 132, 213
shared authority 4, 7, 81, 82, 84, 85–91
Shukra, Kalbir 8
situated learning 11, 105, 180, 185, 191
Sloam, James 112, 149, 150, 164
Smith, Barrett 5
social media 135, 167, 168, 181, 212
Starmanns, C. 188–89
Stitzlein, Sarah 5, 83, 87
student voice 73, 74, 85, 89, 155, 166, 208
Supple, Carrie (Citizenship Foundation) 69
sustainability 10, 135–36, 173–74, 206
Swalwell, K. 203
Sweden 23, 135

T

Talloires Network of Engaged Universities (global coalition) 140
Tam, Henry 212, 214, 222
teachable moment(s) 43, 131, 132
teacher training/development 7, 12, 37, 55, 60, 67, 68, 219, 222
Teaching Civic Engagement (Rutgers University) 134
Torney-Purta, J. 23, 154
Truman's Commission on Higher Education for American Democracy 141
Trump, Donald 2–3, 70, 96, 216, 220
Tryggvason, A. 104–5, 106
Twain, Ann 92

U

UK (or Britain) *see also* England 1, 6, 19, 50–53, 70, 112–14, 122, 172, 175, 183, 223
Ukraine 167
Universities Policy Engagement Network (UPEN) (UK) 140
US 1, 5, 6, 11, 20, 21, 35–47, 52, 93, 99, 141, 172–73, 180, 182, 183, 184, 185, 186, 195–208, 223

V

Vertovec, S. 171
Vogel, Frank 128
Vogt, K. 167
voting 1–3, 9, 11, 19, 55, 73, 81, 84, 116, 120, 123, 124, 182, 183, 185, 187–91, 207, 212, 219, 220, 223

W

Waters, Mick 71
Weinberg, James 18, 55, 164, 165
Welzel, C. 149
Whereas the People: Civics and Citizenship Education report (Australia) 183
Whiteley, P. 152, 183, 186
Wille, A. 128

Y

Young Advisors 117–19
Young Mayor Programme (YMP) (Lewisham, England) 9, 115, 118–24
Youth Act! (project) 69, 70
Youth-Parent Socialization Panel Study (US) 186
Youth Parliament (UK) 117

www.ingramcontent.com/pod-product-compliance
Lightning Source LLC
Chambersburg PA
CBHW051539020426
42333CB00016B/2002